STARTING WITH MERLEAU-PONTY

Continuum's *Starting with. . .* series offers clear, concise and accessible introductions to the key thinkers in philosophy. The books explore and illuminate the roots of each philosopher's work and ideas, leading readers to a thorough understanding of the key influences and philosophical foundations from which his or her thought developed. Ideal for first-year students starting out in philosophy, the series will serve as the ideal companion to study of this fascinating subject.

Available now:

Starting with Berkeley, Nick Jones
Starting with Derrida, Sean Gaston
Starting with Descartes, C. G. Prado
Starting with Hegel, Craig B. Matarrese
Starting with Heidegger, Thomas Greaves
Starting with Hobbes, George MacDonald Ross
Starting with Kant, Andrew Ward
Starting with Kierkegaard, Patrick Sheil
Starting with Leibniz, Lloyd Strickland
Starting with Locke, Greg Forster
Starting with Mill, John R. Fitzpatrick
Starting with Nietzsche, Ullrich Haase
Starting with Rousseau, James Delaney
Starting with Sartre, Gail Linsenbard
Starting with Schopenhauer, Sandra Shapshay
Starting with Wittgenstein, Chon Tejedor

Forthcoming:

Starting with Hume, Charlotte R. Brown and William Edward Morris

STARTING WITH MERLEAU-PONTY

KATHERINE J. MORRIS

continuum

Continuum International Publishing Group

The Tower Building
11 York Road
London SE1 7NX

80 Maiden Lane
Suite 704
New York NY 10038

www.continuumbooks.com

British Library Cataloguing-in-Publication Data
A catalogue record for this book is available from the British Library.

ISBN: HB: 978-1-8470-6280-2
PB: 978-1-8470-6281-9

Library of Congress Cataloguing-in-Publication Data
Morris, Katherine J.
Starting with Merleau-Ponty / Katherine Morris.
p. cm. – (Starting with–)
Includes bibliographical references (p.   ) and index.
ISBN 978-1-84706-280-2 (hardcover : alk. paper) –
ISBN 978-1-84706-281-9 (pbk. : alk. paper) –
ISBN 978-1-4411-7478-9 (pdf) –
ISBN 978-1-4411-1898-1 (epub)
1. Merleau-Ponty, Maurice, 1908-1961. I. Title.

B2430.M3764M67 2012
194–dc23

2011036464

Typeset by Deanta Global Publishing Services, Chennai, India
Printed and bound in India

For my nieces Abby and Emma
and (still) in search of Bitten and Christie,
*who transcend the **a priori** of their species*

CONTENTS

ACKNOWLEDGEMENTS

I have taught Merleau-Ponty in one form or another for many years: in tutorials, in lectures on Sartre and Merleau-Ponty and more recently Merleau-Ponty alone, and in lectures to medical anthropology graduate students on the anthropology of the body and gender. My greatest debt is to all those students in these various forums who, over the years, have raised so many excellent questions and so often forced me to clarify Merleau-Ponty's thinking for myself and for them. My medical anthropology co-lecturers (Karin Eli, Elisabeth Hsu, Caroline Potter) have, among many other things, helped me to understand Merleau-Ponty from their perspective.

A number of people have read and made comments on versions of one or more chapters, for which I am very grateful: Jonathan Cole, Tim Horder, Rasmus Jensen, Kathleen Lennon and Tim Mooney. An early version of Ch. 4 (under the title 'Merleau-Ponty and Gestalt psychology') was presented at a Continental philosophy seminar run by Joseph Schear and Manuel Dries; they and other participants provided very helpful and constructive feedback on that occasion. Special thanks to my omni-talented graduate student Chuanfei Chin, who produced the diagrams (Figures 2a-d) from my impossibly crude sketches. Finally, I thank Tim Horder not only for his comments on several chapters but for his unstinting support throughout the long and sometimes painful gestation of this book.

LIST OF ABBREVIATIONS

Books by Merleau-Ponty:

PP: *Phenomenology of Perception*. (Original French publication 1945.)
There are two versions in English. All page references to *PP* cite both, in
chronological order; I freely use whichever translation seems best, and on
rare occasions my own:
(1962). Tr. C. Smith. Routledge & Kegan Paul: London and Henley.
(2002). Tr. C. Smith. Routledge (Routledge Classics): London and New
York. (Translation slightly modified from the 1962 version.)
SB (1963). *The Structure of Behaviour*. Tr. A. L. Fisher. Beacon Press:
Boston. (Original French publication 1942.)
VI (1968): *The Visible and the Invisible*. Ed. Claude Lefort. Tr. A. Lingis.
Northwestern University Press: Evanston. (Unfinished work. Original
French publication 1964.)

Collections of Merleau-Ponty's essays, etc:

Signs (1964). *Signs*. Tr. R. C. McCleary. Northwestern University Press:
Evanston. (Original French publication 1960.)
SNS (1964). *Sense and Non-Sense*. Trs. H. L. Dreyfus and P. A. Dreyfus.
Northwestern University Press: Evanston. (Original French publication
1948.)
TD (1992). *Texts and Dialogues*. Eds. H. J. Silverman and J. Barry Jr., Tr.
M. B. Smith. Humanities Press: Atlantic Highlands (NJ) and London.

Merleau-Ponty's lectures and lecture notes:

N.B. *CPP* provides some lectures not previously available in English as well
as new translations of lectures which had previously appeared as *CAL*
(new title 'Consciousness and language acquisition') and 'The experience
of others' (trs. F. Evans and H. J. Silverman [1982–3], *Review of Existential
Psychology and Psychiatry* 18, 33–63); it also provides more complete
versions of some lectures in *PrP* ('Phenomenology and the sciences of

man', new title 'Human Sciences and phenomenology', and 'The child's relations with others').

PrP (1964): *The Primacy of Perception*. Ed. J. M. Edie; various translators. Northwestern University Press: Evanston.

CAL (1973). *Consciousness and the Acquisition of Language*. Tr. H. J. Silverman. Northwestern University Press: Evanston. (Original French publication 1964.)

Nature (2003). Ed. D. Séglard. Tr. R. Vallier. Northwestern University Press: Evanston. (Original French publication 1994.)

WP (2008). *The World of Perception*. Tr. O. Davis. Routledge (Routledge Classics): London and New York. (Original French publication 1948.)

CPP (2010). *Child Psychology and Pedagogy: The Sorbonne Lectures 1949–52*. Tr. T. Welsh. (Original French publication 2001.)

Works by others:

CM (1960): E. Husserl, *Cartesian Meditations*. Tr. D. Cairns. Martinus Nijhoff: Dordrecht, Boston and Lancaster. (Page references are to Husserl's page numbers. Original German publication 1929.)

Ideas (1952): E. Husserl, *Ideas*. Tr. W. R. Boyce-Gibson. George Allen & Unwin: London and MacMillan: New York. (Original German publication 1913.)

PRS (1965): E. Husserl, 'Philosophy as a rigorous science'. In E. Husserl, *Phenomenology and the Crisis of Philosophy*. Tr. Q. Lauer. Harper Torchbooks: New York, Evanston and London, pp. 71–147. (Original German publication 1911.)

Crisis (1970): E. Husserl, *Crisis of European Sciences and Transcendental Phenomenology*. Northwestern University Press: Evanston. (Original German publication of Parts I and II 1936; Part III was unfinished at Husserl's death and published posthumously.)

BN (1986): J.-P. Sartre, *Being and Nothingness*. Tr. H. E. Barnes. London: Routledge. (Original French publication 1943.)

BT (1962): M. Heidegger, *Being and Time*. Tr. J. Macquarrie and E. Robinson. Oxford: Blackwell. (Page references are to Heidegger's page numbers. Original German publication 1927.)

GP (1947). W. Köhler, *Gestalt Psychology*. New York and London: Liveright. (Original publication 1930.)

PREFACE

Maurice Merleau-Ponty observes of the history of philosophy that it 'dismantles or embalms certain doctrines, changing them into "messages" or museum pieces'. Others it keeps active, because 'they retain an expressive power which exceeds their statements and propositions. These doctrines are the *classics' (Signs* 10-11). If books as well as doctrines may be called classics in this sense, Merleau-Ponty's *chef d'oeuvre Phenomenology of Perception (PP)* is one such.

Merleau-Ponty, born in 1908, was one of that crowd of 20th-century French intellectuals which included Jean-Paul Sartre and Simone de Beauvoir. Or, rather, he was and he wasn't. He was a contemporary and, like them, attended the prestigious École Normale Supérieure to do his *agrégation* in philosophy. There, he counted among his acquaintances Sartre and Simone Weil; the former, three years his senior, Merleau-Ponty met, as he recounts, 'when the École Normale unleashed its fury against one of my schoolmates and myself for having hissed the traditional songs, too vulgar to suit us. He slipped between us and our persecutors and contrived a way for us to get out of our heroic and ridiculous situation' (*SNS* 41). His friends included Beauvoir and Claude Lévi-Strauss (who was to become a highly influential anthropologist, and to dedicate his celebrated book *The Savage Mind* to Merleau-Ponty's memory). Merleau-Ponty had been outdone in the June 1928 exams by two people, both women: Weil and Beauvoir (Bair 1990: 122), and sought Beauvoir out afterwards 'because he wanted to meet "the girl who had beaten him in the examinations"'(Bair 1990: 124). He shared with Beauvoir not just a Catholic background – to which they both had a troubled relationship – but a taste in literature and a 'fascination with what they called "low-life" while still cherishing self-righteous prudery' (Bair 1990: 124). As for Sartre, '[a]t the École Normale we knew each other without being friends ... We lost sight of each other ... Each of us, nevertheless, was preparing himself, without knowing it, for an encounter with the other' (Sartre 1998: 565). Philosophically, both were drawn to the phenomenology of Husserl and Heidegger, although they worked separately and '[e]ach of us viewed the work being done by the other as an unexpected, and sometimes hostile deviation from his own' (Sartre 1998: 568). Politically, '[i]t took the war to bring us close together', says Sartre (1998: 567). French intellectuals were almost by definition *'engagés'* – that is, 'committed', actively involved in the politics of the day. As the horrors of the Nazi concentration camps were revealed, and after the occupation and liberation of France, Communism seemed a bulwark of uprightness and sanity. (Merleau-Ponty was never a Marxist; as Sartre perceptively comments, 'It was not the idea which he rejected, but the fact that it was a dogma', 1998: 571.) In 1941 Merleau-Ponty joined a short-lived resistance group ('Socialism and Liberty') to which Sartre also belonged. Sartre and Merleau-Ponty co-founded *Les Temps moderne*, a hugely influential political, literary and philosophical magazine, in 1945. Their friendship waxed and waned with the actions of Russia and Cuba and with their complex attitudes towards these actions.

And yet Merleau-Ponty was never quite one of that crowd. By contrast with his flashier contemporaries, there has yet to be a proper biography (at least in English) of Merleau-Ponty.[1] He had no literary ambitions, never wrote plays and novels. Unlike the scandalously unwed Sartre and Beauvoir, Merleau-Ponty got married (to Suzon, a psychiatrist, with whom he had a daughter). He even *looked* out of place: a man who 'had neither the flamboyant nor the dishevelled appearance affected by so many European intellectuals' but instead resembled 'a successful French business executive' (Fisher 1969: 3). Again, very unlike Sartre and Beauvoir, Merleau-Ponty had a normal, indeed a rather distinguished, academic career, teaching at Université de Lyons, the Sorbonne (where he held the Chair of Child Psychology and Pedagogy), and finally holding the Chair of Philosophy at the Collège de France until his untimely death aged 53. He also earned the respect, if not necessarily the philosophical sympathy, of at least some of his British analytic philosophy contemporaries in a way which Sartre did not. Although Mary Warnock paints a bleak picture of this period – '[t]here was deep hostility to the very idea of "continental philosophy" in Oxford and Cambridge in the 1950s' (2002: 85) – Freddie Ayer counted Merleau-Ponty as a friend and was even the one who arranged for *PP* to be translated into English (Ayer 1977: 285); Charles Taylor was 'commissioned to instruct' the participants in J. L. Austin's famous 'Saturday morning meetings' in Merleau-Ponty's *PP* (Warnock 1973: 32 n.1); and there was an exchange with Gilbert Ryle, not long before Merleau-Ponty's death, at a meeting of the Royaumont philosophy society devoted to the attempt to create a dialogue between 'analytic' and 'Continental' philosophers, noteworthy for its illumination of some of the philosophical issues that divided them.[2]

Alas, those British philosophers suffered the worst fate that can befall any philosopher: they went out of fashion. The same was largely true of Merleau-Ponty after his death in 1961, although his friends, admirers and former students across the world have kept his name alive; they have seen to it that his other writings were translated into English and that his unfinished works and lecture notes were published. In France, he was overshadowed, as he was beginning to be even during his lifetime, by such colourful *penseurs* as Jacques Derrida and Merleau-Ponty's former student Michel Foucault. In the Anglophone world, he remained, like the other 'Continental' philosophers, a minority interest. Yet over the past fifteen years or so, things have begun to change. Mainstream Anglo-American philosophers have not only begun to engage seriously with the sorts of issues which occupied Merleau-Ponty, they are beginning to engage with Merleau-Ponty himself. (He even appears to have achieved the dubious distinction of becoming 'trendy' in certain 'cognitive science' circles.) Apparently independently, over roughly the same period, sociology and anthropology have been developing as sub-disciplines the sociology and anthropology of the body, with Merleau-Ponty featuring as a major theoretical player. This by no means exhausts the fields in which Merleau-Ponty is achieving Anglophone acclaim, nor those in which he may yet do so. The major impetus for the present book is to try to exhibit what it is about this modest philosopher that is generating such posthumous enthusiasm.

This book focuses on *Phenomenology of Perception* (1945), although with occasional references to other of his other broadly contemporaneous works, and with a little more breadth of focus in the final Chapter.[3] This may still seem a narrow focus, but *PP* is certainly Merleau-Ponty's best-known and most widely influential work, and its richness and intricacy more than warrant a book-length commentary. Moreover, many, at least, of his subsequent works continued the project that was begun in *PP*: namely (as I will be arguing), of undermining the intellectual prejudices implicit in a particular picture of perception.

The book is aimed at an Anglophone audience (and makes use for the most part of Anglophone material). Reading *PP* in translation, as most of the intended audience will, carries all the dangers of any translation however good; it also potentially brings with it the distortions which occur when any text is transplanted from one 'field of production' (say, a mid-20th-century Parisian field) to very different 'field of reception' (say, an early 21st-century Anglo-American one). (See Bourdieu 1999.) I do my best to inoculate readers against a few of the latter risks.

I hope in this book to give the reader some help in getting started with reading Merleau-Ponty, to forestall some misunderstandings that may get in the way of grasping his way of looking at things, and, most importantly, to give an indication of why that effort is worth it. I try to make *PP* accessible both to undergraduates reading philosophy – whether specifically studying Merleau-Ponty or phenomenology, or reading philosophy of mind and action, philosophy of psychology, philosophy of psychiatry or even philosophy of cognitive science – and to more advanced students or professionals in psychology, psychiatry, sociology and anthropology. By 'making accessible', I emphatically do not mean that the present book should be a substitute for reading *PP*; rather, it is meant to assist readers in grappling with *PP* for themselves.[4]

Reading *PP* is not easy – 'somewhere in the range between formidable and impossible', says Hass (2008: 2), although fortunately he exaggerates a bit. Let me begin by trying to anticipate and allay at least some of the terror that this remark may engender.

First, Merleau-Ponty assumes acquaintance on the part of his readers with a number of thinkers acquaintance with whom cannot be presupposed in many of his Anglophone readers: most obviously, Husserl and Heidegger. Added to this is Merleau-Ponty's 'dog-whistle' style of allusion and of critical engagement, the subject or target often recognizable only by those in the know. In Ch. 1 I try to say enough about these two philosophers to enable the Anglophone reader to get on. Sartre is clearly another important interlocutor; here I confine myself to setting out his solution to 'the problem of others' as a counterpoint to Merleau-Ponty's (in Ch. 5), since many of their fundamental points of convergence and divergence are clearly exhibited there.

Secondly, Merleau-Ponty engages with those with whom he is in disagreement in a characteristic way: he 'cultivated a deliberately nonadversarial dialectical strategy' (Carman 2008: 25), developing others' positions and arguments in such depth and with such sympathy that there are moments where it is unclear at first sight whether he is describing others' views prior to criticism or speaking *in propria persona*. (Even commentators get this wrong.) It is only by getting a grip on the main contours of both his and his interlocutors' thinking that we can make this distinction reliably; I begin to sketch these contours in Ch. 2. I would urge that his ability and willingness to enter into the point of view of the thinkers he is criticizing should be seen as one of his cardinal *virtues*. (Other stylistic quirks, for example his predilection for very long paragraphs and very long footnotes, and his tendency to hide his most important 'findings' in the middle of these very long paragraphs, I won't try to defend.)

Thirdly, Merleau-Ponty engages more than any other phenomenologist with the science of his day: in *PP* in particular with psychologists and neurologists. He does this in such detail that his arguments can at times be difficult for non-scientists to follow. Here I want to suggest that the important point for us is his *exemplification* of a way in which a philosopher may justifiably criticise science. (See the Coda to Ch. 2.) It is vital that he goes into detail since otherwise his targets would protest that he had missed essential elements or accuse him of not really understanding the science. Yet there is a sense in which the details don't matter: he demonstrates what would be necessary for *us* as 21st-century philosophers to criticise those 21st-century scientists who remain in the grip of the intellectual prejudices of Merleau-Ponty's contemporaries.

Fourthly, Merleau-Ponty from time to time introduces or borrows novel and sometimes puzzling terms ('motor intentionality', 'bodily understanding' and so on) to express what he wants to say. There are, as we will see (esp. in Ch. 3), good philosophical reasons for introducing these terms: ordinary language, because of its sedimented history of tradition, leaves no clear space for the concepts to which these expressions refer.

Finally, our own prejudices and preconceptions can get in the way of our understanding him. Many of us are more or less in the grip of what

Merleau-Ponty calls 'the prejudice of objective thought' (see the Codas to Chs. 2 and 6; again, even commentators are not always immune.)

Apart from the final chapter, this book very broadly follows the structure of *PP*, with Chapter 1 taking the reader through the Preface, Chapter 2 through the Introduction, Chapter 3 through Part One, and Chapters 4 and 5 through Part Two.[5] (Chapter 6 looks at aspects of Merleau-Ponty's reception today and at frontiers of further development.) I am attempting to put forward a particular vision of Merleau-Ponty's philosophy, which I outline here

(i) I take him at his word that *PP* is a book about *perception*.[6] This might seem so obvious as not to be worth stating, given the title. It may, conversely, seem to narrow its scope and interest. This latter response, however, is precisely what *PP* seeks to forestall. Perception is 'the paradoxical phenomenon which renders being accessible to us' (*PrP* 17), and '[t]he perceived world is the always presupposed foundation of all rationality, all value, and all existence' (*PrP* 13). To rethink perception is also radically to rethink the *body*. (Merleau-Ponty's reconceptualization of the body is justly celebrated: the so-called '*lived* body' is a prophylactic against the dominant conception of the body as a physical, physiological and anatomical object, a *corps machine*. But this reconceptualization [see Chs. 3 and 4] sometimes eclipses its context: Merleau-Ponty's treatment of perception.) To rethink perception is also to rethink the *world,* since 'the world is what we perceive' (*PP* xvi/xviii): that is, the so-called '*life-world*', the world of everyday experience which is the setting for our ordinary actions (see Chs. 2 and 4). And to rethink perception also entails a reconceptualization of *others*, that is, other human beings (see Ch. 5), since the world thus revealed is intersubjective and since we understand others with our bodies. Thus the scope of a book 'about perception' is immeasurably wider than it might have seemed at first blush. Today's Anglophone students are also truly fortunate to have access to the text of seven radio broadcasts delivered by Merleau-Ponty in 1948, published in English in 2004 as *The World of Perception* (*WP*). These constitute a superb introduction to the breadth and scope, as well as the characteristic flavour, of his 'world-view'.

(ii) I have found it illuminating to treat his analyses of perception as responses to a particular *picture* of perception ('the Picture') which is diagrammed in Chs. 2 and 4 with multiple variations. This picture can appear wholly natural, but actually embodies a number of assumptions. The dominant overall trajectory of *PP* can be seen as an attempt at a root-and-branch upheaval of these assumptions, and thus to enable us to 're-learn to look at the world' (cf. *PP* xx/xxiii).

I also highlight an important sub-trajectory of this argument that represents Merleau-Ponty's specific engagement with the Gestalt psychologists.[7] Merleau-Ponty acknowledges his debt to these psychologists for their correct descriptions of a number of qualities of perceived objects, qualities for which empiricism cannot account: that they are unities, that they are 'impregnated with meaning', that they have a 'physiognomy', etc. (Ch. 2). However, they remain in the grip of many of the assumptions embedded in the Picture; and through their failure to reconceptualize the lived body and the life-world, they deprive themselves of the resources fully to account for their own most profound discoveries (see Ch. 4). Highlighting this sub-trajectory serves two purposes in parallel: it provides a lens through which to examine many aspects of Merleau-Ponty's account of embodied perception, and it offers a paradigm of Merleau-Ponty's critical engagement with science.

(iii) Each chapter includes a Coda which sketches responses to the sorts of questions that students often ask (e.g., 'Is Merleau-Ponty anti-science?'), which forestalls potential misunderstandings (e.g., about what phenomenology is), or which develops central concepts (e.g., Merleau-Ponty's characteristic conceptions of 'normality' or of 'essence'). To treat these within the body of the chapter would have interrupted the flow; but the points sketched in these Codas are vital for understanding what Merleau-Ponty is doing.

(iv) Finally, I want to urge (Ch. 6) that *PP* really is a classic and not a 'museum piece'. Merleau-Ponty himself recognized that *PP* had its limits. For us to acknowledge this is by no means to detract from its brilliance. It is rather an invitation for us to take up where he left off: to think with him, and against him, in new directions, as so many have and as so many more, I trust, will. Indeed, I want to suggest that what he terms 'the prejudice of objective thought' remains in some form deeply embedded not only in many Anglo-American academic disciplines today – including philosophy, sociology, anthropology and psychology – but in 'Western culture', if I may be permitted so grand a term. I submit that it is in part precisely this, and our more-or-less obscure awareness of the dangers it poses for humanity, that lies behind Merleau-Ponty's resurgence in popularity across so many different disciplines.

CHAPTER 1

STARTING WITH MERLEAU-PONTY

Anyone hoping to use the Preface to Merleau-Ponty's *PP* as a way into the body of the book is likely to face a major obstacle. The Preface consists of 15 very dense pages in which Merleau-Ponty addresses an audience already broadly familiar not only with René Descartes and Immanuel Kant – a familiarity that can safely be assumed at least of most Anglo-American students of philosophy – but also with the phenomenologists Edmund Husserl and Martin Heidegger – a familiarity that cannot be so assumed. Thus, the first task of this chapter (§i) will be to say enough about these phenomenological luminaries to enable the reader to get by.[1]

With this background, the general purpose of Merleau-Ponty's preface is straightforward: at least on the face of it, he is attempting a kind of 'reconciling project' addressed to those who suppose Husserl's and Heidegger's approaches to phenomenology to be at odds with one another. Merleau-Ponty aims to show that if we read Husserl as he thinks we should, then Husserl's phenomenology is not only compatible with but actually entails Heidegger's existential philosophy. This project is outlined in §ii.

Intertwined with this reconciling project are glimpses of Merleau-Ponty's unique positive conception of phenomenology; these are highlighted in §iii.

I end this chapter with a Coda that addresses 'what phenomenology is not': it outlines some of the preconceptions which students may have about phenomenology and are liable to get in their way.

i. PHENOMENOLOGY AND EXISTENTIAL PHILOSOPHY: HUSSERL AND HEIDEGGER

Phenomenology is a method of practicing philosophy developed by Husserl.[2] Heidegger made phenomenology into an 'existential philosophy'. Both authors wrote multiple works; for our purposes, the work of Heidegger that is most relevant to the aim of the Preface to *PP* is his 1927 *Being and Time* (*BT*). Husserl is a harder case: many commentators divide his phenomenological corpus, however, contestably, into phases (say, early, middle and late), and since part of Merleau-Ponty's reconciling project is to try to show the *continuity* in Husserl's thinking, we should ideally consider the development of his thought through these phases. For our purposes, however, that would be overkill; we can get most of what we need for understanding Merleau-Ponty's argument from the ('middle') *Ideas* (1913), where many of Husserl's best-known concepts and doctrines were most fully elaborated, and two 'late' works, the *Cartesian Meditations* (1931, based on the *Paris Lectures* delivered in 1929)[3] and the *Crisis* (parts I and II of which appeared in 1936; Merleau-Ponty read the unpublished Part III in 1939), where Husserl signals some of the themes that most gripped Heidegger and Merleau-Ponty, although I will refer to other works from time to time as well.

Edmund Husserl (1859–1938)

Husserl began as a mathematician; he wrote his *Habilitationsschrift* on the concept of a number under Franz Brentano (best known today for his concept of intentionality, on which more in the following paragraphs), and subsequently under the eminent psychologist Carl Stumpf.[4] Husserl developed and modified his conception of phenomenology over the course of a lifetime, beginning in the second volume of his second book *Logical Investigations*. He told Emmanuel Levinas (a noted phenomenologist in his own right, and a contemporary of Sartre and Merleau-Ponty, who attended Husserl's last and Heidegger's first lectures at Freiburg) the story of having been given a pocket-knife as a boy, which he felt insufficiently sharp; he kept grinding it and grinding it until nothing was left of the blade. 'Seemingly, the adult Husserl felt this episode symbolized his philosophical endeavours' (Moran 2000: 67; cf. Spiegelberg 1969: 76n.1).

2

Throughout his writing, Husserl saw himself as following the *spirit* of Descartes' philosophizing: this is clear even from the title *Cartesian Meditations* (although this was based on lectures originally presented to an audience before whom it was virtually obligatory to pay obeisance to the great French philosopher). He characterized that spirit, both ethically and epistemologically, as 'the ultimate conceivable freedom from prejudice, shaping itself with actual autonomy according to ultimate evidences it has itself produced, and therefore absolutely self-responsible' (*CM* 47). Husserl, again like Descartes, always strove for an ideal of rigour not unlike that to be found in mathematics; he wanted philosophy to be, in his terms, a 'rigorous science' – or rather, a *strenge Wissenschaft*, to quote the German title of his 1911 work *Philosophy as a Rigorous Science*: any rigorous and systematic study counts as a *Wissenschaft*, which makes it a broader concept than the modern English concept of science. (Ryle seems to have misunderstood this basic point when he says 'I don't think that philosophy or any part of philosophy can properly be called a "science"', 1971: 168.)[5] As we will see, his unswerving adherence to the idea of a '*strenge Wissenschaft*' may have contributed to his loss of popularity in favour of Heidegger.

The simplest way to introduce Husserl's phenomenology for our purposes is via the four themes which Merleau-Ponty pursues in his Preface.[6]

'*To the things themselves*'. This is regularly described as the 'battle-cry', 'the war-cry' or the 'watchword' of phenomenology, and was present from the beginning (in the *Logical Investigations*). By itself, it does little more than characterize the 'spirit of science': as someone striving for 'genuine science', I 'must neither make nor go on accepting any judgment as scientific *that I have not derived from evidence*, from "experiences" in which the affairs and the affair-complexes in question are present to me as "*they themselves*"' (*CM* 54; cf. *Ideas* §19).[7] It has a positive sense, connecting it to what he calls 'the principle of all principles' (*Ideas* §24) according to which '*whatever presents itself in "intuition" in primordial form . . .is simply to be accepted as it gives itself out to be, though only within the limits in which it then presents itself*'. It also, however, has an important critical use, against enterprises which claim to be scientific but which fail to respect this basic principle. Thus Husserl uses it against what he calls 'naturalism', which supposes that '[w]hatever is is either itself physical, belonging to the unified totality of physical matter, or it is in fact psychical, but then merely as a variable dependent on the physical' (*PRS* 79), as well as the historicism made popular by thinkers such as Dilthey (*PRS* 122ff). Merleau-Ponty's critical use of this 'watchword', as we will see, overlaps with Husserl's; Husserl's anti-naturalism has echoes in Merleau-Ponty's critiques of empiricism.

Intentionality. In some sense, phenomenology for Husserl may be called the systematic study of consciousness. We must not, however, confuse it with *psychology*, which is concerned 'with consciousness from the empirical standpoint', whereas phenomenology is concerned with 'pure consciousness' (*PRS* 91). Nor must we confuse it with *philosophy of mind*, as Ryle does, leading him to wonder why Husserl should accord such a 'privileged position'[8] to philosophy of mind as against all the other branches of philosophy (1971: 181-2). Husserl took from Brentano the basic thesis that consciousness is *intentional*,[9] that is, it has the 'universal fundamental property' of being '*of* something; as *cogito*, to bear within itself its *cogitatum*' (*CM* 72); to perceive or imagine or recollect was to perceive, imagine or recollect *something*, namely what Husserl called the 'intentional object'. Thus, the systematic study of consciousness – 'intentional analysis' – was twofold: it is not confined to exploring 'the modes of consciousness (for example: perception, recollection, retention)' (*CM* 75), something that it *does* share with philosophy of mind; it also produces descriptions of the intentional objects 'as such', be they material objects, melodies or numbers.[10] Moreover, consciousness is not just the subject-matter of phenomenology but also, in the form of 'pure reflection', a key to its *method*.

A central finding is that consciousness '*constitutes*' its objects, differently for each category of object (*CM* §20); this deeply troublesome word is intimately linked to two other important Husserlian terms: *synthesis* and *horizon*. Together, they are getting at the idea that the subject is active in the constitution of the *unity* or *identity* of an object; for example, the identity of a material object such as a die through variations in perceptual perspective:

> I see in pure reflection that 'this' die is given continuously as an objective unity in a multiform and changeable multiplicity of manners of appearing, which belong determinately to it . . . they flow away in the unity of a synthesis, such that in them 'one and the same' is intended as appearing. (*CM* 77-8)

The sides of the die not currently 'genuinely perceived' are none-theless 'co-intended' or 'also meant'; they are inextricably part of the perception of the 'seen' side and form that side's 'horizons' (cf. *CM* §19).

The phenomenological reduction (epoché).[11] Husserl begins by defining what he calls 'the natural standpoint', according to which I find the 'spatio-temporal fact-world' 'to *be out there, and also take it just as it gives itself to me as something that exists out there*' (*Ideas* §30). The phenomenological *epoché* is a matter of 'bracketing' or 'putting out of action' this general thesis of the natural standpoint. In 'putting this thesis out of action', he stresses, 'I do *not* then *deny* this "world", as though I were a sophist, *I do not doubt that it is there* as though I were a sceptic'; rather, I simply bar myself '*from using any judgement that concerns spatio-temporal existence*' (*Ideas* §32). (The phenomenological reduction is often read as a first cousin to Descartes' 'suspension of judgement' on his 'preconceived opinions' at the beginning of the *Meditations*.) The aim of this enterprise is both negative – avoiding presuppositions – and positive – opening up a new realm for exploration: namely, the intentional objects and the different modes of consciousness implied by the fact that conscious-ness is intentional.

We philosophers are almost bound to ask: how does Husserl get rid of those brackets? How does he re-establish contact with the 'external world' whose existence we assume from the natural stand-point? The answer appears to be that he does not; and on this basis he is often read as asserting some variety of *idealism*, according to which, all there *is* is a world of intentional objects 'constituted' by consciousness. It is this implication that seems to put Husserl's philosophy at odds with Heidegger's and that Merleau-Ponty's reconciling project seeks to resist, as we will see.

Essences and the eidetic reduction. The phenomenological reduc-tion becomes in Husserl's hands also an 'eidetic reduction' which gets at the essence (*eidos*, hence the term 'eidetic') of these modes of consciousness and intentional objects. This reduction, which gets us from facts to essences (*Ideas*, Introduction), makes use of the tech-nique of 'free imaginative variation' (see *Ideas* §70), that is, crudely, imagining variations to the object under consideration, and seeing what can and cannot change while the object remains the same object; whatever cannot change without changing the identity of the object is essential.[12]

There are many other Husserlian themes that resonate through-out *PP*; I end by simply flagging up two later themes, which play a role in the Preface to *PP*. One is the *life-world* (*Lebenswelt*), which 'for us who wakingly live in it, is always already there ... the "ground" of all praxis whether theoretical or extratheoretical' (*Crisis* 142) and the linked notion of the *Umwelt* ('environment', 'environing world' or 'surrounding world': see *CM* 160ff.).[13] In Merleau-Ponty's view, the whole of Heidegger's *Being and Time* 'springs from an indication given by Husserl and amounts to no more than an explicit account of ... the "Lebenswelt" which Husserl, towards the end of his life, identified as the central theme of phenomenology' (*PP* vii/viii).[14] The second is his consideration of 'the problem of the other', which occupies the Fifth Cartesian Meditation; as we will see, Merleau-Ponty sees the very fact that Husserl recognizes the existence of other subjects as problematic demonstrates that he is *not* an idealist.

Martin Heidegger (1889–1976)

Heidegger was educated by the Jesuits and was intended for the priesthood. He came across a book of Brentano's while a student at the Gymnasium in Constance, and later, studying theology at Freiburg University, read Husserl's *Logical Investigations*. Once ill health drove him away from the novitiate, he began studying phi-losophy in earnest, mostly, at that time, ancient and scholastic philosophy.

Heidegger got to know Husserl in person when the latter assumed the Chair of Philosophy at Freiburg in 1916. Husserl was full of admiration for Heidegger's 'clarity of vision, clarity of heart and clear sense of purpose', and wrote to him: 'To be young like you! What a joy and a real tonic' (quoted in Safranski 1998: 84). In 1919, Heidegger became Husserl's assistant and began lecturing at Freiburg as a Privatdozent. These lectures were critical of 'Husserl's prioritisation of the realm of the theoretical over the engaged, lived moment in experience' and of his 'flight from historical "factical" existence into transcendental idealism'. He 'rapidly developed a reputation as an extraordinary teacher ... To the post-war genera-tion of students he seemed to be defining and confronting the intellectual crisis which they were experiencing in their own lives'. (Moran 2000: 205)

This notion of 'crisis' requires comment if we are to understand the backdrop to Heidegger's ascendancy over Husserl. The term 'crisis hysteria' has been applied to this period in German history (Spiegelberg 1969: 78), although 'crises' have been sensed at various periods and in various places and we must not assume even that this crisis manifested itself homogeneously. Spengler's *Decline of the West* (2 Vols., 1918–1922) was a prominent articulator of this crisis. At its heart was the status and social role of science. The theoretical puzzles (the theory of relativity, quantum theory) encountered within that seemingly foundational and most secure of all sciences, physics, contributed to the sense of crisis; it seemed that there was 'no longer any good reason for accepting the word of science as the final answer to all conceivable questions' (Spiegelberg 1969: 78). Husserl, as we know, was critical even in his middle period of the 'naturalism' in science, which insisted on seeing everything there is as physical; when coupled with the 'positivism', which confined itself to the collection of 'mere positive facts', it bespoke 'the incapacity and unwillingness of science to face problems of value and meaning' (Spiegelberg 1969: 80): 'Merely fact-minded sciences make merely fact-minded people' (*Crisis* 6). Husserl himself latched onto the *word* 'crisis' in the major work of his later period (as well as the Vienna Lecture); however, unlike Heidegger, he saw the 'crisis' as a crisis *for science* as much as for the rest of us: 'the loss of its meaning for life' (*Crisis* 5). For him, the solution was not to turn away from science but to bring science back to its 'rigorous' roots through the 'rigorous science' of phenomenology. The logic of this move was lost on the students of the time, who found that Heidegger's approach spoke to them more directly. (See also the Coda to Ch. 2.)

Heidegger attained a post at Marburg as Professor Extraordinarius in 1923, and soon after, began work on his masterpiece *Being and Time*. Published in 1927, it was dedicated to Husserl, even though Heidegger told Jaspers that 'if the book was directed *against* anyone it was Husserl' (Moran 2000: 207). Husserl only read it properly after his retirement in 1929, but it shattered their collegial relationship: 'As Husserl saw it, Heidegger had abandoned entirely phenomenology's aspiration to raise and answer transcendental questions, to become a "rigorous science", and has settled instead for a puffed-up anthropology' (Cerbone 2006: 40). To this must of course be added Heidegger's involvement with Nazism, since

Husserl had lost his academic position in the Nazi effort to purge German universities of Jewish intellectuals.

BT is a big book, and in its original plan was to be even bigger; the book we know as *BT* is the first two (of three) Divisions of the first of two envisioned parts. 'Heidegger was of the view that a philosopher has only a single deep thought, which he or she constantly struggles to express' (Moran 2000: 195); Heidegger's 'deep thought' was the question of the meaning of Being, a question that philosophers had 'forgotten' since ancient Greek times. Addressing this question required taking as its starting point the 'vague average understanding' (*BT* 5) of Being possessed by the being which is such that 'in its very Being, that Being is an *issue* for it' (*BT* 12), namely *human beings*. Heidegger's usual term for human beings was *Dasein*, literally 'there-being', reminding us that human beings are *thrown into* the world, at a particular place and time, a place and time not of their choosing.

The requisite method for getting at this vague understanding of the meaning of Being was, according to Heidegger, phenomenology: he quotes phenomenology's watchword 'To the things themselves!', which, as he notes, at first sight appears 'self-evident' and 'the underlying principle of any scientific knowledge whatsoever' (*BT* 28). The issue, however, is the nature of this 'self-evidence', and this leads him into an etymological exploration of the term 'phenomenology' and a 'preliminary conception' (*BT* 28-39), ending in an understanding of phenomenology which differed substantially from that of its founder. He either drops or reinterprets all of Husserl's central concepts.

For example, whereas Husserl's conception of intentionality was a structure of consciousness, Heidegger eschews the term 'consciousness' altogether and makes intentionality into *practical* encounters with 'environmental things' (*Umweltdinge*; see above re: the term *Umwelt* or 'environment'). These environmental things are encountered, primarily and for the most part, as 'ready-to-hand' (*Zuhanden*), rather than simply there to be studied or inspected ('present-at-hand' or *Vorhanden*). The basic state of Dasein is what Heidegger calls *In-der-Welt-sein*: being-in-the-world; this compound expression 'indicates in the very way we have coined it [that it] stands for a unitary phenomenon' (*BT* 53); there is no understanding humans without simultaneously understanding the world in which they dwell, or vice versa. The Being of Dasein is gradually revealed as *care* (cf. *BT* 182); we are not mere spectators: to be in-the-world is for the world to have significance for us. As we will see, Merleau-Ponty, while retaining the word 'consciousness', whole-heartedly embraces the notion of being-in-the-world.

There is a great deal more to Heidegger's analysis, but this is sufficient to enable us to get an inkling of what makes Heidegger's an 'existential philosophy' and how this may appear to put his philosophy at odds with Husserl's. Kant famously called it 'a scandal of philosophy and human reason in general' that there is still no cogent proof for the existence of things outside us that will silence the sceptic (quoted in *BT* 203), and proposed his own proof. Heidegger rejoined that the true 'scandal of philosophy' 'is not that this proof has yet to be given, but that *such proofs are expected and attempted again and again*' (*BT* 205). The starting-point for any such attempted proof, including Kant's, is that that whose existence is to be proved – the 'external world' – is understood as independent of and external to the Being who is attempting the proof – that is, Dasein (*BT* 205); in short such attempts 'presuppose a subject which is proximally *worldless* or unsure of its world' (*BT* 206). The notion of Dasein as being-in-the-world precisely denies that presupposition. The existence of the 'subject' and that of the world are internally related and inextricably interlinked. This *seems* to place him radically at odds with Husserl: Husserl's phenomenological reduction, understood as a bracketing or 'putting out of action' the 'thesis' of the existence of the world, apparently makes the very presupposition which Heidegger rejects. Hence the need for Merleau-Ponty's reconciling project.

ii. MERLEAU-PONTY'S 'RECONCILING PROJECT'

On the face of it at least, Merleau-Ponty looks to Husserl as the fountainhead of phenomenology; yet he also admires certain aspects of Heidegger. The difficulty he faces is that these two great thinkers *appear* to have different and incompatible conceptions of phenomenology: 'Phenomenology is the study of essences . . . But phenomenology also puts essences back into existence . . . It is a transcendental philosophy which places in abeyance the assertions arising out of the natural attitude . . . but it is also a philosophy for which the world is always "already there" before reflection begins'.

One possibility, as he notes, would simply be to say that there are two sorts of phenomenology, Husserl's and Heidegger's, one being an idealism or even a 'transcendental idealism' and the other an 'existential philosophy'; but this will not do: after all, Heidegger's work is at bottom an elaboration of Husserl's notion of the *Lebenswelt*. This, however, seems to imply the intolerable conclusion that 'the contradiction reappears in Husserl's own philosophy'. All this carries the risk that the reader will 'give up the idea of covering a doctrine which says everything, and will wonder whether a philosophy which cannot define its scope deserves all the discussion which has gone on around it'. (*PP* vii/vii-viii)

For Merleau-Ponty, there is only one way out of this impasse: to offer an interpretation of Husserl which both renders him consistent within himself and implies that Husserlian phenomenology, despite its appearance of entailing some form of idealism, is after all an existential philosophy and is, to that extent at least, compatible with Heidegger's.[15] To this end, he takes four 'celebrated phenomenological themes' from Husserl and offers his own distinctive gloss, in the light of which there is no inconsistency either within Husserl or between Husserl and (the relevant aspects of) Heidegger. The main body of the Preface to *PP* is straightforwardly structured around these four themes in this order: 'To the things themselves', the phenomenological reduction, essences and the eidetic reduction, and intentionality. Since the second and third are the most relevant to Merleau-Ponty's reconciling project, I elaborate them here; the first and fourth (and part of the second), most relevant to revealing Merleau-Ponty's own positive contribution, are developed in §iii.

Let us begin by offering some sort of definition of *idealism* and *transcendental idealism*, beginning with the latter. Since Kant is the philosopher most associated with this position, we can begin with a brief sketch (intolerably crude, no doubt, to Kant scholars) of Kant's overall view:

(i) There is an internal 'world' of *phenomena*, that is, the 'world' of experience (represented appearances), which is shaped by the categories of our understanding and hence is entirely transparent to us.

(ii) There is in addition (as a condition of the possibility of the 'world' of phenomena) an external world of *noumena* – things as they are in themselves – which is entirely beyond ('transcends') our experience.

'Idealism' (without the qualifier) may then be characterized as simply accepting (i) while rejecting (ii).

Husserl's failure to 'remove the brackets' of the phenomenological reduction might seem to commit him simply to idealism (without the qualifier); at the same time, he famously asserts that 'Phenomenology is *eo ipso "transcendental idealism"*' (*CM* 86). Yet, neither position is compatible with Heidegger's *existential philosophy*, which we can provisionally characterize thus:

(iii) *The* world is *neither* 'internal' nor 'external'.

Merleau-Ponty's reconciling project consists in showing that Husserl can be understood in such a way as to reject (i) and (ii), and to embrace (iii).

The phenomenological reduction (*epoché*) (*PP* xi-xiv/xii-xvi)

A 'logically consistent transcendental idealism', Merleau-Ponty avers, simply identifies the world as 'precisely that thing of which we form a representation', and thus it 'rids the world of its opacity and its transcendence': hence a) there is nothing to the world *beyond* or *outrunning* our representations, and b) transcendental idealism 'knows nothing of the problem of other minds' (since in a certain sense I and the other are *one and the same*, unified in virtue of representing the world via the same set of categories), thus cannot recognize that the Other is a *paradox*: both 'me' and 'not-me'.[16] The term 'world' here is ambiguous between the ' "world" ' of (i) and the 'world' of (ii). Given that Merleau-Ponty is going to reject the distinction, it *has* to be; but we can for present purposes see these two hallmarks of transcendental idealism as spelling out the implications of (i) above.

Merleau-Ponty's argument then amounts to this: that since Husserl does not fit these two hallmarks; he cannot be a true transcendental idealist. Somewhat disconcertingly, in this section, Merleau-Ponty actually only develops the point that Husserl fails to fit b): he notes that Husserl acknowledged that 'there is a problem of other people, and the *alter ego* is a paradox'. (This was the problem that occupied the Fifth *Cartesian Meditation*.) However, in the next section, we find Merleau-Ponty saying that 'I am in communication with [the world], but I do not possess it; it is inexhaustible' (*PP* xvii/xix) – that is, that the world *does* 'outrun our representations'. For evidence that Husserl too held such a view, we might take his central notion of *horizons* as implying that the world 'outruns our representations',[17] and hence that he also fails to fit a). After all, part of my perception of the die is my awareness of its *unseen* sides: 'Things "seen" are always more than what we "really and actually" see of them' (*Crisis* 51). So, Merleau-Ponty can make a powerful case for saying that Husserl is not an idealist of any sort since he does not fit clause (i) of the definition given above. He concludes that far from being idealistic, the Husserlian *cogito* 'must reveal me in a situation . . . as being-in-the-world'. Instead of being 'a procedure of idealistic philosophy, phenomenological reduction belongs to existential philosophy'. We can read this as entailing that the world is not an 'internal' world: it, and others, outrun our representations. Merleau-Ponty gives a particular twist to the term 'transcendent' that makes it the *equivalent* of 'outrunning our representations' (e.g., 'When I say that things are transcendent, this means that I do not possess them, that I do not circumambulate them', *PP* 369/430). Thus we can say:

(iii'): The world is not an 'internal' world: it, and others, 'transcend' our representations.

Essences and the eidetic reduction (*PP* xiv-xvii/xvi-xix)

Husserl goes beyond the phenomenological reduction to an 'eidetic reduction': 'we cannot subject our perception of the world to philosophical scrutiny . . . without passing from the fact of our existence to its nature [essence]'. However, Merleau-Ponty wants to claim that 'the essence is here not the end, but a means, that our effective involvement with the world is precisely what has to be understood and made amenable to conceptualization'. This is his attempt to reconcile the idea that 'phenomenology is the study of essences' with the idea that 'phenomenology also puts essences back into existence', and thereby to provide a Heideggerean reading of Husserl.

Merleau-Ponty considers the essence of the perceived world and of perception, an example which intersects with the issue of scepticism about the so-called external world.[18] He uses this to critique both what he calls 'sensationalism' (something like Berkeleyan idealism) and transcendental idealism. These two movements of thought try to avoid scepticism, respectively, by claiming that 'after all we never experience anything but states of ourselves', and by regarding the world 'as thought or consciousness of the world'. But these sidestep scepticism by making the world 'immanent in consciousness'; they thereby 'overlook the phenomenon of the world'. Husserl's eidetic reduction, by contrast, is 'the determination to bring the world to light as it is . . . to make reflection emulate the unreflective life of consciousness'. Thus, Merleau-Ponty urges that 'we must not wonder whether we really perceive a world, we must instead say: the world is what we perceive . . . To seek the essence of perception is to declare that perception is, not presumed true, but defined as access to truth'. (Cf. *PP* 374/435-6: 'Perception and the perceived necessarily have the same existential modality . . . Any contention that the perception is indubitable, whereas the thing perceived is not, must be ruled out'.) This amounts to a rejection, on Husserl's as well as his own behalf, of (ii), and can be read positively as entailing:

(iii") The world is not an external world: human beings and the world are internally related, we are Being-in-the-world.

How plausible is this as a reading of Husserl? I have no wish to enter the depths of Husserl scholarship on this topic.[19] Let us simply note that a statement that might appear to entail some type of idealism – '[t]he attempt to conceive the universe of true being as something lying outside the universe of possible consciousness . . . the two being related merely externally by a rigid law, is nonsensical' (*CM* 84) – can straightforwardly be read as entailing (iii").[20] This amounts to reading it in the light of Heidegger's remarks (see earlier) on the true 'scandal of philosophy'.

Note that (iii") (The world is not an external world: human beings and the world are internally related, we are Being-in-the-world) together with (iii') (The world is not an 'internal' world: it, and others, 'transcend' our representations) both entail and give substantive content to our earlier provisional characterization of *existential philosophy*: (iii): The world is *neither* 'internal' nor 'external'. (Cf. 'there is a paradox of immanence and transcendence in perception. Immanence, because the perceived object cannot be foreign to him who perceives; transcendence, because it always contains more than what is actually given', *PrP* 16.) This also helps us make sense of Merleau-Ponty's characterization of the 'chief gain of phenomenology' as having 'united extreme subjectivism and extreme objectivism'. (*PP* xix/xxii)

iii. MERLEAU-PONTY'S DISTINCTIVE CONTRIBUTIONS: FIRST GLIMPSES

Thus far we have seen Merleau-Ponty's endeavours to demonstrate that Husserl is not, after all, an idealist; this argument was made in connection with two of the four 'celebrated phenomenological themes' which form the scaffolding of the Preface. In this section, we look first at Merleau-Ponty's positive understanding of the phenomenological reduction (the second theme; our earlier discussion was focused on how it was *not* to be understood in his view). We then examine Merleau-Ponty's distinctive take on the first theme, phenomenology's watchword 'To the things themselves', which signals the two dominant polemical targets of *PP*, viz. empiricism and intellectualism, and on the fourth theme, intentionality; together these indicate certain uniquely Merleau-Pontyan themes.

The phenomenological reduction: Merleau-Ponty's interpretation (*PP* xiii-xiv/xiv-xvi)

What role does the phenomenological reduction play once we have clarified that it does not require us to be idealists? Merleau-Ponty explains that it is not a matter of *rejecting* 'the certainties of common sense and a natural attitude', but of 'refusing them our complicity', 'putting them "out of play"', 'suspending our recognition' of them, 'being filled with wonder at them' or 'breaking our familiar acceptance of them'. From this perspective, the phenomenological reduction invites comparison, not to Descartes' suspension of judgement on the existence of the external world, but to Wittgenstein's (1968 §129) efforts to render visible what is invisible because of its very familiarity. (Flynn here draws an analogy with the Russian formalists' claim that 'the function of poetic language is to "defamiliarize" language', 2004: 8.)[21] Merleau-Ponty has various strategies for bringing this about, including, most characteristically, the description of pathological experience or of the experience of subjects in strange experimental settings, which illuminates the familiar by way of contrast. (We will see examples in Chs. 3–5; we will also see that there are additional uses to descriptions of 'abnormal' experience.)[22]

'To the things themselves' (*PP* viii-xi/ix-xii)

Merleau-Ponty elaborates phenomenology's watchword by noting that phenomenology 'is a matter of describing, not explaining or analysing'. We have seen already, in a general way at least, what phenomenological description involves. The crucial point here is what phenomenology does *not* involve.

So, first, the insistence that phenomenology is not in the business of 'explanation' indicates Merleau-Ponty's critique of empiricism and what is sometimes called 'scientism' (see the Coda to Ch. 2), what he calls here 'scientific points of view'. According to scientism, I 'am nothing but a bit of the world, a mere object of biological, psychological or sociological investigation'. His objections to this outlook echo Husserl's critique of 'naturalism'. Husserl asserts that all natural science (and he extends this to include psychology) 'is naïve in regard to its point of departure. The nature that it will investigate is for it simply there' (*PRS* 85). Merleau-Ponty also charges scientism with naiveté, adding the charge of *dishonesty* – I almost want to say 'bad faith' (see the Coda to Ch. 6) – because scientism takes for granted, without bothering to mention it, 'the point of view of consciousness', that is, the very humanity of its practitioners, and the fact that '[t]he whole universe of science is built upon the world as directly experienced'. On this basis, Merleau-Ponty offers his first interpretation of the phenomenological battle-cry: 'To return to things themselves is to return to that world which precedes knowledge, of which knowledge always *speaks*, and in relation to which every scientific schematization is . . . abstract'.

Secondly, Merleau-Ponty's denial that phenomenology is in the business of analysing signals his critique of what he here calls 'analytical reflection' (i.e., intellectualism, rationalism and transcendental idealism). He mentions Descartes and Kant by name here, and he forwards two basic objections: first, they *detach* the subject – what they see as the mind or thinker – from the world, rather than seeing the relation between subject and world as 'strictly bilateral'. (If those relations were seen as bilateral, then the certainty of the world would be given with that of the Cartesian *cogito*, 'and Kant would not have talked about his "Copernican revolution"'). Secondly, although in some sense the intellectualists do 'restore' the world afterwards, instead of an account of our actual experience of the world, they offer us 'a reconstruction', a simulacrum, made up of 'judgements, acts or predications'. A particularly telling example is this: Descartes, at the end of the *Meditations*, restores the 'real' world by reassuring us that we can tell it from dreams by virtue of its coherence with itself and with past experience; but this would suggest that 'I ought to be forever hesitant', constantly checking to make sure what I am seeing coheres; yet our conviction of reality is immediate. Moreover, how 'coherent' is the perceived world? 'The real . . . does not await our judgement before incorporating the most surprising phenomena, or before rejecting the most plausible figments of our imagination'.

The truth of the matter, then, is that the relation between subject and world is 'strictly bilateral' (*per* the phrase 'being-in-the-world'), and that '[t]he world is there before any possible analysis of mine', 'not an object such that I have in my possession the law of its making'. So, '[t]ruth does not inhabit the "inner man", or more accurately, there is no *inner* man, man is in the world'.[23] Thus, to return 'to the things themselves' after these intellectualist excursions is, in a sense, to return to *oneself* as 'a subject destined to the world'.

We will learn about empiricism and intellectualism in much more detail in the next chapter, but Beauvoir summarizes them beautifully here:

> Empiricism, like intellectualism, separates the world from consciousness; in order to succeed thereafter in reuniting them, one asked consciousness to abdicate before the opacity of the real; the other dissolved the real in the light of consciousness, and in the end, both failed to give an account of that unique experience: the consciousness of the real. (2004 [1945]: 160)

Intentionality (*PP* xvii-xix/xix-xxii)

The core idea of intentionality for Merleau-Ponty is a matter of *recognizing consciousness itself as a project of the world*, meant for a world which it neither embraces nor possesses, but towards which it is perpetually directed.' This characterization looks like a kind of compromise between Husserl's own characterization of intentionality as the 'universal fundamental property' of consciousness, as being *of* something, and Heidegger's practical encounters with environmental things; but it is a compromise for which Merleau-Ponty finds justification in Husserl himself: he highlights Husserl's distinction between the *intentionality of act,* 'that of our judgements and of those occasions when we voluntarily take up a position' and *operative intentionality,* 'that which produces the natural and antepredicative [pre-conceptual] unity of the world and of our life' (*PP* xviii/xx; cf. *PP* 418/486). Kant, he tells us, only recognizes the first; Husserl's originality lies 'in the discovery, beneath the intentionality of representations, of a deeper intentionality, which others have called *existence'* (*PP* 121 n.5/140 n.54). In other words, Husserl's great discovery was *operative* intentionality, and operative intentionality amounts to Heidegger's pre-conceptual, practical engagement in the world. Eventually, we see that this 'basic intentionality' has two bilaterally related faces: what Merleau-Ponty calls 'motor intentionality' (see Ch. 3iii), in virtue of which '[c]onsciousness is in the first place not a matter of "I think that" but of "I can"' (*PP* 137/159) and the 'non-thetic awareness' which plays a crucial role in perception (see Ch. 4i).

Some distinctively Merleau-Pontyan themes

Merleau-Ponty has often been seen as 'the philosopher of the *ambiguous';*[24] he might with equal justice be called the philosopher of the *'between'*, of the *reciprocal*, of the *indeterminate* and of the *pre-conceptual*. I will not try to define these here, but simply gesture in their direction.

We will see throughout the book a number of examples of what I will sometimes call 'between'-concepts: for example, motor intentionality is 'between' mere movement and thought about movement (see Ch. 3iii); the 'motives' of perception lie 'between' the intellectualist notion of reason and the empiricist notion of cause (see Ch. 4i). In a different sense of 'between', several of his central concepts are explicitly prefixed with 'inter-' (intersubjectivity, the interworld, etc.).

The notion of the reciprocal we have already seen in his complaint that intellectualism fails to recognize that the relation between subject and world is 'strictly bilateral'; it is also present in the notion of 'internal relation' by which he opposes empiricism's strictly 'external' relations of causation and association (see Ch. 2i). We will also (in Ch. 5iv) see a notion of 'bodily reciprocity' which underlies interpersonal understanding.

The ideas of the indeterminate and the pre-conceptual are characteristic markers of Merleau-Ponty's critiques of intellectualism in particular. We have glimpsed the notion of the pre-conceptual in his commitment to the 'primacy of perception': perception is prior to judgements or predications, hence the intellectualists' efforts to reconstruct the perceived world via judgements and concepts are fundamentally misguided. We have also seen it in his lauding Husserl's operative intentionality, which produces 'antepredicative' or pre-conceptual unity, over the intentionality of act which is that of judgements and predications. The notion of indeterminacy (see Ch. 2iii) is connected with the 'horizons' in virtue of which the world 'outruns' or 'transcends' our representations (see earlier) and thence with his insistence on the 'inexhaustibility' of the world ('[t]he world is not what I think, but what I live through. I am open to the world . . . but I do not possess it; it is inexhaustible', *PP* xvi-xvii/xviii-xix) and the unfinished and unfinishable nature of phenomenology: 'The most important lesson which the reduction teaches us is the impossibility of a complete reduction' (*PP* xiv/xv). Again, '[t]he unfinished nature of phenomenology . . . [was] inevitable because phenomenology's task was to reveal the mystery of the world and of reason' (*PP* xxi/xxiii-xxiv).

iv. CODA: WHAT PHENOMENOLOGY IS NOT

There are a number of uses of the term 'phenomenology' in the Anglo-American philosophical literature that have little to do directly with phenomenology as practiced by the phenomenologists, and a number of widespread misconceptions about phenomenology which may positively mislead students; this Coda is intended as a prophylactic.[25]

Appearance and reality. As soon as Anglo-American philosophers learn that phenomenology is to do with 'appearances' (see *BT* 28ff, *BN* Introduction), they are apt to hear this in connection with a ready-made distinction between 'appearance and reality': phenomenology, they will suppose, describes how things appear to us, as *opposed* to how they really are. (This despite J.L. Austin's best efforts to remind us that 'appearance' is by no means always contrasted with 'reality', nor *vice versa*, 1962, esp. §IV.) This reading is all too often combined with a conception of 'how things really are' that is set by *science*. The idea that science has a monopoly on reality is a central dimension of what is often called 'scientism' and is subject to wide-ranging criticism by the phenomenologists (see the Coda to Ch. 2). Nor, however, should we take phenomenology as subscribing to a kind of 'naïve realism' which has nothing to say about illusions; see Ch. 2iii.

'What is it like . . .?' The term 'phenomenology' was used by Thomas Nagel in his seminal 1974 article 'What is it like to be a bat?' and there is a continuous tradition of use among Anglo-American philosophers stemming (although also departing) from Nagel. Nagel himself used the term 'phenomenology' in a sense not too distant from that of the phenomenologists: as a proposed *method,* requiring a *new set of concepts*, to enable us to *describe* the 'subjective character of experience'. However, the term was taken up more or less as a *synonym* for the 'subjective character of experience', so that to talk about the 'phenomenology of pain' is just to talk about the subjective character of the experience of pain. Some philosophers of mind today are moving to replace the term in this usage with the more accurate term 'phenomenality'.

'Qualia'. This post-Nagelian tradition of usage has tended to merge with another tradition in which the subjective character of experience gets reified, that is, transformed into a set of quasi-*things,* often called 'qualia' [singular: quale], which are then taken to have further features: for example, to be atomic, ineffable and accessible (incorrigibly, through introspection) only to the person who has them. (Key reading includes Block 1980, Dennett 1991, and Flanagan 1992, but the literature is vast.) It is difficult to see *any* point of contact between phenomenology proper and this notion of qualia; the phenomenologists will resist both the reification of the character of experience and the idea that introspection is the means for 'accessing' experience. (See Ch. 2 and below.)

'Sense-data', phenomenalism. There is a use of the term 'phenomenology' which originates in the logical positivism of the Vienna Circle, according to which sense-data are the source of knowledge. These sense-data (taken up by Ayer and other Anglophone empiricists via the logical positivists) were supposed to be atomized elements of experience, more 'basic' than the physical objects in terms of which we ordinarily describe our experience. This conception has

a tenuous historical connection to phenomenology proper, inasmuch as Rudolf Carnap, a leading light of the Vienna Circle, attended some of Husserl's lectures. However, the notion of such experiential atoms is as distant as it could possibly be from the phenomenological conception; indeed it bears a marked resemblance to the first conception of sensation attacked by Merleau-Ponty in the Introduction to *PP* (see Ch. 2ii).[26] Since the term 'phenomenalism' (easily enough confused with 'phenomenology') generally refers to the view that objects are collections of actual and possible *sense-data*, the same point applies.

   '*Phenomenological reflection as introspection*'. There seems to be a widespread belief – usually on the part of critics – that *introspection* is the central methodological tool of phenomenology. (This supposition may stem in part from the fact that the focus of phenomenology is *experience*, together with a confusion about what phenomenologists mean by 'experience', e.g., the idea that experience consists of 'qualia'; see *supra*.[27]) This is explicit in both Ryle (1971: 176–77) and Dennett (1991: 44), for example, and Dennett builds his well-known critique of what he takes to be phenomenology on this foundation. Husserl himself expended considerable effort *distinguishing* between introspection and reflection (e.g., *PRS* 115 ff.).[28] I leave the final word, however, to Merleau-Ponty. He refers to the notion (prevalent among those he refers to as 'classical psychologists' as well as many philosophers) that the 'object' which they study is "'without extension" and "accessible to one person only"' graspable only 'by means of a special kind of act, "internal perception" or introspection'. He notes that these 'objects' (impressions, sensations, sense-data) were *inexpressible*, so that 'the imparting of philosophical intuitions to others . . . reduced itself to a sort of incantation designed to induce in them' comparable experiences; meanwhile 'the philosopher himself could not be clearly aware of what he saw in the instant, since he would have had to think it, that is fix and distort it' (*PP* 57/66). However, '[t]he return to the phenomenal', that is, to the description of phenomena as practiced by the phenomenologists, 'presents none of these peculiarities' (*PP* 57/67).

CHAPTER 2

'INTELLECTUAL PREJUDICES' IN ANALYSES
OF PERCEPTION

The substantial Introduction to *PP* identifies certain fundamental
assumptions common to both empiricist and intellectualist psychologists and philosophers, assumptions that show up in their analyses of
perception and, as Merleau-Ponty argues, distort them.[1] Freeing ourselves from these assumptions clears the way to the 'return to phenomena' heralded in the title and the last chapter of the Introduction.

Merleau-Ponty, beginning in the Introduction, also engages with
the Gestalt psychologists.[2] These psychologists (in particular Max
Wertheimer, Kurt Koffka and Wolfgang Köhler) developed their theories, mainly in Germany, over roughly the same period as Husserl was
developing phenomenology, and to some degree in dialogue with
Husserl.[3] They worked within the same academic culture, 'one in
which the relation between philosophy and psychology was . . . problematic and conflicted' (Carman 2008: 20), and, like the later Husserl
and Heidegger (see Ch. 1), they developed their theories in response
to a perceived 'crisis'.[4] Merleau-Ponty credits Gestalt psychology
with 'its overcoming of the classical alternatives between objective
psychology and introspective psychology' (*SB* 183), which invites
comparison with Merleau-Ponty's remark that 'the chief gain of *phenomenology* is to have united extreme subjectivism and extreme objectivism' (*PP* xix/xxii, italics added). Most famous for their researches
on perception (and visual perception in particular), they, correctly in
Merleau-Ponty's view, focused our attention on a number of features
of the perceived world for which (as both they and he argue) empiricism has great difficulty accounting: for instance, the fact that even the
simplest item of perception is structured into *figure* and *background*.
(He refers to them as 'the very psychologists who described the world

as I did', *PrP* 23.) Since much of Merleau-Ponty's argument both here and later takes off from these features, §i sketches those 'Gestalt qualities' which are of particular importance for making sense of the critical parts of Merleau-Ponty's Introduction, many of which were also identified by Husserl.

I find it helpful in thinking about Merleau-Ponty's critiques of empiricist and intellectualist assumptions to begin with what is literally a *picture* (or set of linked pictures) of perception (Figures 2a–c below).[5] The first version – the Empiricist Picture (Figure 2a) – often strikes students as rather natural and obvious; indeed, I hope that it will. Figure 2a allows us to see graphically the assumptions made by empiricism; it also enables us to locate precisely the criticisms of the Empiricist Picture made by the Gestalt psychologists and by Merleau-Ponty himself.[6] The Empiricist Picture and these initial criticisms are brought out in §ii. Figures 2b and 1c are intellectualist variants on the Empiricist Picture; they, and Merleau-Ponty's initial criticisms of intellectualism, are treated in §iii. Figures 2a–c allow us to see graphically that the Intellectualist Pictures really are *variants* on the Empiricist Picture, that is, that there is a good deal they have in common. They also allow us to see graphically which assumptions remain unchallenged at this stage and hence to discern where Merleau-Ponty is going to dispute not just empiricism and intellectualism, but also Gestalt psychology and any other approaches to perception that share these assumptions (Chs. 3–5 develop these further criticisms). Finally, §iv highlights another Gestalt notion: that of a field, which will help orient us with respect to the notion of 'the phenomenal field' (*PP* Introduction: Ch. 4).

In the Introduction and elsewhere, Merleau-Ponty is highly critical of a number of *scientific* theories (scientific psychology here, both neurology and psychology in the remainder). This will raise a number of questions in the reader's mind: Is Merleau-Ponty 'anti-science'?[7] Does he see science as having anything to offer phenomenology? What gives him, a philosopher, the right to criticize science? And, are his criticisms of the science of his day not simply outdated? These questions are addressed in the Coda to this chapter.

i. GESTALT QUALITIES

What I am loosely labelling 'Gestalt qualities' are those qualities of the perceived object identified by the Gestalt psychologists and embraced by Merleau-Ponty not only as (roughly) correct descriptions of perceptual experience, but because they resist empiricist treatment. Many readers will be familiar with the sorts of pictures and diagrams with which the Gestalt psychologists illustrated some of their discoveries; perhaps the most famous are the so-called ambiguous pictures, for example, this one:

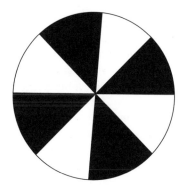

Figure 1 The double cross

Such pictures may undergo what the Gestalt psychologists call a 'reversal', what is popularly known as a 'Gestalt switch'. This particular ambiguous picture is an example of *figure-ground ambiguity*; the 'switch' is going from seeing a black cross (a figure) on a white background to seeing a white cross (another figure) against a black background. Note that in each case the background is seen to *continue beneath* the figure; additionally, although I have described the background as 'white' in the first case and 'black' in the second, the whiteness of the white cross is clearer and brighter than that of the background of the black cross, and conversely the blackness of the black cross is deeper and more solid than that of the background of the white cross. The figure is given as more 'solid' than the background, so that when one cross is playing the role of the figure, 'the area of this cross has a character of solidity and substantiality', while the background appears comparatively 'empty' or 'loose' or 'undifferentiated' (*GP* 120). Such reversals depend on a more fundamental Gestalt principle:

(i) *Figure-ground structure.* It is not just ambiguous pictures that exhibit this structure: 'a figure on a background is the simplest sense-given available to us' (*PP* 4/4). Even a simple white patch is always a figure on a background: all the points on the white patch 'belong together' as a 'circumscribed unit' from which the background is excluded, the background itself being undifferentiated (*GP*: 137)

(ii) *Significance.* A consequence of figure-ground structure is that even the simplest perception, such as the aforementioned white patch, is, in Merleau-Ponty's terms, *charged with meaning*

All the points in the patch have a certain 'function' in common: that of forming themselves into a 'shape'. The colour of the shape is more intense and as if it were more resistant than that of the background; the edges of the white patch 'belong' to it . . . the patch appears to be placed on the background and does not break it up. Each part arouses the expectation of more than it contains, and this elementary perception is therefore already charged with a *meaning.* (*PP* 4/4, cf. 13-14/15-16)

A remark on this notion of meaning: it is not one with which analytic philosophers would have much truck, as they tend to confine their use of the word 'meaning' to words and sentences (see Morris 2003: 163-4, Wrathall 2005: 114). This was one subject of the interchange between Merleau-Ponty and Ryle at Royaumont. Ryle had criticized Husserl – 'a bit naughtily' (*un peu méchamment*) in Merleau-Ponty's view – for having 'padded and inflated' the use of the word 'meaning' beyond 'that which a linguistic expression signifies'. Merleau-Ponty wanted to know whether Ryle would allow a distinction between *meaning* and *word-meaning* (Merleau-Ponty 1962: 93). Ryle's response was to say that he was perfectly well aware that one could say that the halo around the moon 'means' rain tomorrow or that the footprint in the sand on Robinson Crusoe's island 'meant' that Crusoe was not alone,[8] and '[f]ar be it from me to forbid anyone to use the words "to mean" or "meaning" in this enlarged sense', but this use of the word 'meaning' 'isn't of interest to the philosopher'. (Ryle 1962: 97). In one breathtaking sentence, Ryle dismisses the greater part of the life-world, 'the seat and as it were the *homeland* of our thoughts' (*PP* 24/28), as of no philosophical interest.

(iii) *Gestalten and 'horizons'.* The term *Gestalt,* though difficult to translate, indicates the idea that the objects of perception are '*segregated wholes*' or 'unities', and the object-horizon structure (which we touched on in our outline of Husserl in Ch. 1) is the correlate of this unity.[9] We can distinguish between:

'*Outer horizons*', indicating the figure-ground structure already sketched. Every perception of an object has a 'zone of *background intuitions*' which refer to what Husserl terms the 'outer horizons' of the object. These horizons are 'also "perceived", perceptually there, in the "field of intuition" . . . yet [are] not singled out, [are] not posited on their own account' (*Ideas* §35). Thus the object, say a lamp, stands out as a unified thing against the background.[10]

'*Inner horizons*', indicating the fact that objects are always given perspectively; at any given moment I 'genuinely see' only one side (in Husserl's terms, a 'profile' [*Abschattung*]) of the lamp; it could not be otherwise, since 'to see [is] always to see from somewhere' (*PP* 67/77). And 'there belongs to every external perception its reference from the "genuinely perceived" sides of the object of perception to the sides "also meant"' (*CM* §19): '[t]he hidden side is present in its own way . . . I am given, together with the visible sides of the object, the nonvisible sides as well' (*PrP* 14). Thus the lamp is given as a unified object, not simply a profile or a surface.

'*Temporal horizons*', strictly part of the inner horizons: 'my perceptual field itself . . . draws along in its wake its own horizon of retentions, and bites into the future with its protentions' (*PP* 416/484). 'Retention' and 'protention' are Husserlian terms indicating the horizon of the past and the horizon of the future respectively. If one were to move around the lamp, bringing a hitherto unseen profile into sight, the perception of the previous profile is 'retained': otherwise we would seem simply to be faced with disparate and unconnected fragments of perception, that is, not a unified object. Conversely, prior to moving around the lamp, the currently unseen profile is 'protended' or anticipated.[11]

(iv) '*Physiognomy*'. Perception, as Merleau-Ponty puts it, is 'physiognomic' (*PP* 132/152-3), so that 'the object "speaks" and is significant' (*PP* 131/151). As Beauvoir comments in her review of *PP*, 'one must not give these words a figurative or symbolic meaning . . . The most savage desert, the most hidden cave still secrete a human meaning' (2004: 162). This indicates an aspect of significance that goes beyond the significance of the white patch on the homogeneous background: it is an *immediate practical recognizability*: immediate, in that we *just recognize* a word, someone's handwriting or a fountain pen without having to *work out* what the thing is (as we *just recognize* someone's face from their literal physiognomy); 'practical' in the sense of not being 'intellectual' ('[t]he Gestalt of a circle is not its mathematical law but its physiognomy', *PP* 61/70). It is also 'practical' in the sense that the object, in virtue of this physiognomy, 'speaks to' our practical capabilities (see §iv below and Ch. 3iv and v).

(v) *Internal relations between qualities.* A further aspect of unity is that the various qualities of an object which one might be inclined to think of as separate or 'atomised' are given as inseparable. We might be tempted to think of the colour and the texture of a carpet as distinct 'atomic' qualities, but 'this red would literally not be the same if it were not the "woolly red" of a carpet' (*PP* 4-5/5; cf. *PP* 313/365, *SNS* 51); 'One sees the hardness and brittleness of glass . . . the springiness of steel [etc.]' (*PP* 229/267).

(vi) *The constancies* (colour constancy, shape constancy, size constancy, etc.). According to the Gestalt psychologists, perceived objects maintain their apparent size, shape, colour, etc. – and hence their unity – through variations in distance, orientation, lighting and so on. 'Suppose, while standing at a street corner, we see a man approaching us. Now he is ten yards away, and presently five . . . We shall be inclined to say that at both distances his visual size was approximately the same' (*GP* 44). Again, '[w]hen dining with friends, in what shapes do we see the plates on the table, to the left, to the right and opposite us? We shall be inclined to say that they are circular, just as our own plate' (*GP* 45). The sides of a perspective drawing of a cube are 'squares seen askew', not diamonds (*PP* 264/308).

One final quality has a special importance to Merleau-Ponty; it follows from the notion of horizons, although he has stressed it more than any other phenomenologist has.

(vii) *Indeterminacy.* 'The present still holds onto the immediate past *without positing it as an object* . . . The same is true of the imminent future' (*PP* 69/80, italics added); thus the immediate past and immediate future are part of our experience, horizonally, without being determinate. 'The region surrounding the visual field is not easy to describe, but . . . it is neither black nor grey. There occurs here an *indeterminate vision*, a *vision of je ne sais quoi*'. The background to the figure, as we have seen, possesses a kind of 'looseness' or lack of differentiation or indeterminacy; again, the hidden sides of the lamp are present in their own way, and, 'to take the extreme case, what is behind my back is not without some element of visual presence'. Thus, '[w]e must recognise the indeterminate as a positive phenomenon' (*PP* 6/7). See §iii.

ii. THE EMPIRICIST PICTURE

Because Merleau-Ponty's critique of empiricist accounts of perception takes off from the Gestalt psychologists' critique, we can begin there.

Empiricist psychology of the period under discussion may usefully be divided into two main camps: *Behaviourism* and *Introspectionism*. Both camps were characterized by a desire for psychology to be '*scientific*' (at least in part through doing experiments and looking down, as Husserl notes, on what they thought of as 'armchair psychology', *PRS* 92, 97). Merleau-Ponty subjects Behaviourism to severe criticism in his first book, *The Structure of Behaviour*, developing the critiques of the Gestalt psychologists: the well-known behaviourist James Watson reduces behaviour 'to the sum of reflexes and conditioned reflexes between which no intrinsic connection is admitted. But precisely this atomistic interpretation fails even at the level of the theory of the reflex', and *a fortiori* in connection with higher levels of behaviour, 'as Gestalt theory has clearly shown' (*SB* 4-5); likewise, Pavlov's notion of the conditioned reflex (*SB* 94ff.).[12] Köhler argues further that Behaviourism and Introspectionism have essentially the same structure (see also *PP* 7/8).We will however be focusing on Introspectionism rather than Behaviourism for present purposes, since Behaviourists do not really have a theory of *perception*.[13]

Before we describe experience, say the Introspectionists, 'we must learn to make the all-important distinction between *sensations* and *perceptions*, between the bare sensory material as such and the host of other ingredients with which this material has become imbued by processes of learning' (*GP* 43). The sensation is 'the genuine sensory fact', by contrast with those 'mere products of learning' (*GP* 44). This fundamental move *can* seem deeply attractive: it is easy to persuade ourselves that we cannot, strictly speaking, *see* a *book*, 'since this term ['book'] involves knowledge about a certain class of objects to which the present specimen belongs, about the use of such objects, and so forth' (*GP* 43). When we add to this move a bit of basic information about physics, optics and physiology of seeing – that it involves light, that is electromagnetic radiation, causally impacting on our retina, projecting an 'image' on the retina, simulating the rods and cones and so on – it can seem irresistible to assert that the 'genuine sensory fact' causally depends solely on the image on the retina, and that everything else which we *say* we see is not, strictly speaking, *seen* since it brings in further knowledge. We can diagram the Empiricist Picture of vision thus:

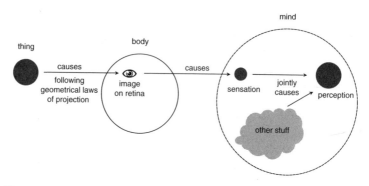

Figure 2a The Empiricist Picture

The Introspectionists thus insist that if we are to explore vision, we must try to ignore the *meaning* that comes about through knowledge and learning and to focus only on the actual sensations. 'The procedure by which this is achieved is called *introspection*' (*GP* 44). Consider the constancies of size and shape outlined in §i. From the Introspectionists' point of view, these so-called constancies are 'mere illusions, which must be destroyed if the true sensory phenomena are to appear'; we can overcome them if we 'assume the right analytical attitude' (*GP* 47) or by certain laboratory techniques and apparatus.[14] Our inclination to say that the plates across the table look circular is unacceptable to the Introspectionist, and to make this clear 'we must repeat the observation in the laboratory' (*GP* 44). The experimenter sets up two screens, on one of which – oblique to the direction of the eye – is a circle, on the second – perpendicular to the direction of the eye – is an ellipse. We will insist that the first looks circular, the second elliptical. He then sets up a third screen with two holes in it, 'through which we can see both forms, but which excludes the data by which the angles of the planes could at first be recognized. Now ... both look like ellipses. Thus the Introspectionist seems to have made his point' (*GP* 46) – and, adds Köhler, now 'you know what introspection means' (*GP* 45).

Köhler labels the distinction between the sensation and the perception as the *'empiristic hypothesis'*; he labels the posited direct dependence of the sensation on the retinal image as the *'constancy hypothesis'*, according to which 'the characteristics of true sensory experience depend only upon corresponding characteristics of peripheral stimuli' (*GP* 55). (This label carries the potential for confusion; we must not confuse *'the constancy hypothesis'*, an empiricist assumption which both Köhler and Merleau-Ponty criticize heavily, with *'the constancies'* – size constancy, shape constancy, etc. – which they take, contrary to empiricist psychologists, to be part of our perceptual experience.) Köhler's main concerns are the fact that these 'hypotheses' are never tested (see the Coda below), and the fact that '[o]nce an experience has had the misfortune of being . . . interpreted' as influenced by learning, the Introspectionists 'seem to take no more interest in its existence' (*GP* 51). As a consequence, they occupy themselves wholly with the *non-meaningful* layer of perception, viz., the sensation, thereby excluding from scientific study a rich realm of potential material: 'if this attitude were to prevail, such experiences as form the matrix of our whole life would never be seriously studied' (*GP* 51).

Merleau-Ponty's critique of empiricism draws directly on Köhler's, although it goes a great deal further. Like Köhler, he rejects the notion of sensation (*PP* Introduction: Ch. 1, 'The "sensation" as a unit of experience', is devoted to this task); and he embraces the phrase 'constancy hypothesis' as the shibboleth of empiricist (and even much intellectualist) psychology. Ch. 2 of the Introduction then considers the sorts of 'auxiliary hypotheses' which empiricist psychologists deploy in order to retain the constancy hypothesis in the face of recalcitrant phenomena (its title, '"Association" and the "projection of memories"', indicates two such auxiliary hypotheses).[15]

The "sensation" as a unit of experience. Merleau-Ponty's critique of apparently 'immediate and obvious' notion of sensation is more thoroughgoing than Köhler's: he begins by distinguishing three *different* conceptions of the sensation.

First, we might consider 'pure sensation' as 'the experience of an undifferentiated, instantaneous, dotlike impact' (*PP* 3/3). Not only does this correspond to nothing in our actual experience, it *could not* do *so*, argues Merleau-Ponty: 'a figure on a background is the simplest sense-given available', as we have seen, hence even the simplest sense-given has this structure and is thus 'charged with meaning' (*PP* 4/4).

A second attempt to define the sensation – the idea that 'to see is to have colours or light, to hear is to have sounds, to sense is to have qualities' (*PP* 4/5) – is equally untenable for different reasons. First, 'red and green are not sensations, they are the sensed . . . quality is not an element of consciousness but a property of the object' (*PP* 4/5); thus this conception of the sensation commits 'the experience error', by making properties of the object elements of consciousness (*PP* 5/5). And secondly, 'the quality is as rich and mysterious as the object', citing, for example, the internal relations *between* qualities which we noted in §i: 'this red would literally not be the same if it were not the "woolly red" of a carpet' (*PP* 4-5/5), so cannot be analysed down into the sensation of red *and* the sensation of wooliness.

At this stage, we must at least agree that there is (at least outside the laboratory)[16] no *experience* of sensation. But there is a third notion of sensation which invokes it as an *explanatory* concept located in the 'causes and objective origins' of experience (*PP* 7/8); this is the Introspectionists' concept of sensation. This conception begins by assuming that the world consists of 'fully developed and determinate' qualities and then assumes that the world 'passes on to the sense-organs messages which must be registered, and then deciphered in such a way as to reproduce in us the original text', so that 'we have in principle a point-by-point correspondence and constant connection between the stimulus and the elementary perception'. This, as Merleau-Ponty notes, is the 'constancy hypothesis' identified by Köhler as a fundamental assumption of empiricist psychology. Like Köhler, he shows that this conception 'conflicts with the data of consciousness' (*PP* 7/8); he cites 'colour constancy' as an example: 'a coloured area appears to be the same colour over the whole of its surface, whereas the chromatic thresholds of the different parts of the retina ought to make it red in one place, orange somewhere else, and in certain cases colourless', and concludes (like Köhler) that 'the "sensible" cannot be defined as the immediate effect of an external stimulus'.

By themselves, of course, such cases *refute* neither the sensation as a theoretical posit nor the constancy hypothesis. It is open to the psychologist to attempt to *explain away* these recalcitrant cases by invoking 'additional factors' as auxiliary hypotheses (*PP* 8/9). Some of these additional factors are considered in the next chapter of the Introduction.

'Association' and the 'projection of memories'. Merleau-Ponty's main concern in Ch. 2 of the Introduction is with the qualities of figure-ground (*PP* 13-15/15-18), the unity of the object (*PP* 15-17/18-20) and objects' possession of a 'physiognomy' (*PP* 17-22/20-26). Empiricist psychologists use 'association' and other items from the empiricist repertoire (e.g., resemblance, contiguity) to try to explain the first two and 'the projection of memories' to explain the third. However, as Merleau-Ponty argues, their explanations are hopeless.

We have seen already that even a simple white patch on a background is 'charged with meaning'. In order for the 'atomic sensation' 'to become integrated into an "outline" which is bound up with the "figure" and independent of "background"', it would have to cease to exist as a sensation (*PP* 14/16). If the empiricist should try to argue that we perceive the patch as having a certain *shape* (say, circular) in virtue of the fact that, through an 'association of ideas', the present data call up previous experiences which have taught me what a circle is, the answer is that any such association of ideas 'can restore only extrinsic connections' (*PP* 14/17).

We have also seen that objects are perceived as unities or 'wholes'. Merleau-Ponty pours cold water on the suggestion that the parts of a thing are held together through an association 'arising from their interrelatedness observed while the object is in movement', since we have never seen houses or mountains in motion and yet we perceive them as unities (*PP* 15/18). Nor will the empiricists' recourse to resemblance and contiguity succeed in explaining how wholes get grouped together (*PP* 16/19). This cannot begin to work, since to speak of resemblance or continuity is to speak of resemblance or continuity between things *already* perceived as unities; thus 'the unity of a thing in perception is not arrived at by association [even combined with resemblance and contiguity], but is a condition of association' (*PP* 17/19-20).

Empiricist psychologists may bring in the idea of 'projections of memory' to explain (for example) the speed at which people read: they reason that 'in the reading of a book the speed of the eye leaves gaps in the retinal impression, *therefore* the sense-data must be filled out by a projection of memories'. Here Merleau-Ponty reminds us that the words on the page have a *physiognomy*, and that no 'projection of memory' could happen in the first place *without* 'what is seen' 'so organiz[ing] itself as to present a picture to me in which I can recognize my former experiences'. But it was precisely this physiognomy, this 'self-organizing' of the perceived object, that the appeal to the projection of memories was supposed to explain (*PP* 19/22-3). Hence 'the "projection of memories" is nothing but a bad metaphor hiding a deeper, ready-made recognition' (*PP* 20/23). In short, '[w]hen we come back to phenomena we find, as a basic layer of experience, a whole already pregnant with an irreducible meaning: not sensations with gaps between them, into which memories may be supposed to slip' (*PP* 21-2/25).

What we have so far is detailed confirmation of the Gestalt psychologists' argument that empiricism, even with these auxiliary hypotheses, cannot make sense of the Gestalt properties outlined earlier. Empiricism 'succeeds in constructing only a semblance of subjectivity: it introduces sensations which are things, just where experience shows that there are meaningful patterns' (*PP* 11/12). We turn now to intellectualism.

iii. INTELLECTUALIST VARIANTS ON THE EMPIRICIST PICTURE

One central characteristic of intellectualism quite generally is its insistence that the *subject* is active in perception; hence, intellectualists are bound to feel uncomfortable with an empiricist picture which makes perception nothing but the causal outcome of retinal impingements plus 'learning'. With this much, Merleau-Ponty is in total agreement; but in the end, intellectualism is no better than empiricism and indeed shares many of its assumptions. There are two different versions of intellectualism which Merleau-Ponty considers, what we might call 'popular' and 'sophisticated'; they share the notion that *judgement* is central to perception.

Judgement and "the disunity of the senses". Merleau-Ponty begins (*PP* 32-6/37-42) by looking at a conception of perception popularized by intellectualist psychologists (cf. *PP* 46/54), according to which, perception *is interpretation* (cf. *PP* 37/42) or involves *judgement* or even *inference*. Judgement is introduced by these psychologists 'as *what sensation lacks in order to make perception possible*' (*PP* 32/37).

To take an example beloved of such intellectualists, the perception of *relief* (three-dimensionality) cannot depend wholly on the sensation, since sensation depends on the image on the retina and that image is two-dimensional. The 'popular intellectualist' psychologists may say that we arrive at the perception of relief by *inference* from 'the apparent size of the object, the number of objects interposed between it and us, the disparity of retinal images, the degree of [ocular] adjustment and convergence' and so on (*PP* 47/54). Thus 'relief seems obvious; yet it is *concluded* from an appearance which bears no resemblance to relief, namely from a difference between the appearances presented to our two eyes by the same things' (the intellectualist psychologist Alain, quoted in *PP* 33 n.1/38 n.17, emphasis added). We might diagram the conception of (visual) perception held by this version of intellectualism as a variant on Figure 2a.

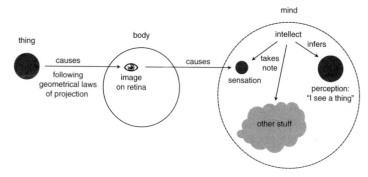

Figure 2b Popular intellectualist variant on the empiricist picture

We can see instantly that Figure 2b retains both the sensation and the constancy hypothesis which links the sensation to the image on the retina; thus all the critiques of empiricist psychology of perception will return to haunt this Picture. Moreover, the idea that we *infer* relief from 'the apparent size of the object, the number of objects interposed between it and us, the disparity of retinal images, the degree of [ocular] adjustment and convergence' seems to presuppose that we are 'expressly aware' of these items – yet normally we are not (*PP* 47/54; this example returns in Ch. 4i). Can a more sophisticated version of intellectualism do any better?

'Sophisticated' intellectualism (*PP* 36-41/42-8) looks more like the familiar philosophy of Descartes and Kant. This approach simply does away with the sensation altogether, and thereby the idea that perception is interpretation, since 'there is nothing prior for it to interpret' (*PP* 37/43), and asserts that perception is thought or judgement about perceiving (*PP* 38/44), or perhaps better, that it is the thought or judgement *that* one is perceiving (i.e., that one's bodily sense-organs are being causally affected by something in the world), a conception that readers may recognize from Descartes.

Sophisticated intellectualism distances itself further from both empiricism and popular intellectualism by criticizing another assumption implicit in Figures 2a and b: what we can call *the disunity of the senses*.[17] These figures represent *visual* perception: at its centre is the retina. Other sense modalities – touch, hearing and so on – would be diagrammed in a parallel fashion, with different sensory organs playing the central role. What does this imply about how these sense-modalities are related? Both empiricism and popular intellectualism reply that each sensory modality gives rise to different sensory data or sensations and thus that there must be 'purely visual data', 'purely tactile data' and so on (cf. *PP* 217-18/252-3). As Merleau-Ponty notes, this is entailed by the constancy hypothesis, 'because our body includes as a matter of fact sets of visual and auditory apparatus which are anatomically distinct and to which isolatable contents of consciousness are supposed [according to that hypothesis] to correspond' (*PP* 114/131-2). The empiricist imagines that ideas of whole objects are arrived at through a process of association, which, as we have seen, is hopeless. The popular intellectualist supposes that the subject interprets or makes a judgement about these disparate sensations so as to arrive at perceptions of whole objects; it will begin with these separate data and bring them together into an interpretation or 'act of intellectual synthesis': thus 'this lemon is a bulging oval shape with two ends *plus* this yellow colour *plus* this fresh feel *plus* this acidic taste' (*WP* 45).

We can see immediately that these accounts are incompatible with the internal relations between qualities noted in §i; the qualities of the lemon cannot be atomized: 'It is the sourness of the lemon which is yellow, it is the yellow of the lemon which is sour' (Sartre, quoted in *WP* 48). There is a correlate of this: that *the senses form a unity*. The very notion of a Gestalt *entails* that the senses form a unity: 'There never are isolated stimuli. There are only those stimuli which, together with more stimuli of the same – or other – sense modalities, form organized total patterns' (Katz, quoted in Mirvish 1983: 458).[18] 'My perception is therefore not a sum of visual, tactile, and audible data, I perceive in an undivided way with my whole being; I grasp a unique structure, a unique way of being, which speaks to all my senses at once' (*SNS* 50; cf. *PP* 119/137).

Here the sophisticated intellectualists will agree, although not on these grounds: while acknowledging that there are different sense-modalities, they will see this diversity as merely *a posteriori*; what is *a priori* is the unity (see the Coda to Ch. 4). (This is clear in Kant; recall too that the arch-intellectualist Descartes' fundamental project was to demonstrate that the intellect, conceived as one mental faculty, was more reliable than *the senses*, thought of, *en bloc*, as another mental faculty.) Thus, a diagram of their view might look like this; note that there is no causal connection between mind and body and that we no longer have the *retina* in the centre, but simply 'the senses'.

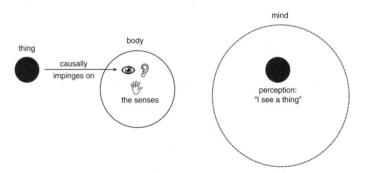

Figure 2c Sophisticated intellectualist variant on the empiricist picture

Sophisticated intellectualism clearly represents an advance over empiricism and popular intellectualism. What then could there be left to object to? Chapters 3–5 are devoted to further critiques of *all* versions of the Picture. For now, we will highlight just one difficulty, which emerges in Merleau-Ponty's discussion of attention: namely, that 'the thing' remains the same in all versions of the diagram, and this 'thing' is supposed to be *determinate*. And this assumption renders impossible a true account of the function of *attention*.

The indeterminate. Objective thought interferes with our recognition of 'the indeterminate as a positive phenomenon' (*PP* 6/7). Merleau-Ponty invites us to imagine constructing, 'by the use of optics and geometry, that bit of the world, which can at any moment throw its image on our retina'. Objective thought would say that we ought therefore to perceive 'a segment of the world precisely delimited, surrounded by a zone of blackness' (*PP* 5/6). But we do not: 'The region surrounding the visual field is not easy to describe, but . . . it is neither black nor grey. There occurs here an *indeterminate vision*, a *vision of je ne sais quoi*'. This example is by no means isolated; horizons too are indeterminate, and since the horizonal structure of perceived objects is part of the very essence of perception (see the Coda to Ch. 4), the world is *shot through* with indeterminacy.

The term 'indeterminate' is arguably a little too vague for Merleau-Ponty's descriptive purposes: 'not-fully-determinate' may actually be better. (In some cases, the term 'ambiguous' is more suitable than 'indeterminate', and is one Merleau-Ponty also employs from time to time.) To say that the region surrounding the visual field is 'neither black nor grey' is to say that it is a colour which 'does not allow itself to be placed satisfactorily in the white-black series', like a piece of white paper seen in shadow (*PP* 304-5/355, cf. *PP* 226/263); but if one were, for example, to attempt to paint it, one would use shades from the greyish end of the palette. Thus, although the description 'neither black nor grey' itself sounds vague, it actually captures some positive content of the experience: 'neither pink nor red', for instance, just would not do it. Likewise, the background to the lamp (its outer horizons) is not pure undifferentiated chaos: it is given to me as a complex array that includes a variety of colours, some broad horizontal lines, a general impression of lots of verticalities; when I focus on it, the new figure – the bookcase – was a possibility *already immanent in the 'indeterminate' background*, whereas, say, a blossoming rose bush was not: there is positive content in the indeterminate background that allows some resolutions and not others. (Think about the line on the eye chart at the optician's, the one where you begin to have trouble making out the letters; the first letter on that line, say, could be either an E or an F, or possibly a T, but could not be an O or a G.)

The importance of indeterminacy (or not-full-determinacy) for Merleau-Ponty cannot be overstated. It is, as we have noted, the correlate of the horizonal structure of perception, which is essential to perception. We have already seen the role that the horizonal structure of perception played in establishing the basic premise of existential philosophy: that the world is neither internal nor external, since it implies that the world always outruns or transcends our representations (Ch. 1ii). This will prove to have implications for the *cogito* (Ch. 5ii). Indeterminacy also plays a central role in Merleau-Ponty's account of *illusion*, the occurrence of which has historically been a primary driver of many empiricist arguments for 'sense-data' (a species of sensation: see the Coda to Ch. 1) as well as intellectualist arguments for the epistemological priority of the intellect over the senses. Consider, for example, Descartes' well-known example (from Meditation 6) of the tower which 'looks round' at a distance but 'looks square' when close up. Merleau-Ponty's argument here is that distance by its very nature involves a type of indeterminacy (see Ch. 4i): a tower at a distance cannot be as thoroughly explored with the gaze as when it is nearby, so that the 'round' tower 'appears only in a field of confused structure in which connections are not yet clearly articulated' (*PP* 296/346). Thus, the tower does not 'look round' at a distance *in the same sense* as it 'looks square' when close to: these are not two *conflicting* appearances. Moreover, there is no sharp dividing line between 'correct' and 'illusory' perception (*PP* 297/346): as I walk toward the tower, as its shape becomes more and more open to exploration by my gaze, there will come a moment when something about the shape (a vaguely glimpsed angle against the white of the sky, say) raises a question, I feel 'that the look of the object is on the point of altering', there is a kind of uneasiness which suddenly resolves itself as the tower becomes square (cf. *PP* 17/20). At this stage I have a 'precise hold on the spectacle', but even so, this hold is never 'all-embracing', because indeterminacy is intrinsic even to 'correct' perception (*PP* 297/346). Since both empiricism and intellectualism reject indeterminacy, he argues, they cannot make sense of illusions.

'Attention'. The notion of *inattention* is invoked by empiricist and popular intellectualist psychologists to *explain away* indeterminacy (or, in a certain sense, 'ambiguity'). 'The object, psychologists would assert, is never ambiguous, but becomes so only through our inattention' (*PP* 6/7). Insofar as they begin from the constancy hypothesis, they reason that '[e]ven if what we perceive does not correspond to the objective properties of the source of the stimulus . . . the "normal sensations" are already there. They must then be unperceived, and the function which reveals them, as a searchlight shows up objects pre-existing in the darkness, is called attention' (*PP* 26/30). So, for example, if someone touches some part of my body, I am being touched in a precise place and so (according to the

constancy hypothesis) my tactile sensation must locate the point precisely, but I may not perceive that precise location until I *attend* to the sensation (cf. *PP* 29/34). Again, the perceived object is never indeterminate: if an object comes into my visual field, 'there is a moment when the approaching object begins absolutely to be seen, but we do not "notice" it' (*PP* 6/7).

Merleau-Ponty sees this as misdescribing not only the world but *attention*. 'To pay attention is not merely further to elucidate pre-existing data, it is to bring about a new articulation of them by taking them as *figures* . . . [it is] the active constitution of a new object which makes explicit and articulate what was until then presented as no more than an indeterminate horizon' (*PP* 30/35).[19] Although attention can be deliberate, in its central role it is *called forth* (*PP* 28/32) or *awakened* (*PP* 26/31) by the object (or we are or *appealed to compellingly, PP* 28/33), and brings about 'a passage from indistinctness to clarity' (*PP* 27/32, cf. *PP* 31/36). Neither empiricism nor intellectualism can make this role for attention intelligible: empiricism lacks the resources to make sense of how a perception awakens attention, since it has at its disposal only external relations (*PP* 27/31); intellectualism – and this applies to all versions thereof – cannot see the need 'to analyse the act of attention as a passage from indistinctness to clarity, because [for it] the indistinctness is not there' (*PP* 27/32). The objectivist conception of attention is 'no more than an auxiliary hypothesis, evolved to save the prejudice in favour of an objective world', that is, a world in which objects are, *inter alia*, determinate (*PP* 6/7).[20]

In sum, with sophisticated intellectualism, '[w]e pass from absolute objectivity to absolute subjectivity, but this second idea is no better than the first and is upheld only against it, which means by it. The affinity between empiricism and intellectualism is thus much less obvious and much more deeply rooted than is commonly thought' (*PP* 39/45). Empiricism and intellectualism are 'the dual expression of a universe perfectly explicit in itself' (*PP* 41/48).

iv. 'THE PHENOMENAL FIELD'

The final chapter of the Introduction to *PP* signals the way forward: having cleared away some of the fundamental assumptions with which psychologists and philosophers have traditionally approached perception, we are free to begin to explore the territory that has opened up before us: *the phenomenal field.* To understand this concept (as well as the notion of a 'transcendental field' which the phenomenal field becomes through phenomenological reflection), it is helpful to have at hand another pair of correlative concepts drawn from Gestalt psychology: the notion of a field and the notion of a 'physiognomy' understood as 'practical significance'.

Fields. The Gestalt notion of a field derived from the electromagnetic field theory in physics. And as Tiemersma (1987: 419) notes, 'the entire book [*PP*] appears to be penetrated by field-theoretical terminology'.[21] In physicists' hands, the crucial point about fields is a reconceptualization of space (and indeed time): 'space is no longer a void in which bodies or corpuscles exist', but an extension with 'dynamic properties', structured by forces with directional 'vectors' such that the identity of any one structure 'depends on all the other parts of the field and their structures' (Tiemersma 1987. 424; cf. *CPP* 346). Gestalt psychology adopted and adapted this notion of a field; the one who did this most systematically is arguably Kurt Lewin, who employed the term 'life space' to designate 'the totality of facts which determine the behaviour of an individual at a certain moment' (1936: 12).[22]

According to Lewin, objects within our 'psychobiological environment' are not motivationally neutral; they have 'valences'. Valences 'determine the direction of the behaviour' (Lewin 1935: 77), those with a positive sign effecting approach, those with a negative sign effecting withdrawal (p. 81). Valences are one important type of force within the person's 'field of force', which Guillaume (whose books on Gestalt psychology helped to introduce it to the French-speaking world) also calls the 'phenomenal field' (N.B.); they are driving forces, but there are also restraining forces, or barriers, which define the boundaries of regions of freedom of movement (1935: 80-1). Lewin delights in representing these forces diagrammatically with vectors, that is, arrows converging when the valence is positive and diverging when it is negative (cf. 1935: 91), and in representing the 'locomotions' determined by the combination of forces in play within the field of force by paths, that is, directed dotted lines in his diagrams.

Guillaume offers some helpful illustrations (some, we might note, involving what we *ordinarily* call 'fields': battlefields, playing fields, etc.): if I am simply lying tranquilly on the beach, the phenomenal field that extends around me is 'homogeneous, uniform'. 'But suddenly, a cry of alarm splits the silence, at some distance, to my left:

the field is now centred on that point which becomes an attracting pole; it contains a vector directed from my position toward that point.' Again, a battlefield contains 'a gradient of danger and of difficulty'. (1937: 133). On a playing field, 'in addition to its permanent orientation, the incessant displacements of the team of players give variable positive and negative values to different parts from moment to moment, creating zones of resistance and open zones which orient their efforts'; cf. Merleau-Ponty's own oft-quoted example: 'For the player in action the football field is . . . pervaded with lines of force (the "yard lines"; those which demarcate the "penalty area") and articulated in sectors (for example, the "openings" between the adversaries) which call for a certain mode of action and which initiate and guide the action' (*SB* 168-9).

Physiognomies revisited. Lewin's notions of 'valences' and 'barriers' (forces within the 'field of force') may be seen as instances of Merleau-Ponty's 'physiognomies'. They manifestly exhibit an important aspect of meaningfulness or significance: in them, perception and (potential) action are so intertwined as to be inextricable. 'A description of the objects within our behavioural environment would be incomplete and inadequate if we omitted that some of these objects were attractive, others repulsive, and others indifferent' (Koffka 1935: 353). 'A handle wants to be turned . . . chocolate wants to be eaten, a mountain to be climbed, and so forth' (Koffka 1935: 353); 'an object looks attractive or repulsive before it looks black or blue, circular or square' (quotation from Koffka, *PP* 24/28); '[t]he light of a candle changes its appearance for a child when, after a burn, it stops attracting the child's hand and becomes literally repulsive' (*PP* 52/60). Koffka makes further distinctions within this general category of qualities with such 'practical significance', distinguishing between 'demand characters' (Lewin's 'valences') and 'functional characters'.[23] 'The demand characters will, as a rule, come and go with the need. The functional characters will, as a rule, be permanent' (Koffka 1935: 392). Thus, a letter-box makes demands on us only when we want to post a letter, but it remains as something to-post-letters-in (and not merely a blue or yellow or red box) even when we are not in the letter-posting business. 'Demand characters' are freely rendered by Guillaume in terms of 'appeals', 'attractions', 'exigences', 'solicitations', etc. (Guillaume 1937: 132), and one sees much of this friendlier sort of language in Merleau-Ponty (e.g., *SB* 67).[24]

In the light of these twin notions of the phenomenal field and physiognomies understood as practical significances, we can find our way into the final chapter of the Introduction. It begins by noting that empiricism had 'emptied' sense-experience 'of all mystery'; what we now glimpse is 'an experience in which we are given not "dead" qualities, but active ones' (*PP* 52/60). In place of both empiricism's 'association' and intellectualism's 'intellectual construction', we have the idea of the 'constitution' of a 'significant grouping' or Gestalt (*PP* 53/61). '[W]hat we discover by going beyond the prejudice of the objective world is not an occult inner world', but a 'world of living experience': *the phenomenal field* (*PP* 58/67).

So, the phenomenal field *is* the life-world, shot through with 'lines of force', 'peopled' by demands and resistances, barriers and solicitations. Finally, phenomenological reflection 'transforms the phenomenal field into a transcendental one' (*PP* 63/74). Merleau-Ponty is here using the notion of *'transcendental'* in the transformed sense we identified in Ch. 1ii: the point is not that there is an external world that 'transcends' all possible experience, it is rather that the 'world of living experience' – the phenomenal field – 'transcends our representations': 'reflection never holds, arrayed and objectified before its gaze, the whole world' (*PP* 61/71).

v. CODA: MERLEAU-PONTY AND SCIENCE

In the Introduction to *PP* and indeed throughout the book, Merleau-Ponty critically engages with the scientific psychology of his day, as well as with neurology (in Part I; see Ch. 3). In later works (see Ch. 6iii and iv), he does the same thing with the 'social sciences' of sociology, anthropology and linguistics as well as with biology. How *does* Merleau-Ponty see the relationship between philosophy and science?

Is Merleau-Ponty 'anti-science'?

The thrust of his critique of 'scientific' psychologies as they have emerged in this chapter is not to dismiss science but, on the contrary, to show that their own assumptions have led *them* to be *un*scientific in a number of respects. In this sense, despite not embracing Husserl's term 'rigorous science' to apply to phenomenology, he is rather closer than most other phenomenologists to the spirit in which Husserl treated science (see Ch. 1i).

- *Naturalism and 'scientism'.* Recall Husserl's definition of natural-ism: this is the supposition that '[w]hatever *is* is either itself physi-cal, belonging to the unified totality of physical matter, or it is in fact psychical, but then merely as a variable dependent on the phys-ical' (*PRS* 79).[25] Merleau-Ponty himself occasionally uses the term 'scientism' to similar effect, for example, criticizing the 'scientistic or positivistic ontology' of the psychologists he engages with (*PrP* 24; see also *CPP* 338): the notion that 'the real world is the physical world as science conceives it' (*PrP* 23). Other Merleau-Ponty com-mentators define 'scientism' in a broadly similar way: for example, as 'the assumption implicit in most sciences that their theories . . . constitute a truer account of reality than one . . . based on direct experience' (Fisher 1969: 9). Merleau-Ponty certainly rejects natu-ralism or scientism in this sense: 'in asserting that there is philoso-phy we thereby take something away from the scientist; we take away his monopoly on truth. But this is the only way in which I would limit the role of science' (*PrP* 35). There is a slightly differ-ent sense of the term 'scientism', according to which its *methods of inquiry* are 'the only valid mode of knowing' (Fisher 1969: 9). This too Merleau-Ponty rejects: 'It is not a matter of denying or limiting the extent of scientific knowledge, but rather of establish-ing whether it is *entitled* to deny or rule out as illusory all forms of enquiry that do not start out from measurements and comparisons' (*WP* 34-5, italics added; cf. *CPP* 338). Not only are such assump-tions unproven, they are by their nature *unprovable.* (Any attempt to prove them by scientific methods would be question-begging; the attempt to prove them by other methods would acknowledge that there *are* other methods and hence would be self-undermining.) They are, we might say, matters of faith; yet few scientists would care to admit to accepting such fundamental things on faith. (And faith may be '*bad* faith'; see the Coda to Ch. 6.)
- *Invalid inferences grounded in unjustified 'hypotheses'.* There are several places, similarly, where Merleau-Ponty (as well as Köhler) charges scientific psychologists with making *obviously invalid inferences* – again, hardly best scientific practice: 'the experiences revealed by introspection [e.g., the plate's looking elliptical under the experimental conditions outlined above] depend upon the

attitude of introspecting. One cannot show that they also exist in the absence of this attitude' (*GP* 52, cf. *PP* 8/9: 'If attention, more precise instructions, rest or prolonged practice finally bring perception into line with the law of constancy, this does not prove the law's universal validity'). Merleau-Ponty and Köhler also offer a diagnosis of the *source* of such obviously invalid inferences, namely what Merleau-Ponty terms 'the prejudice in favour of the law of constancy'. (The term 'prejudice' is scrutinized in the Coda to Ch. 6.) He quotes the intellectualist Alain as follows: 'I have met a person who was not prepared to admit that our eyes present us with two images of each thing; it is, however, sufficient to fix our eyes on a fairly close object such as a pencil to see that the images of distant objects are immediately doubled'; Merleau-Ponty comments: 'That does not prove they were double beforehand', and adds that '[h]ere can be seen the prejudice in favour of the law of constancy which demands that phenomena corresponding to bodily impressions be given in places where they are not observed' (*PP* 33 n.3/38 n.19). Of course, if the law of constancy had itself been given appropriate scientific support, such inferences *could* be justified; but, as Köhler comments, these psychologists seem to have no interest in submitting their assumptions to scientific scrutiny: 'The customary thing to do with an hypothesis is to test it. Does Introspectionism test its empiristic assumptions? We see no evidence that it does, or intends to'. Indeed 'many psychologists tend to lose their temper when their empiristic convictions are called hypotheses . . . When a scientific discussion tends to assume this direction, it has always touched upon some particularly deep-rooted presupposition which one does not want to see regarded as an open issue' (*GP* 53).

- *Inappropriate use of 'auxiliary hypotheses'.* A good deal of the Introduction is devoted to exhibiting empiricism's and popular intellectualism's use of 'auxiliary hypotheses' (association, the projection of memories, inattention, etc.) to explain away phenomena that did not fit the constancy hypothesis. In itself, the use of auxiliary hypotheses is a perfectly acceptable part of scientific procedure; it becomes scientifically problematic only if a) no reason is proffered to accept the hypothesis that created the lack of fit with the phenomena; and/or b) there are available alternative hypotheses that do not require such auxiliary hypotheses. (If a scientist begins with the hypothesis that the sun and the planets go around the earth and on this basis finds the motion of the planets bizarre and puzzling, there is no objection to his positing 'epicycles' to explain planetary behaviour. However, if someone else can explain these motions much more simply and clearly by starting with the hypothesis that the earth and the other planets go around the sun, then in the absence of some very powerful reason for the first scientist to stick to his geocentric hypothesis, his positing of epicycles as auxiliary hypotheses begins to look unscientific.) We have seen that no reasons are offered for accepting the constancy hypothesis in the first place; we have also seen that many of these psychologists' auxiliary hypotheses presuppose what they set out to explain, so do not serve their purpose anyway. It remains open to them to try to come up with further auxiliary hypotheses which will actually do the job. However, there is an alternative 'way of looking at things' – Gestalt psychology – 'which reverses the relative positions of the clear and the obscure' and 'will be seen to be justified by the abundance' of phenomena which it elucidates' (*PP* 23/26-7). In these circumstances, the more *scientific* procedure would surely be to consider giving up the constancy hypothesis and beginning with Gestalten.

Phenomenology and science: mutual benefits?

Merleau-Ponty explicitly considered the relationship between philosophy and the human sciences' (psychology, sociology, anthropology, history, linguistics etc.) in later essays and lectures, in particular 'The philosopher and sociology' (in *Signs*) and his Sorbonne lectures 'Phenomenology and the Human Sciences' (in *CPP*) (a version of which appeared much earlier as 'Phenomenology and the Sciences of Man' in *PrP*). He observes that at the beginning of the twentieth century 'there was an abstract fashion of conceiving philosophy that excluded psychology and a scientistic fashion of conceiving psychology that excluded philosophy' (*CPP* 338), and makes parallel remarks about sociology and philosophy (*Signs* 98-9). He is optimistic that this segregation is on the verge of collapse,[26] and proposes that '[e]very science secretes an ontology; every ontology anticipates a body of knowledge' (*Signs* 98), which immediately gives us our cue: on the one hand, scientific discoveries can provide facts that (in a way that needs careful spelling-out) bear on philosophy. At the same time, the philosopher may be better placed than the scientist to bring out into the open, and to assess, the ontology which the science in question 'secretes'.

- *How scientific facts bear on philosophy.* Merleau-Ponty argues that the philosopher has no 'right' to *ignore* what science says about the world and experience, which are after all what the philosopher too is investigating (*Signs* 102; cf. *PrP* 91); '[p]sychology and philosophy are nourished by the same phenomena' (*PrP* 24). Nor should it, for sometimes science reveals undreamed-of possibilities. This is what Husserl discovered upon reading the anthropologist Lévy-Bruhl's *Primitive Mythology*. The 'contact with an alien culture' afforded by this book provided an 'impulse' to Husserl's 'philosophical imagination', and prompted him to reflect that 'the imagination, left to itself, is unable to represent the possibilities of existence which are realised in different cultures' (*PrP* 90), since it is, inevitably, culturally and historically situated.[27] We have seen already that Merleau-Ponty is very willing to embrace many of the findings of the Gestalt psychologists; we will see in Ch. 4 that he is *more* willing to embrace the discoveries of the Introspectionist psychologists than are the Gestalt psychologists: they can actually serve to illuminate aspects of perceptual experience that Gestalt psychology screens out. We will also see in Ch. 3 how certain abnormal cases from neurology and neuropathology throw up possibilities (e.g., phantom limbs) that the philosophical imagination alone would be unlikely to come up with: 'the philosopher could not possibly have immediate access to the universal by reflection alone' (*Signs* 107). Thus, scientific discoveries may have an important role to play in the performance of the phenomenological reduction (see Ch. 1; the various methodological roles of such abnormal cases are highlighted in Ch. 3). However, for a philosopher to admit that 'his "ideas" and his "certainties" . . . cannot truly be known by just being scrutinised and varied in thought' is not to 'abdicate his office and hand his rights over to empirical investigation and the positive disciplines' (*Signs* 108).
- *Why philosophy has the right to criticize science.* First, no human science worth its salt is a 'mere inventory of actual facts' (*PrP* 91); only a human scientist wearing 'the blinders of Baconian or "Millian" induction' (*Signs* 99), in other words, only an 'objectivist' or 'scientistic' human scientist (cf. *Signs* 101) actually proceeds like that. To the extent that the human scientist gets rid of those 'blinders', he is *philosophizing*: the human scientist 'philosophises every time he is required to not only record but comprehend the facts' (*Signs* 101); and here a philosopher clearly

has a right to intervene in the dialogue: he 'is not disqualified to reinterpret facts he has not observed himself, if these facts say something more and different than what the scientist has seen in them' (*Signs* 101). For example, the fundamental problematic of sociology and social anthropology is, we might say, a version of *the problem of the other* (see Ch. 5); likewise '[h]istory is other people' (*PrP* 24). The expression of the emotions in 'primitive peoples' is not immediately intelligible to us (*PP* 184/214); and a philosopher may urge, as Merleau-Ponty does, that the issue is how we can 'understand someone else without sacrificing him to our logic or it to him' (*Signs* 115; cf. *Signs* 122). Just for example, we learn from anthropology that 'in such and such cultures children treat certain cousins as their "kin", and facts of this sort allow us ultimately to draw up a diagram of the kinship structure in the civilisation under consideration' (*Signs* 100, here alluding to anthropologists such as Lévi-Strauss; see Ch. 6iii). But 'only the philosophical consciousness of intersubjectivity enables us to understand [such] scientific knowledge' (*Signs* 111). Without a comprehension of 'the style of kinship which all these facts allude to and *the sense in which* certain subjects in that culture perceive other subjects of their generation as their "kin"' – in other words, without the sort of understanding which phenomenology brings– 'the formulas which sum up these correlations could just as well represent a given physical or chemical process of the same form' (*Signs* 100). Thus, without the understanding provided by philosophy, Lévi-Strauss' theories are nothing but an 'algebra of kinship in need of completion by the meaning of the familial for humans' (Descombes quoted in Carman 2008: 217).We will see in Ch. 4 that according to Merleau-Ponty, Gestalt psychology 'secretes' a quite specific ontology, namely a phenomenological ontology that is entirely at odds with its own explicit naturalistic pronouncements (cf. *CPP* 317); here too, the philosopher has a right to extract the implicit ontology and to draw attention to its incompatibility with what Gestalt psychology actually asserts.

- *Why science needs philosophy.* In the end, philosophy 'is not defined by a peculiar domain of its own', it is 'not a particular body of knowledge'; in a sense, it is science's *conscience*; it is 'the vigilance which does not let us forget the source of all knowledge' and is 'necessary' to the human sciences 'as a constant reminder of its tasks' (*Signs* 110). This pronouncement will strike scientists as both pious and vague, and so it should strike all of us were it not for the fact that it is merely the epitome of Merleau-Ponty's critical efforts. His careful and detailed critical engagement with Gestalt psychology is a *paradigm* of the potential for philosophy to act as 'a constant reminder of psychology's tasks'. It may also be taken as a *model* for us philosophers to follow if we undertake to engage critically with the science of our contemporaries.

CHAPTER 3

THE BODY

Merleau-Ponty's justly fêted reconceptualization of the body is an essential component of his critique of the assumptions implicit in all versions of the Picture (Figures 2a–c in Ch. 2). We have already highlighted several of these assumptions; but there is a further, absolutely central one: namely, that the *body* of the perceiver, represented in the Picture by the retina (or other sense-organs, or the senses *en bloc*), is conceived simply as one more *object* in a causal chain. By the end of *PP* Part I, one's own body should be restored to its proper place: '*my point of view on the world*', not '*one of the objects of that world*' (cf. *PP* 70/81).

The notion that the body is nothing but an object is so deeply engrained in modern Western culture that it is worth saying something at the outset about the phenomenological tradition's critique of this conception. The epitome of the objectification of the body is Descartes' conception of the body as a biological *machine*, explicable on purely mechanical principles. This conception continues today, both in medicine (see Ch. 6i) and in much Anglo-American philosophy of mind. A central problem in the philosophy of mind is the so-called mind/body problem: How are we to understand the relationship between the mind (consciousness, etc.) and the body? (Or, as this problem is usually expressed today, between the mind and the *brain*?) However, as Sartre argued (and Merleau-Ponty continues this argument), any attempt to unite consciousness with 'a certain living thing composed of a nervous system, a brain, glands, digestive, respiratory, and circulatory organs' will 'encounter insurmountable difficulties' (*BN* 303). (And to replace that thing, the body, with one of its parts, the brain, hardly makes those difficulties *more* surmountable!) Descartes himself admitted this when he asserted that the mind or soul (an immaterial substance) was in life 'united' with the body-machine, but that 'what belongs to this union is known only obscurely by the intellect'; 'it is the ordinary course of life and conversation . . . that teaches us how to conceive the union', that is, it really is not *conceivable* (1991: 227). The requisite move, seldom made by Anglo-American philosophers, is to *re-examine the conception of the body* which one is attempting to 'unite' with consciousness.

Prior to Sartre and Merleau-Ponty, Husserl had already made a crucial distinction between 'the lived body' (*Leib*) and 'the body-object' (*Körper*).[1] The Cartesian conception of the body treats it as pure *Körper*. The phenomenologists are most renowned for their elaboration of the *Leib*. The lived body is 'the *medium of all perception*; it is the *organ of perception* and is *necessarily* involved in all perception' (*Ideas* II §18). Husserl's point here is *not* that we in fact need eyes to see and ears to hear. It is rather that perception, being necessarily perspectival, implicitly refers to a 'zero-point of orientation' (*Ideas* II §18) – a 'centre', as Sartre would later put it – which is the *Leib*. For human reality, Sartre tells us, 'to be is to-be-there [*Dasein*, in Heidegger's terms]; that is, "there in that chair", "there at that table", [etc.]' (*BN* 308). The lived body is the 'thereness' of human reality, and the body as it is lived in everyday dealings with the world is the centre of the field of perception and action – the *unperceived* and *unutilizable* centre, as Sartre puts it, since in such everyday dealings the body is always in the background, at the horizon. This is sufficient for us to begin to see how their description of the lived body sidesteps the 'mind/body problem' altogether. To say that consciousness is a *relation* between the centre of the perceptual-cum-instrumental field and the objects in that field, that is, between the lived body and the world, is already to *answer* the question of how consciousness and the (lived) body are related; there is no *problem*.[2] However, many Anglo-American philosophers will still require some 'softening up' before being prepared to consider such a route; that will be one task of this chapter.

A good place to begin, even if not quite where Merleau-Ponty himself begins, is with *PP* Part I.2, where Merleau-Ponty argues that many properties, which 'classical' (i.e., empiricist and intellectualist) psychologists,[3] likewise many philosophers,[4] ascribe to the body, are incompatible with treating it as an object if properly thought through; for instance, the fact that we feel pain in our bodies and the fact that we normally do not have to look in order to know how our limbs are positioned. The only reason that these psychologists and philosophers have not drawn the obvious conclusion is their immersion in objective thought. See §i, which at the least, will function as a softening-up exercise.

The remainder of *PP* Part I[5] is enormously complex, with several philosophical tasks being accomplished in tandem. The most illuminating way of presenting Merleau-Ponty's phenomenology of the body may be to tease out and develop perspicuous examples of each of these philosophical tasks, although they are not wholly separable. I pick out four here:

i) *A better account.* One of Merleau-Ponty's tasks is to show 'that one's own body evades, even within science itself, the treatment to which it is intended to subject it' (*PP* 71-2/83), that is, its treatment as an *object* by neurologists and physiologists. This is what justifies the preponderance in *PP* Part I of examples from the neurological literature, for instance, phantom limbs. At bottom, his argument is a straightforward one that objective thought cannot account for these phenomena, his phenomenological approach can, so it is to be preferred.

ii) *A better vocabulary.* In the course of his arguments, Merleau-Ponty develops a new vocabulary, for example, 'motor intentionality', which is more suited than our (or the neurologists') existing vocabulary to describe what is going on in abnormal, and ultimately normal, cases. Although this point requires careful formulation, our existing vocabulary may be said to carry objectivist assumptions from which we need to distance ourselves with new expressions.

iii) *Using the 'abnormal' as a kind of refutation of objective thought.* Schneider, a brain-injured war veteran, exemplifies many of the ways in which we 'normal' people *would* experience our bodies and the world *if* objective thought were true. The argument in a nutshell is this: we do not, so it is not. (The example developed here is his inability just to recognize ordinary objects unless engaged in a familiar task, so that he needs to work out what he is being presented with from sensory clues; this may look like an anomalous example in this chapter, but in fact it is closely tied both to the previous and to the next example).

iv) *Using the 'abnormal' to shed light on the 'normal'*. Such abnormal cases are also used for a different philosophical purpose: subserving the phenomenological reduction by bringing to light (be it through contrast or more directly) what is ordinarily invisible because of its very familiarity. The main example developed is that of motor habits or motor skills; Merleau-Ponty's treatment of these embodied capacities has wider philosophical implications and has proved extremely influential even outside philosophy.

Central examples of these four tasks are considered in §§ii–v respectively. Although this approach to *PP* Part I may appear indirect, it actually reveals a great deal about Merleau-Ponty's conception of the body *en route*, which is summed up just before the Coda. The Coda considers the question of whether the distinction between 'normal' and 'abnormal' evidently presupposed in Merleau-Ponty's procedure here is a problematic one.

i. 'SPECIAL OBJECT' VS. BODY SCHEMA

Merleau-Ponty notes that those classical psychologists who have talked about the body recognize it as a very *special* object, in virtue of a number of unusual characteristics. (He here describes them in the psychologists' rather than his own terms; many of these descriptions will prove to be phenomenologically problematic.) These include the fact that my own body is 'constantly perceived', that it has 'the power to give me double sensations', that it is an 'affective object' (Merleau-Ponty's example here is pain) and the fact that 'kinaesthetic sensations' are confined to one's own body. (Kinaesthesia is related to what is commonly called 'proprioception'; [6] one is often supposed to be the means by which we are aware of the motion of our own body, the other the means by which we are aware of posture and the position of our limbs, but both terms are sometimes used to cover both functions. They are closely linked to what Merleau-Ponty calls the 'body schema', one of the central concepts in his reconceptualization of the body).[7] These characteristics ought to encourage these psychologists to acknowledge the body, not as a *special* object but as *not an object*.

For illustrative purposes, I want here to expand on the last characteristic.[8] Merleau-Ponty's comments on kinaesthetic sensations are unfortunately rather brief. The issue with which he begins is the experiential difference between moving one's own body (say, my moving my arm) and moving objects with one's body (say, my moving my coffee mug onto the floor). The psychologists under scrutiny tried to account for the difference by 'arguing that these [kinaesthetic] sensations present the body's movements to us globally, while attributing the movements of external objects to a mediating perception and to a comparison between successive positions' (*PP* 93-4/107). Merleau-Ponty naturally objects to the talk of sensations, but that is not his point *here*. What these psychologists were striving to express was 'the originality of the movements which I perform with my body: they directly anticipate the final situation, for my intention initiates a movement through space merely to attain the objective initially given at the starting-point' (*PP* 94/107-8). As with the other features highlighted in *PP* I.2, this feature of the body ought to make these psychologists reconsider their conception of the body as an object, but it does not.

A thinker who may be familiar to readers and who holds a not dissimilar view to these classical psychologists is William James[9]: 'The only ends which follow *immediately* upon our willing seem to be movements of our own bodies', he asserts, and goes on to inquire about the 'mechanism of production' of such movements (1890 II: 486).[10] Part of his answer is that we have acquired a stock of kinaesthetic images of 'kinaesthetic impressions', 'which come up from the parts that are actually moved'; once our kinaesthetic imagination has been thus stocked 'with as many distinctive feelings as there are movements possible to perform' (1890 II: 488), these make us conscious of movements (including passive movements) and of our 'attitude' or posture (1890 II: 488).[11] James further claims that we have an 'absolute need' of such sensations to guide us in 'the successful carrying out of a concatenated series of movements . . . we need to know at each movement [in the series] just where we are in it, if we are to will intelligently what the next link shall be' (1890 II: 490-91).[12]

What ought to strike us most forcibly here is James' insistence that we need something (e.g., a sensation) to *tell us* how our limbs are positioned or where we are in a sequence of movements. This is certainly what struck Wittgenstein: 'The idea "there *must* be a feeling of position – how else do we know where our limbs are?" is very compelling', and he goes on: 'It is important in philosophy to know when to stop – when not to ask a question. There need be no "how"; *we know* how our limbs are situated' (1988: 90). Merleau-Ponty will embrace this idea that the knowledge in question is immediate (the body schema [see below] 'presents us immediately with our bodily position', *PP* 143 n.3/166 n.108). He will however go further to suggest that *we know* how our limbs are situated may sound overly intellectualistic, at least if we are thinking of the sort of everyday case which James is describing, where we are for example playing tennis and concentrating on the position of the ball and the other player. It would be better to say, as we will see in a moment, that our *body* knows how our limbs are positioned and how they are moving in the normal run of things. (This does not of course imply that it would *always* be problematic to say that 'I know how my limbs are situated', if for example I am deliberately concentrating on my posture or the way I am moving.[13] Such explicit thematization of the body would be a species of 'analytical perception' [see Ch. 4i], which, like all analytical perception, interrupts unity: it interferes with the flow and musicality of everyday moving; I cannot simultaneously play good tennis and keep explicit track of where my feet are. What primarily interests Merleau-Ponty for present purposes is the usual case where the position and motion of our limbs are unthematized.)

Kinaesthesia and proprioception have begun to figure in recent Anglo-American philosophy in large part due to popularizations (by neurophysiologists such as Oliver Sacks and more recently Jonathan Cole) of neurological cases of what Sacks terms 'proprioceptive blindness' or what Cole calls the loss of 'movement and position sense in the body and limbs' (2009: 344).[14] Sacks' patient Christina, suffering from an acute polyneuritis, suddenly found herself unable to stand unless she looked at her feet. 'When she reached out for something, or tried to feed herself, her hands would miss, or overshoot wildly . . . She could scarcely even sit up – her body "gave way"' (Sacks 1985: 44). 'She could at first do nothing without using her eyes, and collapsed in a helpless heap the moment she closed them . . . Her movements, consciously monitored and regulated, were at first clumsy, artificial.' Gradually, with practice, 'her movements started to appear more delicately modulated, more graceful, more natural (though still wholly dependent on the use of her eyes)' (1985: 47). Again, Cole's patient Ian, in whom an autoimmune reaction had induced a loss of myelinated sensory nerve fibre function below the neck, could not tell without looking how his limbs were situated or whether they were moving. Initially he was unable to control the movements of his limbs, until 'he discovered that if he saw the part he was trying to move, and thought about moving, then he could – slowly – move it' (Cole 2009: 344). Like Christina, Ian gradually learned to sit, stand and eventually walk, 'though still dependent on intense mental attention to movement, since automatic movement was no longer possible' (2009: 344).[15]

What should we say about such cases? Should we follow Sacks in describing these unfortunate individuals as 'proprioceptively blind'? Everything depends on how exactly we conceptualize proprioception. In Merleau-Ponty's rare uses of the term 'proprioception' (e.g., *SB* 89), he evidently uses it in the sense in which he uses 'interoceptivity' in *PP* (75-6/87); in these cases, he is *criticizing* its use to refer to a literal 'sixth sense' rather comparable to Descartes' 'internal senses'.[16] (Hence, he caricatures interoceptivity as 'message-wires sent by the internal organs to the brain, which are installed by nature to provide the soul with the opportunity of feeling its body', *PP* 76/87.) One need not understand proprioception in this way, but many philosophers do, because they want it to answer the 'How do we know?' question; thus understood, it suffers from the same problems as kinaesthetic sensations. At the least, it cannot be *just another* sense modality: Sacks calls it 'our hidden sense', and describes its operations as being 'automatic and unconscious' (1985: 42; this would however on the face of it rule out our *ever* being explicitly aware of how our limbs are situated). Christina's own gloss on Sacks' interpretation of her condition is striking, however, and suggests a way of understanding proprioception that might be more acceptable to Merleau-Ponty: 'This "proprioception" is like the eyes of the body, the way the body sees itself. And if it goes, as it's gone with me, *it's like the body's blind.*' She reasons, 'So *I* have to watch it – be its eyes' (Sacks 1985: 46). Thus, she suggests, first, that whereas *she* sees, hears, feels, tastes and smells, it is her *body* that 'propriocepts' – or used to, before her neurological disaster – and secondly, that the body is not (normally) an object: her body became an object for her only *after* the onset of her neurological difficulty.[17]

The notions of kinaesthesia and proprioception are linked to an absolutely central aspect of Merleau-Ponty's reconceptualization of the body: the 'body schema'.[18] This notion begins precisely as a way for classical psychology (i.e., empiricist and popular intellectualist psychology) to *avoid* the conclusion that the body is not an object. Unable to conceive that the peculiarities they had identified (in *PP* Part I.2) could be 'structural characteristics of the body itself', they transformed them into '"distinctive characteristics" of those *contents* of consciousness which make up our representation of the body' (*PP* 95/109):[19] it is this *representation* that they call the 'body schema' and it is this, they imagine, that tells me 'where each of my limbs is' (*PP* 98/113) and allows me to keep track of them as I move them.

Merleau-Ponty shows that this conception of the body schema hoists itself by its own petard. For classical psychologists, the term 'body schema' was nothing more than 'a convenient name for a great many associations of images' (*PP* 99/113). Such a conception cannot make sense of the phenomenon of allocheira (literally, 'other hand': a condition in which the subject feels in one hand stimuli applied to the other). The question is: what makes the two hands *equivalent* on this conception of the body schema? To take an example from normal experience, how can this conception make sense of the relative ease with which we transfer from a right-hand to a left-hand gear-shift? After all, if you have only ever moved the gear-shift with your right hand, all the 'associations' in the body schema will be between the sensations (visual and tactile) produced by the gear-shift and the kinaesthetic sensations produced in your *right* hand, and it ought to take as long to learn to shift with the left hand as it originally did to learn to shift with the right, but it manifestly does not. Both the abnormal and the normal case imply that 'the spatiality of the body must work downwards from the whole to its parts, the left hand and its position must be implied in a comprehensive bodily *purpose*' (*PP* 99/113), a purpose that makes it the *pragmatic equivalent* of the right hand.

Merleau-Ponty's own definition of the body schema emerges from his development of the Gestalt psychologists' definition: 'a total awareness of my posture in the intersensory world, a "form" in the sense used by Gestalt psychology', as Konrad proposed, adding that this body schema was 'dynamic' (*PP* 100/114). Merleau-Ponty expands on this: to say that the body schema is 'dynamic' is to say that 'my body appears to me as a posture having a certain actual or possible task in view', it is 'polarized by its tasks': it '*exists towards*' them, it 'collects itself together' in pursuit of its aims (*PP* 100-101/115; more in Ch. 4 on the term 'aims'). We see the body almost literally polarized in his description of leaning with both hands on his desk: 'only my hands are stressed and the whole of my body trails behind them like the tail of a comet' (*PP* 100/115). *This* is the proper meaning of 'body schema': in the end, it is nothing less than 'a way of stating that my body is in-the-world' (*PP* 101/115). We could also put it that the body schema is what Merleau-Ponty repeatedly terms a '*system of equivalents*': it is a 'system of equivalent gestures' (*PP* 315/367), an 'immediately given invariant whereby the different motor tasks are instantaneously transferable' (*PP* 141/163), in which (for example) my left hand and my right hand are 'pragmatic equivalents' as in the example above; in which, when I am imitating someone facing me, *his* right hand is immediately the equivalent of *my* left hand (*PP* 141/163); and in which there are multiple 'equivalent' ways of achieving the same task. (E.g., if I am sitting at my desk and want to reach my copy of *PP*, I can either lean forward and stretch my arm a little, or remain sitting back so as not to disturb the cat and stretch my arm further, cf. *PP* 149/172.) My body schema does all these things for me without my having to think about them. Moreover, as we will discover in Ch. 4iii, the body schema is also 'a ready-made system of equivalents and transpositions from one sense to another' so that the different senses – sight, touch, hearing and so on – 'translate each other without any need of an interpreter' (*PP* 235/273); thus the motor and the perceptual are both 'supported by the prelogical unity of the bodily schema' (*PP* 233/270), as indeed are the relations *between* the motor and the perceptual.

It becomes increasingly implausible to continue to deny that the body's peculiarities are its own, and to try to explain them away by peculiarities in our conscious representation of the body. This should, it seems to me, be sufficient at least to *problematize* the ontological status of the human body.

ii. A BETTER ACCOUNT: CARTESIAN PHYSIOLOGY VS. EMBODIED BEING-IN-THE-WORLD

One philosophical task to be performed in *PP* Part I.1 is to show that phenomenology can offer a better account than objectivist thinking of the phenomenon of *a phantom limb*. Merleau-Ponty argues that 'modern physiology' is at bottom Cartesian:[20] that the phantom limb, from that perspective, clearly involves both the mind and the body; that any objectivist account of it faces exactly the same problems that Descartes faced in bringing mind and body together; and that we must therefore reject objectivism. In addition, he offers his own account, an embodied version of Heideggerean being-in-the-world, an account which precisely avoids these difficulties.

According to Merleau-Ponty, 'modern physiology' is essentially *Cartesian,* equally treating the body as a machine. Descartes himself did not discuss phantom limbs *per se* (only pains *in* phantom limbs); however, modern physiology borrows his distinction between the external and the internal senses under the rubrics 'exteroceptivity' and 'interoceptivity' (*PP* 75-6/87). From this perspective, if a stimulus is applied to the stump of an amputee, 'the subject will feel a phantom leg, because the soul is immediately linked to the brain and it alone' (*PP* 76/87-8).

The term 'phantom limb' was coined by the surgeon Silas Weir Mitchell who encountered many veterans wounded in the American Civil War; WWI provided a further occasion to study this phenomenon. Such studies, however, show that phantom limbs depend on 'psychic' determinants as well as physiological ones (*PP* 76/88). For example, a phantom limb can suddenly appear in an amputee who had none if he finds himself in circumstances recalling those in which the wound was received (*PP* 76/88); and a phantom limb may gradually shrink and be absorbed into the stump 'as the patient consents to accept his mutilation' (quoted in *PP* 76/88). This is bound to be a difficulty for Cartesian physiology, just as the union of mind and body was notoriously problematic for Descartes: physiologists can have no clear explanation of 'how the psychic determining factors and the physiological conditions gear into each other'. It cannot possibly make sense to speak of 'a mixture of the two', unless they can somehow 'be integrated into a common middle term' (*PP* 77/89). However, as Merleau-Ponty argues, the phenomenological notion of being-in-the-world provides just such a middle term: it 'can effect the union of the "psychic" and the "physiological"' (*PP* 80/92; cf. 88-9/102).

As a way into this solution, let us consider for ourselves how we might try to think about phantom limbs. Many will be inclined to say that the amputee's limb is straightforwardly *absent* – it has, after all, been amputated – but that the phantom limb is a *representation* of the lost limb as straightforwardly *present* (cf. *PP* 80/93). Both halves of this seemingly obvious statement are challenged by Merleau-Ponty when he asserts that a phantom arm 'is not a representation of the arm, but the ambivalent presence of an arm' (*PP* 81/94). This implies three things:

a) To call the phantom limb a *representation* of the arm is too intellectualistic; the amputee surely does not *believe* that he still 'has an arm': 'the awareness of the amputated arm as present . . . is not of the kind "I think that . . ."' (*PP* 81/94). By the same token, the 'refusal of mutilation' to which physiologists find themselves referring is not a 'deliberate decision', as intellectualism would imply.

b) At the same time, the amputated limb is *not* straightforwardly absent but *present* – *practically* rather than intellectually: 'To have a phantom arm is to remain open to all the actions of which the arm alone is capable' (*PP* 81/94). The world of manipulatable, 'physiognomic' objects still 'flows toward' the amputee, the piano or the writing-desk continues to 'appeal to' his arm and thus to solicit his actions (cf. *PP* 82/94). Thus, '[t]he refusal of the deficiency is only the obverse of our inherence in a world' (*PP* 81/94).

c) But the arm's 'practical presence', as indicated by the world, is *ambivalent*: 'in concealing his deficiency from him, the world cannot fail simultaneously to reveal it to him': 'utilizable objects, precisely in so far as they present themselves as utilizable, appeal to a hand which I no longer have' (*PP* 82/95). When the amputee tries to respond to the piano's solicitation, his attempt falls short.

The deeper meaning of the conjunction of b) and c) is the ambiguity *of the body*: 'our body comprises as it were two distinct layers, that of the habit-body and that of the body at this moment' (See §§iii and v below.) In the case of the amputee, manipulatory movements remain in the habit-body but have 'disappeared' from body at this moment (*PP* 82/95). As Beauvoir lucidly summarizes this: 'the phenomenon of the phantom limb becomes intelligible if one defines the body as our manner of being in the world . . . One then understands that the world, which has been constituted by my body as handleable, remains that way at the moment, even if I have lost the power to handle it' (2004: 160).[21] In this way, 'being-in-the-world'

has brought together the physiological and the psychological and made intelligible the phenomenon of the phantom limb in a way in which neither the Cartesian physiologist nor the objectivist philosopher could manage.

iii. A BETTER VOCABULARY: 'MOTOR INTENTIONALITY' AND THE 'POWER OF PROJECTION'

PP I.3 introduces us to Johann Schneider, a war veteran with occipital lobe damage who was extensively studied by the Gestalt-oriented A. Gelb (a psychologist) and K. Goldstein (a neurologist). Traditional psychiatry, we are told, would class Schneider as a case of 'psychic blindness' (*PP* 103/118) or 'apperceptive visual agnosia'. One prominent symptom, and the one that most occupies Merleau-Ponty, is 'a dissociation of the act of pointing [*Zeigen*] from reactions of taking or grasping [*Greifen*]: the same subject who is unable to point to order to a part of his body, quickly moves his hand to the point where a mosquito is stinging him' (*PP* 103/118). This dissociation between pointing and grasping is an instance of a more general dissociation between 'abstract' and 'concrete' movements, that is, between movements which are not as opposed to those which are 'relevant to an actual situation' (*PP* 103/118; the latter encompasses both movements such as mimicking a salute, where it is obvious what an appropriate context *would be*, and movements such as tracing a circle in the air, where it is not).[22] So Schneider cannot, with his eyes closed, bend and straighten a finger to order, but is able, even with his eyes closed, to take his handkerchief out of his pocket to blow his nose. Indeed he is employed in manufacturing wallets and his production rate is not far off that of the normal employees (*PP* 103/118).

The very idea that there might be such a distinction to be drawn between concrete and abstract movements seems surprising: after all, physiologically, the movements to be performed are indistinguishable. (This is a prime example of the ways in which scientific discoveries can expand the philosophical imagination; see the Coda to Ch. 2.) That someone could retain the ability to perform the one while having lost the ability to perform the other might seem positively paradoxical: 'If I know where my nose is when it is a question of holding it, how can I not know where it is when it is a matter of pointing to it?' (*PP* 104/119). At any rate, it seems clear that objective thought will have difficulty making sense of it, although I will not review the arguments here.[23] Merleau-Ponty's strategic move is to argue that the solution to the paradox must lie in the fact that 'knowledge of where something is can be understood in a number of ways', and that we need 'to create the concepts necessary to convey [this]' (*PP* 104/119). Two concepts in particular emerge in the course of his discussion: *motor intentionality* and *the power of projection* ('[t]he normal function which makes abstract movement possible', *PP* 111/128) or *the power to reckon with the possible* (*PP* 109/125).[24] To a first approximation, the first, I will suggest, is preserved in Schneider and accounts for his ability to perform concrete movements; the second is what is needed to engage the first *if* what is at issue is an abstract movement, and it is this power of reckoning with the possible which in Schneider is impaired or lost.[25]

Motor intentionality is explicitly introduced as one of Merleau-Ponty's 'between' notions: 'something *between* movement as a third person process and thought as a representation of movement' (italics added). He goes on to explain it as 'an anticipation of, or arrival at, the objective' which is 'ensured by the body itself' (*PP* 110/127). It is in virtue of this that when it comes to concrete movements like grasping, Schneider's movement 'is magically at its completion' from the outset (*PP* 104/119). Again, when bitten by a mosquito, Schneider 'does not need to look for the place where he has been stung . . . because between the hand as a scratching potentiality and the place stung as a spot to be scratched a directly experienced relationship is presented' (*PP* 105-6/121). And again, when asked to do a familiar task such as sewing a wallet, he does not need to look for his hands 'because they are not objects to be discovered in objective space . . . but potentialities already mobilized by the perception of scissors or needle . . . [T]he task to be performed elicits the necessary movements from him by a sort of remote attraction' (*PP* 106/122).[26] Motor intentionality is the link between the 'potentialities' of the body (which it possesses due to its motor skills or habits: see §v below) and the 'calls', 'solicitations', and 'elicitations' – the 'demand characters' – of objects (Ch. 2iv and §iv below).

When it comes to abstract movements, however, something more is needed to mobilize or engage this motor intentionality: to allow him to 'convert the thought of a movement into actual movement'; without this, 'the order remains a dead letter' and 'does not communicate anything to him as a mobile subject' (*PP* 110/126); his 'intentional arc' 'goes limp' (*PP* 136/157). This 'something more' is the 'power of projection' or the 'power of reckoning with the possible'. (Merleau-Ponty also calls it the function of 'summoning', 'in the sense in which the medium summons an absent person and causes him to appear', *PP* 112/129.) Likewise, what underlies Schneider's 'sexual inertia' (*PP* 155/179) is the loss of 'his power of projecting before himself a sexual world' (*PP* 156/181). This power is what enables normal individuals to 'play-act', to extricate their bodies 'from the living situation to make them breathe, speak and, if need be, weep in the realm of the imagination' (*PP* 105/120); play-acting is precisely what abstract movement demands, but Schneider is 'incapable of play-acting' (*PP* 135/156). Concrete movement is 'centripetal': it takes place in the realm of the actual, whereas abstract movement is 'centrifugal': it takes place in the realm of 'the virtual or the non-existent' (*PP* 111/128). (There are different cases here: if normal subjects are asked to mimic a salute, they tend to abbreviate it; Schneider can manage it, but 'his whole body is involved in it' and he adds other 'external marks of respect'; this is because he can perform these movements 'only provided that he places himself mentally in the actual situation to which they correspond', *PP* 104/119-20. If asked to trace a circle in the air – where the normal 'actual situation' for performing this action is far less obvious and clear-cut – 'he first "finds" his arm, then lifts it in front of him as a normal subject would do to find a wall in the dark and finally he makes a few rough movements . . . if one of these happens to be circular he promptly completes the circle', thus incidentally demonstrating, *pace* the intellectualists' account, that Schneider is not *intellectually* impaired: he *understands* the order to touch his arm, 'since he recognizes the inadequacy of his first attempts, and also since, if a fortuitous gesture produces the required movement, he is aware of it and can immediately turn his piece of good fortune to account', *PP* 110/126.) Unlike Schneider, the normal subject 'is not open merely to real situations' (*PP* 108/124); he is 'in possession of [his] body independently of any urgent task to be performed' (*PP* 112/129.) We can perhaps think of what Schneider lacks as a kind of 'bodily imagination' (an expression which one could easily imagine Merleau-Ponty coining; he does offer the expression 'concrete liberty', *PP* 135/156).

One thing needs qualification, however: to say that motor intentionality is preserved in Schneider while he has lost his power to reckon with the possible is undoubtedly too crude. In normal subjects, even when they are absorbed in familiar concrete tasks, motor intentionality is *inseparable* from the power of projection; by the same token, in normal subjects, concrete and abstract movements are not sharply separated. If I am making a dress on a sewing machine, my behaviour exhibits a flexibility or plasticity that enables me to deal with obstacles (whether expected: the bobbin runs out, or unexpected: the capacitor starts smoking) without 'losing my stride', to consider the possible effect of a different stitch length than the one I am using, to transpose my skills onto an unfamiliar sewing machine with little loss of fluency, to be interrupted in the midst of the performance and pick it up again where I have left off . . . ;[27] and such plasticity reveals the power to reckon with the possible as *part and parcel* of normal motor intentionality. One suspects that Schneider's performance lacks just these kinds of plasticity.[28] Thus, strictly, Schneider has lost *both* his motor intentionality *and* his power of projection, but he retains a simulacrum of motor intentionality that looks *so like* genuine motor intentionality (as long as he is not challenged by obstacles and interruptions or required to take the initiative) that we can actually learn from his case what genuine motor intentionality is (see §v).[29]

The point of this section is, however, to call attention to Merleau-Ponty's *novel concepts* which get far closer to allowing us to describe Schneider's difficulties than the concepts available to the empiricists and intellectualists. As we will see (§v), Merleau-Ponty introduces other novel concepts: e.g., 'bodily understanding' ('A movement is learned when the body has understood it', *PP* 139/160, cf. *PP* 143/165); 'motor significance' and a 'motor grasping' of that significance (*PP* 143/165, cf. *PP* 110/126); the 'knowledge in the hands' of the accomplished typist, 'forthcoming only when bodily effort is made' and impossible to formulate 'in detachment from such effort' (*PP* 144/166). We made the point earlier that such puzzling vocabulary may be seen as necessary in order to break out of the objectivist philosophical traditions embodied in certain words. Merleau-Ponty says of his new vocabulary that 'it will appear absurd' – for instance, to say that 'the body understands' will sound nonsensical 'if understanding is subsuming a sense-datum under an idea, and if the body is an object' (*PP* 144/167) – but that is just the point. Much of our vocabulary for describing human beings is deeply objectivist and deeply Cartesian. A little less crudely, these words have *philosophical* traditions of usage, which give them a 'horizon of significance' (cf. *PP* 370/431); 'because it has been used in various contexts . . . the word gradually accumulates a significance which it is impossible to establish absolutely' (*PP* 388/452), and almost equally difficult to overturn. If Heidegger chose to eschew the word 'consciousness' altogether, if the other phenomenologists take it up, but avoid the word 'mind', it is because of these traditions of usage which are all but bound to mislead their readers. Other strategies for avoiding the objectivist connotations of such terms include inventing wholly new terminology (e.g., Heidegger's 'Being-in-the-world') and – as Merleau-Ponty does here – combining old terms in ways that are bound to have a ring of self-contradiction precisely because of the traditions of usage of the constituent terms.

iv. USING THE ABNORMAL I: 'DECODING' VS. 'PHYSIOGNOMY'

Merleau-Ponty also uses abnormal cases such as Schneider in the service of two rather different philosophical tasks. One may be called polemical, the other more purely phenomenological (we will look at examples of the latter in §v below), although, as we will see, the polemical use also subserves the phenomenological. Polemically, such cases may function as a kind of refutation of objective thought. In a number of respects, Schneider *exemplifies* objectivist theories; for instance, we saw in §i that there is an objectivist tendency to suppose that we know the disposition of our limbs through sensations, and Schneider may seem to *confirm* this: he cannot just tell whether he is lying down or standing up, but 'concludes' (*PP* 107/123) this from the sensations (of the pressure of the mattress on his back, or of the ground on his feet), or 'tries, by means of preparatory movements, to make his body into an object of present perception'. However, Merleau-Ponty immediately cautions us that '[n]othing would be more misleading than to suppose the normal person adopting similar procedures, differing merely in being shortened by constant use' (*PP* 108/124). On the contrary: the very fact that Schneider is *abnormal* – the fact that he has to go through this procedure to *discover* how his limbs are disposed when asked, whereas we do not – is a kind of refutation of the objectivist view. (And as we have seen, when engaged in concrete activities as opposed to the artificial experimental situation just described, Schneider does *not* need to look for his hands, 'because they are not objects to be discovered in objective space', as the objectivist supposes, *PP* 106/121.)

Since we have discussed kinaesthesia and proprioception at some length already, I want to introduce a *prima facie* different example of such a 'refutation' from this same chapter. Schneider, we learn, 'does not recognize any object merely by looking at it' (*PP* 113/130) except in the context of familiar activities.[30] When shown a fountain pen with the clip turned away and asked what it is, he begins by identifying its qualities: '"It is black, blue and shiny . . . it has the shape of a stick. It may be some sort of instrument . . . " The pen is then brought closer and the clip is turned towards the patient. He goes on: "It must be a pencil or a fountain pen."' As Merleau-Ponty observes, '[t]he sensory givens are limited to suggesting these meanings as a fact suggests a hypothesis to the physicist. The patient, like the scientist, verifies mediately and clarifies his hypothesis by cross-checking facts, and makes his way blindly towards the one which co-ordinates them all' (*PP* 131/151).[31] Schneider cannot recognize a letter which he himself has written when it is read out to him, and 'even states that without a signature one cannot know whose a letter is' (*PP* 132 n.2/152 n.69); 'the world no longer has any *physiognomy* for him' (*PP* 132/152), again except when he is engaged in a familiar task.

Such 'a laborious decoding of stimuli and deduction of objects' (*PP* 109/125) is precisely what, according to the objectivist conception, perception consists in. But here too, Merleau-Ponty warns us, '[t]here can be no question of simply transferring to the normal person what the deficient one lacks and is trying to recover'. The procedures that Schneider employs to replace normal functions 'are equally pathological phenomena' (*PP* 107/123). As we saw in Ch. 2, '[i]n the normal subject the object "speaks" and is significant, the arrangement of colours straight away "means" something' (*PP* 131/151); perception *for us* is 'physiognomic' (*PP* 132/153), even when we are not performing a relevant task. In the terms introduced in Ch. 2, for *us* the world possesses both 'demand characters' (solicitations, invitations to act) and 'functional characters' ('affordances'). Likewise, even for the amputee of §ii, the piano continues to possess both a demand character and a functional character: it continues to solicit his hands' actions when he feels like playing even if he is no longer able to respond to that solicitation, and to afford playing when he is merely considering the piano in abstraction from any such desire. By contrast, the objects in Schneider's world still possess demand characters (the piece of leather presents itself to him as 'to be cut up', the lining as 'to be sewn'; they 'offer themselves to the subject as poles of action', *PP* 106/122), but have lost their functional characters. (There is, we might say, concrete perception as well as concrete movement.) As Merleau-Ponty points out, he does not even recognize Prof. Goldstein's house unless he has the express intention of going there (*PP* 134-5/155).[32] The deficiencies in his 'power to reckon with the possible' (§iii above) translate into deficiencies in his *world*. And conversely, we learn once again that the body is not an object: 'In order that we may be able to move our body towards an object, the object must first exist for it, our body must not belong to the realm of the "in-itself"' (*PP* 139/161).

Thus, Schneider's mode of arriving at the tentative conclusion that he is faced with a fountain pen serves as a kind of *refutation* of objectivist accounts of perception. 'A *kind* of refutation', because, as Merleau-Ponty is always acutely aware, it is always open to the objectivist to come up with auxiliary hypotheses, such as the process' having been 'shortened by constant use', or – the last refuge of the intellectualist – being 'unconscious', to explain away the differences between us and Schneider in this regard; but it does at least place the onus of proof firmly upon the objectivist.

v. USING THE ABNORMAL II: HABITS, SKILLS AND BODILY KNOWLEDGE

The polemical task just outlined also serves a phenomenological function: here the abnormal case sheds light on the normal *by way of contrast*. Because *we* do not engage in 'a laborious decoding of stimuli and deduction of objects' but rather just recognize objects even outwith a concrete task, our consideration of Schneider brings out the 'physiognomic' nature of normal perception. Schneider served a similar function in §iii, where his lack of 'the power of projection' revealed this power in us. In these cases, Schneider's deficits call attention to aspects of normal embodied existence which might well have remained hidden because of their familiarity were we not faced with someone who *lacked* them.

But to the extent that Schneider *preserves* certain aspects of normal embodiment, the abnormal can shed light on the normal more directly. Again, we have already seen an example of this: Schneider's preservation (however approximate and truncated) of motor intentionality when performing a familiar task. For instance, the fact that his hands are 'potentialities already mobilized by the perception of scissors or needle' (*PP* 106/121) fits normal individuals as well as Schneider: 'to move one's body is to aim at things through it; it is to allow oneself to respond to their call, which is made upon it independently of any representation' (*PP* 139/160-1). This is a delicate strategy either to describe or to execute.[33] In the first place, Merleau-Ponty just got through telling us that we cannot simply 'transfer' to the normal person 'what the deficient one lacks and is trying to recover'. In the second place, we have seen that Schneider's motor intentionality is itself *defective*, precisely because he lacks the power of projection with which motor intentionality is normally seamlessly interwoven. The fact remains that our exploration of Schneider brought into the line of our phenomenological vision a fundamental aspect of normal human embodiment that we might well have missed had we not been investigating Schneider's way of being-in-the-world, as our exploration of the amputee brought our phenomenological attention to the distinction between the habit-body and the body at this moment. In this section, I want to develop a closely related example that is – in this same delicate sense – revealed via Schneider directly rather than by way of contrast.

The example I have in mind is that of 'motor habits'. A word on the term 'habit' before we get stuck in: we are apt to hear this term as referring to 'addictions' like smoking, or annoying 'tics' like cracking one's knuckles, and this is not what Merleau-Ponty means. Nor does he use the term primarily to refer to what Ryle calls 'mere habits' or 'blind habits', dispositions induced by drill and repetition like being able to recite the alphabet; its primary reference is to what Ryle calls 'competences', 'skills' or 'intelligent capacities' (Ryle 1949: 42ff; cf. Dreyfus 1996: 2). They include motor skills required for the performance of 'actions necessary for the conservation of life', for instance an infant's being able to suckle or the child to walk; those 'elaborating upon these primary actions and moving from their literal to a figurative meaning', for instance, knowing how to dance; and those whose meaning 'cannot be achieved by the body's natural means' and thus requiring an instrument, such as being able to wield a hammer, or knowing how to drive a car, play the organ or sew a wallet (*PP* 146/169).[34]

The acquisition of a motor habit '*dilates*' our being-in-the-world, through the 'incorporation' of such instruments *into the body*.

(Merleau-Ponty elaborates this with some delightfully dated examples: the woman who is able, 'without any calculation', to navigate through low doorways without breaking the feather off her hat,[35] or the man who 'without comparing the width of the opening with that of the wings' can safely negotiate his car through a passageway. The woman 'feels where the feather is just as we feel where our hand', the man negotiates the passageway 'just as I go through a doorway without checking the width of the doorway against that of my body', *PP* 143/165.) And as Merleau-Ponty points out, the acquisition of a motor habit or a motor skill 'presents great difficulties to traditional philosophies' (*PP* 142/164). To know how to type is not 'to know the place of each letter among the keys', as the intellectualist might say, nor is it 'to have acquired a conditioned reflex for each one, which is set in motion by the letter as it comes before our eyes', as the empiricist might insist. (To say that 'the perception of a letter written on paper aroused the representation of the same letter, which in turn aroused the representation of the movement needed to strike it on the machine' is to use 'mythological language'; cf. also *SB* 121.) What happens is rather that 'patterns are formed as I look, and these are endowed with a typical or familiar physiognomy. When I sit at my typewriter, a motor space opens up beneath my hands, in which I am about to "play" what I have read' (*PP* 144/167), and in which I can *improvise* (*SB* 121).

Merleau-Ponty offers as a general characterization of the acquisition of a habit or skill 'a rearrangement and renewal of the corporeal schema', i.e. the body schema sketched in §i (*PP* 142/164). Thus, to acquire a motor skill is to live one's *body* differently, for it to acquire new and further 'systems of equivalents'. It is simultaneously to live the *world* differently. Habit, as 'the basic function which sets boundaries to our field of vision and our field of action' (*PP* 152/175), 'is both motor and perceptual, because it lies . . . between explicit perception and actual movement' (*PP* 152/175). He gives the example of a blind man's learning to find one's way about with a stick: 'Once the stick has become a familiar instrument, the world of feelable things recedes and now begins, not at the outer skin of the hand, but at the end of the stick' (*PP* 152/175-6). 'Whether a system of motor or perceptual powers, our body is not an object for an "I think", it is a grouping of lived-through meanings' (*PP* 153/177).

*****

The Picture of perception introduced in Ch. 2 presupposed that the body is an object, effectively a Cartesian machine, and this fundamental assumption has now been called into question. We began by pointing to certain familiar facts – e.g., that we do not normally need to look in order to 'know' the situation of our limbs – that started to cast doubt on this fundamental presupposition and brought to light the central notion of the body schema. The remainder of this chapter, while focusing on Merleau-Ponty's philosophical *tactics*, gradually expanded this non-objectivist conception of the body.

- Showing that phenomenology offered a better account of the phantom limb than Cartesian physiology revealed our *embodied being-in-the-world*, by means of which we can simply *sidestep* the problem of uniting the physical with the psychological.
- Inventing a better vocabulary to characterize Schneider's paradoxical situation of both knowing and not knowing where his nose was revealed *motor intentionality* and *the power of projection* as interwoven features of normal embodied being-in-the-world.
- Exhibiting Schneider's need to 'decode' stimuli like a scientist confirming a hypothesis, as a kind of refutation of the objective thought that insists that *all* perception is like his, revealed that normal perception is *physiognomic*, whether or not we are engaged in a task relevant to the particular physiognomy of the object.
- Schneider's preservation of his motor habits and motor skills brought this absolutely fundamental but seldom-thematized aspect of embodied being-in-the-world to phenomenological attention.
- These features of embodied existence are intertwined. Motor intentionality, interwoven with the power of projection, is that in virtue of which our body's potentialities, brought about through the acquisition of motor habits, collected together as the 'habit-body' and sedimented in the body schema, respond to the world's physiognomies.

In a sense, this could all be summed up by saying that Merleau-Ponty makes *bodily* Heidegger's claim that *temporality* is the ontological meaning of the being of human reality.[36] As Merleau-Ponty puts it, 'the ambiguity of being-in-the-world is translated by that of the body, and this is understood through that of time' (*PP* 85/98).[37] The habit-body and its motor skills, the body of the present moment and its motor intentionality, what might be called the 'futural' body and its power of projection – these correspond to the past, the present and the future and are strictly inseparable.[38] In the first place, the motor habits that collectively constitute the 'habit-body' may be seen as literally *incarnating the past*: the practice that went into our acquiring the motor skill in question.[39] Thus, the body 'is not enclosed in the instant, but implies an entire history, and even a prehistory' (Beauvoir 2004 : 163). To borrow a phrase from Merleau-Ponty's former student, the prominent sociologist and anthropologist Pierre Bourdieu, habits are 'history turned into nature' (1977: 78), or rather (a phrase used by both Ryle and Bourdieu) 'second nature' (see Ch. 6). It is in virtue of the body's capacity to acquire habits that the past has a *weight* (cf. *PP* 442/514), and the weight of the past, we might say, both enables us to go forward and holds us back, it creates both momentum and inertia.[40] On the one hand, without the capacity to acquire habits, we could not learn from experience, we could not acquire the skills and competences which enable us to do things that we could not do before. On the other, habits can be difficult to change, so that if I have learned to play tennis a bit inefficiently, correcting my bad postural habits is difficult.[41] In the second place, motor intentionality may be understood as 'the power to reckon with the *actual*'[42] (by contrast with the power of projection as the power to reckon with the possible or the virtual), as well as the power to reckon with the present as opposed to the future. And in the third place, the 'futural' body's power of projection is its ability to project itself into a bodily imagined future or a non-actual possible situation. Most importantly, these three 'layers' of bodily existence *are internally related*.

In fine, my body is 'my point of view on the world', not 'one of the objects of that world' (cf. *PP* 70/81).

vi. CODA: NORMAL AND ABNORMAL

In this chapter, I have illustrated Merleau-Ponty's strategies of using the abnormal both polemically – as a kind of refutation of objective thought – and phenomenologically – to illuminate the normal by way of contrast (and even, with appropriate caveats, directly). These strategies may however raise the question of whether Merleau-Ponty is presupposing an objectionable dichotomy between 'normal' and 'abnormal'. To address this concern, we must first ask *what* distinction is being drawn; once this is clearer I think that there are fewer grounds for finding it objectionable. (This is not to say that there are none; Ch. 6 returns to this.)

There is a bland everyday use in which the term 'normal' just means something like 'typical' or 'ordinary'. Both Schneider and the amputee with a phantom limb are *surely* atypical or non-ordinary, although, as I will urge, Merleau-Ponty's use of 'normal' and 'abnormal' is stronger than this. There are two other uses that sophisticated readers might have in mind:

- One is the purely statistical use of the words 'normal' and 'abnormal'. Certain measurable properties – height, weight, IQ, etc. – are distributed in the population according to a bell-shaped 'normal' curve, and anyone whose height, weight, IQ etc. falls into the 'tails' of this curve is 'abnormal'. It is clear that this *is not* Merleau-Ponty's notion of 'normal' and 'abnormal'.
- A second use stems from Foucault. For Foucault, the notion of 'abnormality' – deviation from a norm of conduct, say in a classroom (gripping one's pencil too tightly) or in the army (dressing sloppily) – is just the reverse side of 'disciplinary practices' – techniques which make possible 'the meticulous control of the operations of the body' (1979: 137) – which aim at making the body 'docile' and thereby bringing the 'abnormal' conduct into line (i.e., 'normalize' it); this process is supported by structures (in his paradigm cases, literally *architectural* structures) which facilitates the constant possibility of surveillance. When this set of notions is taken out of formal institutions (schools, armies, prisons etc.) and dispersed into wider society, we seem to arrive at a vision of a 'surveillance society' in which deviation from the norm is likewise to be 'corrected' by 'disciplinary practices' aimed at creating 'docile bodies'. (Feminists have made extensive use of this expanded notion; see Ch. 6ii.) The notion of normality on which Merleau-Ponty is drawing is clearly not *this* either.

We can, I submit, get closer to Merleau-Ponty's notion with certain distinctions drawn by Georges Canguilhem.[43] Canguilhem is an interesting figure in this context: he was a contemporary of Merleau-Ponty's – he was born in 1904 and attended the École Normale

Supérieure in the same year as Sartre – and both he and Merleau-Ponty taught Foucault. We can begin to get a feel for Canguilhem's outlook by pursuing an example: obesity.

- Obesity – or, better, *fatness* – is one of the qualities of the body which current '**social norms**' (Canguilhem 1978 sec. II.ii) and in particular the 'norms of femininity' rule *against*. Medics however would be horrified by the suggestion that the current 'war against obesity' is nothing but an instance of Foucauldian normalization. (It is also clearly not a statistical notion, given, for example, that more than 50% of Americans are of 'abnormally high' weight.)
- Medics may then go on to talk about 'body mass indices' (BMIs). (An individual's BMI is calculated as his weight in kilograms divided by his height in metres squared; *very* roughly, an individual with BMI of less than 20 is categorized as 'underweight'; 20-25 'normal'; 25-30 'overweight'; 30-35 'obese'; 35-40 'morbidly obese'; and some use the term 'supermorbidly obese' for those with BMI over 40.) The BMI indexes not simply 'fatness' as a social 'abnormality' but a whole range of important health issues: diabetes, heart disease, osteoarthritis and so on; that is, those whose BMI classifies them as obese or morbidly obese are *statistically* more likely to suffer such health consequences. However, as Canguilhem urged, such '**laboratory norms**' must not take precedence over '**clinical norms**'; the former are matters of measurement and examination by laboratory instruments, the latter are grounded in '**vital norms**'. Thus laboratory norms only count as *norms* – with 'normative force' – by reference to vital norms. That is, 'BMI of over 40' is just a number; it is only '*bad*' because an individual with such a BMI usually lives a miserable and constricted life, that is, in terms of the vital norms in terms of which '*pathology is a lived reality*', a reality in which 'the organism can no longer react creatively to new elements of its surroundings'.[44]
- I submit that we should understand the norms underpinning Merleau-Ponty's distinction between normality and abnormality as at least *akin* to Canguilhem's 'vital norms'. (Merleau-Ponty's notion of essence provides a different but compatible angle on the 'normal/abnormal' distinction; see the Coda to Ch. 4.) Schneider's pathology and that of the amputee with a phantom limb are 'lived realities' in which their ability to 'react creatively to new elements of their surroundings' is at least impaired. Instances of

'abnormal' experience in experimental set-ups, e.g., subjects wearing Stratton's 'inverting spectacles' (see Ch. 4v), while not what we would usually call 'pathological', nonetheless are surely 'vitally abnormal' at least at the beginning of the experiment, when 'the visual field appears both inverted and *unreal* because the subject does not live in it and is not geared to it' (*PP* 251/293).

- Note that 'normal'/'abnormal' on this conception is not a *dichotomy*: we can acknowledge that there is a *spectrum* of cases between normality and abnormality; to say this is not to abolish the distinction (any more than to acknowledge that there is a spectrum of cases between being in the prime of life and being dead abolishes the distinction between them). Certainly, many of Merleau-Ponty's descriptions are of individuals at the extreme ends of this spectrum – both extremely abnormal and 'extremely normal'. His description of the 'knowledge in the hands' of the expert typist, who knows where the letters on the typewriter are 'as he know where one of his limbs is', and beneath whose hands 'a motor space' simply opens up, is a description of an *expert* typist (one who has *already* acquired the motor habit in question to a high level of proficiency), who, moreover, is not ill, tired, drunk or simply having an 'off day'.[45] There is a whole range of experiences *between* this and the experience of someone who has never before met with a typewriter: that of the novice who still has to find each key, that of the chronically clumsy person, that of the expert typist when very tired, and so on. Likewise, there is a whole range of experiences between, say, Schneider's or the amputee's and that which Merleau-Ponty describes as 'normal'. (We all experience the momentary disjuncture of the habit-body and the body of this moment from time to time, e.g., when we wake up in a strange hotel room and 'automatically' reach for the radio switch, only to find that it is not there.) These in-between experiences could be the focus of phenomenological explorations in their own right.[46] But they do not *undermine* the normal/abnormal distinction upon which Merleau-Ponty relies, and there is a philosophical point to his focus on the extreme ends of the spectrum, which is to break the grip of the picture which only sees the extremely abnormal end of the spectrum and takes *that* to be the *normal*.

CHAPTER 4

THE BODY AND THE PERCEIVED WORLD

I have presented the dominant argumentative trajectory of *PP* as a thoroughgoing critique of the assumptions embedded in the Picture. This trajectory is intertwined with an important sub-trajectory: Merleau-Ponty's engagement with Gestalt psychology.[1] In Ch. 2, we concentrated on Merleau-Ponty's positive debts to the Gestalt psychologists: they accurately described many perceptual qualities; they correctly argued that empiricism could not account for these qualities; they correctly rejected the disunity of the senses (i.e., the separateness of visual, tactile and auditory 'sensations') implicit in the Empiricist Picture of perception; and they rightly rejected both the sensation and the 'constancy hypothesis', which lay at the heart of the Empiricist Picture (as well as some of its intellectualist variants). At a more abstract level, Merleau-Ponty drew from Gestalt psychology the distinction between 'ordinary' or 'normal' and 'analytical' attitudes in perception.[2] (A paradigm of the 'analytical' attitude is the sort of experimental set-ups whereby the Introspectionists purported to reveal 'what was really seen' [see Ch. 2ii], e.g., by getting the subject to look through a hole in a screen. See §i.)

However, Merleau-Ponty was far from simply appropriating Gestalt psychology's principles and discoveries[3]; he argued that it had not put the question marks about the Picture deep enough down: it had failed to see 'that psychological atomism is only one particular case of a more general prejudice: the prejudice of determinate being or of the world' (*PP* 50 n.1/58 n.45). If we were to diagram the Gestalt psychologists' explicitly announced picture of perception, it might look something like this:

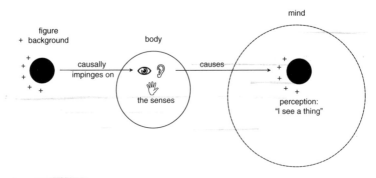

Figure 2d The Gestalt psychologists' picture

We can see that this version of the Picture still has much in common with the versions treated in Ch. 2: (i) The arrows in the diagram are causal; it is not that Merleau-Ponty wants some of these arrows to become *rational* (e.g., inferential), as they are in the popular intellectualist variant on the Picture (Figure 2b). Rather, he wants us to question the 'either causal or rational' *dichotomy*. (ii) Although Figure 2d has replaced 'thing' with 'figure-plus-background', this remains for the Gestalt psychologists a determinate object – a molecule rather than an atom, as it were (cf. Dillon 1988: 69), but still a determinate object. (iii) A third assumption implicit in all versions of the Picture including Figure 2d is that the body is a thing, an object in a causal chain; this was the assumption to which Ch. 3 above was devoted to undermining. Accepting assumptions (i)–(iii) is nothing less than misconceiving the perceived world, the body and the relations between them. Rejecting them undermines the whole structure of the Picture.

Merleau-Ponty argues that fully to account for Gestalt psychology's most profound results requires us to *reject* all of these assumptions. Thus, there is 'a whole philosophy implicit in the criticism of the "constancy hypothesis"' (*PP* 50 n.1/58 n.45): 'acceptance of its account of perception is not merely the substitution of one psychological theory for another, but a rejection of the whole objectivist framework for thinking about human experience' (Matthews 2006: 27–8). However, not only does Gestalt psychology *fail to see* 'that the return to perceptual experience, in so far as it is a consequential and radical reform, puts out of court all forms of realism' including scientism or naturalism (*PP* 47/54; see the Coda to Ch. 2), its explicit pronouncements *commit* it to naturalism by committing it to the assumptions (i)–(iii)[4]; 'by this very fact it betrays its own descriptions' (*PP* 47/54).[5] This explicit commitment therefore comes 'at the price of an internal contradiction' (*PrP* 24).

This chapter begins by setting out some important background: the notion of 'motive' (as something between 'cause' and 'reason') by means of which Merleau-Ponty resists assumption (i), together with a correlative notion of 'non-thetic awareness' (§i); it develops these notions in connection with the distinction noted above between the normal and the analytical attitudes in perception, and in application to one prominent example: the perception of depth or distance. In relation to this example and in the remainder of the chapter, we explore some important (and needless to say, inseparable) aspects of the relations between the body and the perceived world; the aim is to clarify how the Gestalt qualities revealed in Ch. 2 (as well as more global spatial qualities such as up/down orientation) connect with the aspects of the lived body revealed in Ch. 3. Chapters 3iv and v have already accomplished part of this task (although this was not the main aim of Ch. 3): the perceived physiognomy of the letters on the keyboard 'calls out to' the body of the typist in virtue of the latter's having acquired the motor skills of typing, and the body's immediate response to that call exhibits its motor intentionality. This chapter deepens these connections by developing a handful of further examples in some detail. §ii looks at the constancies (focusing on the case of colour constancy); §iii at the unity of the sensory qualities, the senses and the intersensory object; and §iv at orientation. The cumulative effect should be not only to reinforce the rejection of assumptions (i), (ii) and (iii), but also both to 'reawaken our experience of the world' and to 'rediscover' the body as our 'natural self' (*PP* 206/239).

A further criticism of Gestalt psychology is brought out in the Coda; it provides an opportunity to consider Merleau-Ponty's construal of certain fundamental philosophical distinctions (essence/accident; *a priori/a posteriori* and so on).

i. SOME BACKGROUND AND THE EXAMPLE OF DEPTH

The relations in Figures 2a and 2d are *causal*; in other versions of the Picture, some of these relations are *rational*: for example, the subject is imagined as drawing an *inference* from, say, the apparent size of the object, the number of objects interposed between it and us, the degree of ocular convergence and so on, to the *judgement* that the object is near or distant. The Picture therefore presupposes that perception comes about *either* causally *or* rationally, and this dichotomy reflects objective thought's general tendency to define 'pure concepts which are mutually exclusive': it hangs together with the 'thought vs. extension' dichotomy (as the essences, respectively, of the Cartesian mind and the Cartesian body), 'the vocal *sign* as a physical phenomenon arbitrarily linked to certain thoughts' vs. '*meaning* as a thought entirely clear to itself', and so on (*PP* 49/57). What we need, Merleau-Ponty argues, is a concept that is neither that of an objective cause nor that of an explicitly articulated reason, and the concept which Merleau-Ponty puts here is that of *motive.* Correlatively, we need to reject the objectivist dichotomy between our being completely unaware of something and our being explicitly and expressly aware of it; here Merleau-Ponty puts the notion of 'non-thetic (or non-positional) awareness'. This is the mode of our awareness of the 'motives' of perception. We begin by clarifying these notions in application to the example of depth or distance, before bringing out the body's role in all this.

Motives and non-thetic awareness. The notion of *motives* for *perception* may seem strange, and I will begin by offering a couple of objects of comparison. First, the context where we perhaps find the word 'motive' most natural is in connection with *actions*. It is noteworthy that psychologists and philosophers have traditionally conceptualized *these* motives as either causes or reasons. Actions are seen either as the *causal* outcome of objective stimuli combined with object-like internal states (desires conceived of as inner things) or as the outcome of a process of practical *reasoning*, one of whose premises is the motive. The term '*motive*' properly (phenomenologically) understood, lies between these two traditional ways of understanding the sources of action[7]: the motives for action are states of the world, aspects of the situation in which I find myself; so, for example, the news of the death of my aunt motivates ('moves') me to book a flight so as to attend her funeral. Motives in this sense are neither 'causal' nor 'rational'. What *causal* story can be told that will link a phone call from my uncle with my going online to find a flight to Boston? The motive 'acts only through its *significance*' (*PP* 259/301, italics added): the meanings of the words he utters and that of the words I type into Google, the significance of the death of a relative in my culture and of this particular aunt to me, for starters. Yet, a *rational* story would equally be otiose: of course we can say that the news 'provides a reason' for my booking the flight, but only as a figure against the background of the entire situation. The practical reasoning that would get me from 'My aunt has died' to 'I must go to her funeral' would require me (impossibly) to make explicit all the implicit background significance of, again, the death of a relative in my culture and this particular aunt to me, etc. I neither do nor could go through any such reasoning; instead, I simply 'take up the situation' (*PP* 259/302) with which I am confronted. It follows too that the 'relation between the motivating and the motivated' is *reciprocal* (*PP* 259/302): I book the flight 'because of' the news; but the situation I confront would not be the situation that it is unless it moved me to book the flight. (Of course, there is a *possible* situation in which I learn of my aunt's death but am not moved to go to her funeral; that would however not be *my* situation.) The news of my aunt's death and my booking the flight are two 'moments', inseparably linked, within the whole situation (cf. *PP* 309/360).

This first object of comparison enables us to see what a relation that is neither causal nor rational would look like and to make sense of the idea (which will carry over to the motives for perception) that motivating and motivated are internally related through being linked 'moments' in the situation. The second object of comparison actually offers an *instance* of what might be understood as perception's being 'motivated'. When we look at a painting, listen to a piece of music, or read a poem, what often strikes us first are, for example, the delicacy and luminosity of the lighting, the grave melancholy of a theme, the relentless power of a particular poetic image. It may be only afterwards, perhaps with the assistance of a critic or teacher, that we are able to point to the features of the work – the use of a particular palette, the shift from a major to a minor key, the repetition of a particular vowel sound – which in some sense 'explain' or are 'responsible for' the presence of the qualities which first struck us. (In fact, they are no more separable than motivating and motivated are: we can say that the artist's palette 'is responsible for' the luminosity of his painting, but only in the context of the entire painting.) If we ask ourselves whether we perceived these 'explanatory' features before the teacher or critic pointed them out, we are inclined to say 'yes and no'. What struck us immediately were the luminosity, the melancholy and the power; yet we were not

*un*aware of the palette, the key and the repetition: what the critic or teacher points out does not come as a complete surprise (cf. *PP* 326/380). We might propose saying that the features pointed out by the critics 'motivate' the perception of the qualities which first struck us; and if we want a label for our mode of awareness of those features prior to the critic's having 'called them to our attention', we might propose Merleau-Ponty's term 'non-thetic'.[8]

We come even closer to Merleau-Ponty's conception, and begin to lead into our example, by thinking about the creation of perceived distance in paintings. We may see in the painting the road winding 'into the distance'; we then reflect (perhaps at the instigation of a teacher) that the 'effect' is 'achieved' by the painter's having made the two sides of the road gradually converge. Again, one tree looks further away than the others; this is 'because' it is painted smaller and there are houses and a field 'between' it and the others, and so on. Here, we may say that the convergence of the painted sides of the road, the size of the painted tree, the intervening objects painted between the one tree and the others 'motivated' the perception of the distance into which the road winds and of the further tree, and that we were non-thetically aware of them prior to our explicit reflection.

The perception of depth or distance is an example which Merleau-Ponty clearly deems important and to which he devotes a good deal of time: '[m]ore directly than the other dimensions of space, depth forces us to reject the preconceived notion of the world' (*PP* 256/298; cf. *PrP* 172f.). Objective thought cannot allow that we strictly speaking *see* depth.[9] According to the empiricist psychologists (as well as empiricist philosophers such as Berkeley), depth (distance, relief, three-dimensionality) could not possible be seen since 'our retinas receive only a manifestly flat projection of the spectacle' (*PP* 254-5/297). The sophisticated intellectualists will say that 'distance, like all other spatial relations, exists only for a subject who synthesizes it and embraces it in thought' (*PP* 255/297). The 'popular intellectualist' psychologists will say that we arrive at the perception of depth or distance by *inference*, as we have seen. They take the illusion of depth produced by the stereoscope (*PP* 257-8/300) as evidence that we use binocular disparity to infer depth. (The stereoscope is a device that presents photographs of two marginally different scenes separately to the two eyes, creating the illusion of seeing a single, three-dimensional scene.) They will set up screens, which hide the intervening objects, show that in this set-up perceived distance shrinks, and cite this as evidence that intervening objects operate as 'signs' of distance (*PP* 48/56). And so on.[10]

We referred at the beginning of this chapter to the distinction between the 'analytical' and the 'normal' attitude in perception. The experimental set-ups with the stereoscope or the screen are paradigmatic methods of inducing the analytical attitude. One can easily enough assume this attitude without the help of experimenters; for example, if you hold a pen at arm's length and slowly bring it towards your face, keeping the pen in focus but attending to what your two eyes are doing, you will notice that they are rotating inwards; this is ocular convergence. Painters too learn to adopt the analytic attitude: they may hold up their paintbrush at arm's length alongside the distant tree in order to focus on its 'apparent size' and to compare its apparent size to that of the farmer in the field (cf. *WP* 41). The issue between Merleau-Ponty and the Gestalt psychologists concerns what we ought to *do* with discoveries made within the analytic attitude. The Gestalt psychologists will of course rightly insist, against both empiricists and intellectualists, that we *do* perceive depth and distance. They recognize that 'I am not expressly aware of the convergence of my eyes or of apparent size'; they are also cognizant of the 'precocity' of the perception of depth (cf. *CPP* 146): an infant perceives depth before it is capable of the sort of sophisticated reasoning that the popular intellectualists propose.[11] Yet, these factors clearly 'enter into the perception of distance' *somehow* (*PP* 257/300); so the Gestalt psychologists conclude that these things 'are not signs, but conditions or causes' of the perception of depth, of which we are unaware (*PP* 257-8/300; cf. *PP* 47/55).

For Merleau-Ponty, the Gestalt psychologists' consignment of ocular convergence, intervening objects, etc. to the realm of 'conditions and causes' signals their inability to transcend the 'either cause or reason' dichotomy. This is where Merleau-Ponty puts 'motives': 'the silent language whereby perception communicates with us', in which 'interposed objects, in the natural context, "mean" a greater distance' (*PP* 48/56). (Pursuing our analogy with painting, we might say that the classical psychologist, in calling attention to such features as apparent size, intervening objects, etc, plays a role analogous to that of the art teacher or critic.) The Gestalt psychologists' inference from 'not expressly aware' to 'unaware' signals their inability to transcend a correlative dichotomy; for Merleau-Ponty, the right inference to draw from the fact that we are not, in the normal attitude, *expressly* aware of ocular convergence, intervening objects, etc., is that we are *non-expressly* ('non-thetically' or 'non-positionally') aware of them (*PP* 258/301, cf. *PP* 49/57). These motives 'are tacitly known to perception in an obscure form, and they validate it by a wordless logic', 'a *logic lived through* which cannot account for itself, and . . . an *immanent meaning* which is not clear to itself' (*PP* 49/57).

And as with action, so with perception: here too the relation between the motivating and the motivated is reciprocal or internal. The fact is that I never perceive *distance*, I perceive a man (say) in a particular setting *who is* distant. And apparent size (likewise ocular convergence and so on) appears (thetically) only in the analytical attitude which excludes that setting and which deprives the man of his existence as an intersensory thing (see §iii): 'is not a man *smaller* at two hundred yards than at five yards away? He becomes so if I isolate him from the perceived context and measure his apparent size'. Otherwise he is just '*the same man seen from farther away*' (*PP* 261/304). Distance and its motives (ocular convergence, intervening objects and apparent size) are 'moments of a comprehensive organization of the field' (*PP* 259/302; cf. *PP* 261/305).

The body's role. The key to grasping the body's role in the perception of distance lies in the fact that the spectacle is *broken up* and the life-world *disrupted* by the analytical attitude, rather as focusing on how our feet are placed or how our arm is moving interferes with the flow of our tennis stroke and renders smooth and seamless action impossible (cf. Ch. 3i). Experiences in which the motives of perception become the objects of explicit awareness are 'unstable, and alien to natural perception' (*PP* 225/262). We need to acknowledge *both* the role of motives in depth perception *and* the importance (for the inhabitability of the everyday life-world) of their remaining *at the level of non-thetic awareness*.

Note first that the non-thetic awareness of the motives of perception is not an intellectual but a *bodily* awareness. We can begin by distinguishing two facets of this, which the treatment so far has run together.

(i)   First, the body is (via the proprioception or kinaesthesis which we introduced in Ch. 3i) 'aware' of *itself*. Of obvious particular relevance for the present example, it is aware of the convergence or divergence of the two eyes as they rotate in their sockets. As we will see in various ways in this chapter, 'perception and experience of one's own body are mutually implied' (*PP* 130 n.1/150 n.66; cf. *PP* 205/237).

(ii) Secondly, the body is also 'aware' of the apparent size of the object focused upon, of the intervening objects and so on. Note that that 'and so on' is crucial; the motives of perception can no more be completely spelled out than can be the entire situation in which my uncle's phone call and my booking the flight to Boston were but two moments.[12]

These sound like very different 'objects' of bodily awareness: one 'inside', the other 'outside'; they are brought together in the idea of a 'comprehensive bodily *purpose*' (*PP* 99/113). The two eyes converge or diverge *because* the body is *focusing the eyes* on the near or distant object. And focusing is a 'prospective activity' (*PP* 232/289), a 'purposive' activity which has an aim: one focuses *in order to see the thing*. (More on focusing in §iii.) The body is, moreover, attempting to explore the object – with touch, if it is near enough, or if out of reach, with its *gaze*. The exploratory gaze has the same aim as focusing: *to see the thing*. (To fix the gaze, as opposed to exploring *with* the gaze, is to step into the analytical attitude and hence to 'separat[e] the region under scrutiny from the rest of the field, interrupting the total life of the spectacle', *PP* 226/263.)[13] The natural or normal attitude of perception may be defined as one in which 'I make common cause with the gaze' and 'surrender myself to the spectacle' (*PP* 227/263).

All of the other 'motives' of perception figure in this exploratory gaze – not as objectively measurable or countable items (indeed it is only by adopting the analytical attitude that I can even answer the question of *how big* the man in the distance looks or *how many* intervening objects there are, cf. *PP* 260/303; *PP* 31/36, *PP* 11/13) but in relation to 'a certain "scope" of our gestures, a certain "hold" of the body on its phenomenal surroundings', with the body aiming at the 'best hold' it can have (*PP* 266/311). The gaze is 'the natural correlation between appearances and our kinaesthetic unfoldings . . . experienced as the involvement of our body in the typical structures of the world' (*PP* 310/361-2). From this perspective, to say that the man who is two hundred yards away is further away than the same man twenty yards away is just to say that he 'is a much less distinguishable figure, that he presents fewer and less identifiable points on which my eyes can fasten . . . he is less strictly geared to my powers of exploration'; increasing distance 'expresses merely that the thing is beginning to slip away from the grip of our gaze' (*PP* 261/304). Thus, depth or distance 'cannot be understood as belonging to the thought of an acosmic subject, but as a possibility of a subject involved in the world' (*PP* 266-7/311).

We can express this more philosophically rigorously by saying that this non-thetic awareness of motives is, like motor intentionality (Ch. 3iii) and inseparable from it, is a facet of '*operative intentionality*' (*PP* 50/57: 'operative reason'; see also *PP* 232-3/270). We know that operative intentionality (see Ch. 1iii) is 'that which produces the natural and antepredicative unity of the world and of our life' (*PP* xviii/xx). It is the *body* which 'brings about the synthesis' (*PP* 232/270), so that instead of perceiving ocular disparity, intervening objects, apparent size and so on, I perceive a unified object within a total spectacle, and hence a world in which I can live. Thus, *the thing* is 'the goal of a bodily teleology' (*PP* 322/376); '[t]he human body . . . has running through it a movement towards the world itself' (*PP* 327/381).

We can perhaps appreciate this purposive bodily 'synthesis' better by an analogy that picks up on our earlier analogy with painting; it is one which Merleau-Ponty himself invites with his striking use of virtually identical phrases of both the body and a painting: the *body* is 'a grouping of lived-through meanings which moves towards its equilibrium' (*PP* 153/177), and 'the whole' of a *painting* 'strives towards its equilibrium' (*PP* 262/305-6).[14] The painter, as we have seen, learns to take the analytical attitude: he makes himself thetically aware of the motives of perception (apparent size, intervening objects, etc.); he 'interrogates' the mountain with his gaze, asking it to 'unveil the means' 'by which it makes itself a mountain before our eyes' (*PrP* 166).[15] '[T]he poplar on the road which is drawn smaller than a man, succeeds in becoming really and truly a tree only by retreating toward the horizon' (*PP* 262/306); the sides of the road must converge in the painting if the road is to retreat into the distance (cf. *PP* 261/304). The painter must *incorporate* these 'means' by which a mountain becomes a mountain or a tree a tree into his painting, yet they must remain *hidden* if we, the viewers, are to see the mountain or the tree and not the apparent size, the intervening objects or the convergence of parallel lines (*PrP* 167). Achieving this is the 'equilibrium' of a painting. In other words, the painter needs to learn explicitly what the body has always 'known' non-thetically; the painter must achieve by technical skill what the body achieves 'naturally' through its operative intentionality: to *use* that 'knowledge' but *conceal* it, so as to present us with a world of unified objects which we can inhabit. Achieving this is the 'equilibrium' of the body.

ii. THE CONSTANCIES: THE EXAMPLE OF COLOUR

In Ch. 2, we introduced our critiques of Figure 2a with the notion of 'shape constancy'. Psychologists in the grip of the Empiricist Picture of perception insisted that a circular shape seen at an angle really *looked* elliptical (because the projection on the retina *was* elliptical); the Gestalt psychologists insisted that, on the contrary, it continued to look circular: hence 'shape constancy'. Similarly, whereas empiricist psychologists would insist that a man in the distance really looked smaller than when he was close up (because his projection on the retina *was* smaller), the Gestalt psychologists, cleaving to the notion of 'size constancy', would say that he looks the same size. Again, the empiricist psychologists will say that that part of a white piece of paper in shadow looks grey (here they will refer to rods and cones, no doubt), whereas the Gestalt psychologists will speak of 'colour constancy', and so on. It may seem from everything we have said so far that Merleau-Ponty sides whole-heartedly with the Gestalt psychologists on this point; once again, he does not.

Note first that in fact although the Gestalt psychologists use the term 'constancy', they do not really mean it. Their claim is not actually that the apparent shape of the plate remains constant when it is tilted, or that the apparent size of the man remains constant as he moves further away, but rather simply that 'the apparent size of a retreating object does not vary proportionately to the retinal image, and that the apparent shape of a disc turning round one of its diameters does not vary as one would expect according to the geometrical perspective' (*PP* 259-60/302). The apparent shape (according to the Gestalt psychologists) is actually some kind of *compromise* between its apparent shape when seen from above and what geometrical perspective would suggest, the apparent size is a compromise between the apparent size when within reach and the projection on the retina (*PP* 260/303). Likewise, so-called 'colour constancy' just means that, for example, a piece of paper seen in gaslight looks *closer* to the colour that it would look in daylight than we would expect from a photometer reading (cf. *PP* 307/357), because, *inter alia*, 'the eye "takes the lighting into account"'(Guillaume quoted in *PP* 309 n. 1/360 n.22).

We focus in this section on colour constancy; Merleau-Ponty makes three (interrelated) criticisms. First, Gestalt psychology, in giving up *constancy,* has actually abandoned its fundamental insight that should have allowed us to see 'colour in living perception' as 'a way into the thing' (*PP* 305/355). Secondly, their story still makes the 'apparent colour' a determinate colour that is to be explained as the causal outcome of various factors. And thirdly, the idea that 'the eye "takes the lighting into account"' is meaningless without a reconceptualization of the body.

So, first, Merleau-Ponty wants us to be able to speak of 'colour constancy' in a way that does not *conflict* with the fact that a 'piece of white paper seen in shadow . . . is not purely and simply white' but a kind of steely grey, or better, 'it "does not allow itself to be placed satisfactorily in the white-black series"' (*PP* 304-5/354-5). What remains constant – the object's 'real' colour (*PP* 304/354) – is to be understood in terms of 'a *colour function* which may remain the same even when the qualitative appearance is modified' (*PP* 305/355, italics added; cf. *PP* 306/357, 311/363). A colour has a physiognomy, a 'functional character' (see Ch. 3v), a 'concrete essence' (see the Coda): my fountain pen 'is black'; this blackness is not so much a 'sensible quality' as 'a sombre power which radiates from the object' even when it is reflecting the sun's rays. This 'real colour' 'persists beneath appearances as the background persists beneath the figure' (*PP* 305/356), and it is *this* which is 'constant'. And corresponding to the perceptual physiognomy of colour is a 'motor physiognomy' whereby a colour is 'enveloped in a living significance' (*PP* 209/243), 'a type of behaviour which is directed towards it in its essence' (*PP* 211/245). Although these correspondences show up in their purest form in abnormal subjects with diseases of the cerebellum (*PP* 209-11/242-45), we are all dimly aware that blue and green are 'restful', red and yellow 'stimulating' ('anyone who has had to choose carpets for a flat knows that a particular mood emanates from each colour', *WP* 46), and no doubt that sombre power radiating from the object which we call blackness has its own motor physiognomy. Merleau-Ponty invites us to 'rediscover how to live these colours as our body does, that is, as peace or violence in concrete form' (*PP* 211/245).

Regarding the second line of criticism, many of the conclusions of the previous section carry over to the phenomenon of colour constancy. Colour constancy too has its 'motives': 'the decisive factor in the phenomenon of colour constancy . . . is the articulation of the totality of the field, the wealth and subtlety of its structures' (*PP* 308/358), including in particular the structure 'lighting-thing lighted' (*PP* 306-7/357). As with the motives of the perception of distance, Gestalt psychology's move is to relegate the articulation of the field and the lighting to the role of 'causes' or 'conditions' of constancy; what we need to see instead is that they 'motivate' it, hence to see them as 'moments' of the phenomenon of constancy and internally related to it (*PP* 309/360).

As before, the phenomenon of colour constancy disappears when this articulation is disrupted by the analytical attitude. Suppose that I look at a table spread with sheets of paper, some of which are in shadow. 'If I do not analyse my perception but content myself with the spectacle as a whole, I shall say that all the sheets of paper look equally white'. But if I fix my gaze or look at the sheets in shadow through a match-box lid, that is, disrupt the articulation of the field, they 'change their appearance: this is no longer white paper over which a shadow is cast, but a grey or steely blue substance, thick and not definitely localized' (*PP* 225-6/262). Again, a feebly lighted white wall which in some sense appears white 'to the unhampered vision' 'appears a bluish-grey if we look at it through the window of a screen which hides the source of light' (*PP* 307/357); hiding the source of light disrupts the 'lighting/thing-lighted' structure, and looking through the screen disrupts the entire articulation of the field, since when we look through the screen we no longer perceive 'subordinated wholes, each with its own distinctness, standing out one against the background of another' (*PP* 308/359): in the analytic attitude, 'we no longer see real bodies, such as the wall or the paper' (*PP* 307/358). A painter can achieve the analytical attitude, for example, by squinting his eyes so that the colours he sees 'are determined by the quantity and quality of reflected light' (*PP* 307/357); he thereby 'does away with the field's organization in depth and with it, the precise contrasts in lighting, so that there are no longer any determinate things with their own colours' (*PP* 308/359).

This brings us to the third line of criticism. We can hardly let the Gestalt psychologists get away with saying that 'the eye "takes the lighting into account"' and leaving it at that. It is the body schema that 'contrives' the organization of the field (since 'my body is the general power of inhabiting all the environments which the world contains, the key to all those transpositions and equivalences which keep it constant', *PP* 311/363), and the body's operative intentionality that 'takes the lighting into account' while, crucially, keeping its own operations hidden, so that in the normal attitude of perception we see not lighting but things which have their 'own' colour (*PP* 307/357). Lighting and reflection 'play their part only if they remain in the background as discreet intermediaries, and *lead* our gaze instead of arresting it' (*PP* 310/361). The gaze is precisely 'an apparatus capable of responding to the promptings of light in accordance with their sense' (*PP* 310/361-2); it '"knows" the significance of a certain patch of light in a certain context; it understands the logic of lighting' (*PP* 326/380).

And as before, the painter learns explicitly what the body and that 'annex' to the body schema, the gaze, have always 'known' non-thetically: his 'interrogation of painting' looks toward the 'secret and feverish genesis of things in our body' (*PrP* 167). When the painter interrogates the mountain with his gaze, he finds '[l]ight, lighting, shadows, reflections, color' which 'exist only at the threshold of profane vision'; and his gaze 'asks them what they do to suddenly cause something to be and to be *this* thing' (*PrP* 166). We have all seen the play of shadows and the play of light, but in ordinary life, 'it hides itself in making the object visible. To see the object, it is necessary *not* to see the play of shadows and light around it' (PrP 167). Cézanne said that 'If I paint all the little blues and all the little maroons, I capture and convey his glance. Who gives a damn if they want to dispute how one can sadden a mouth or make a cheek smile by wedding a shaded green to a red' (quoted in *SNS* 16; cf. *PP* 197/230). The logic of the cheek's smile is understood not by the intellect but by the body, and the painter must achieve by technical skill and explicit awareness what ordinarily 'works in us without us', that is, through the efforts of our body, if he is to present us with a real mountain or a real hand or a real smile (*PrP* 167).

iii. THE UNITY OF THE SENSES AND INTERSENSORY UNITY

Recall from Ch. 2 that the Empiricist Picture of perception (as well as the Popular Intellectualist Picture) involved the atomization of the senses and thereby the atomization of qualities, so that 'this lemon is a bulging oval shape with two ends *plus* this yellow colour *plus* this fresh feel *plus* this acidic taste' (*WP* 45), perceived separately by sight, touch, and taste. The Gestalt psychologists rejected this, insisting that there are never 'isolated stimuli', and thence embracing the unity of the senses. Readers may have been left with the impression that Merleau-Ponty would accept this whole-heartedly. In fact, he insists that we must maintain *both* the unity *and* the diversity of the senses (*PP* 221/257). I may 'take up an attitude' (the analytical attitude) wherein 'instead of living the vision, I question myself about it' (*PP* 227/264). Again, in certain unusual experiences, the senses open out onto different spaces; for example, on those rare occasions when we deliberately absorb ourselves totally in one of the senses (say, sight), we might experience a 'purely visual space'. This justifies talk of the diversity of the senses. However, again, in the analytic attitude 'the world is atomized into sensible qualities, [and] the natural unity of the perceiving subject is broken up' (*PP* 227/264); such an attitude is 'unstable, and alien to natural perception ... which opens on a world of inter-acting senses' (*PP* 225/262, cf. 233/270). Normally, '[t]he senses intercommunicate by opening on to the structure of the thing' (*PP* 229/266). This justifies talk of the unity of the senses.

As with his remarks on the motor physiognomy of colour, Merleau-Ponty here uses a particular type of 'abnormal' experience to shed light on the normal in a different way than those revealed in Ch. 3. This is the experience of synaesthesia. Merleau-Ponty reports on experiments with mescalin, in which 'the sound of a flute gives a blu-ish-green colour, the tick of a metronome, in darkness, is translated as grey patches' whose spatial intervals correspond to the intervals of time between the ticks, and so on (*PP* 228/265). Subjects under its influence 'speak of hot, cold, shrill, or hard colors, of sounds that are clear, sharp, brilliant, rough, or mellow, of soft noises and of pene-trating fragrances' (*SNS* 49-50). Again, 'S.', the patient at the centre of Luria's classic study *The Mind of a Mnemonist* (1987 [1968]), not only possessed a remarkable memory but experienced synaesthesia. He saw puffs of steam or splashes when he heard certain sounds (Luria 1987: 22); a particular acquaintance had a 'yellow, crumbly voice' (Luria 1987: 24). We are inclined to think of synaesthetic experience as *abnormal*; and yet Merleau-Ponty describes the influence of mescalin as 'surrendering the subject to his vitality' (*PP* 228/265), and even asserts that synaesthetic perception is the *rule* rather than the exception; 'we are unaware of it only because scientific knowledge shifts the centre of gravity of experience, so that we unlearn how to see, hear, and generally speaking, feel' (*PP* 229/266).[16]

We need to rediscover the unity of the senses in the unity of the intersensory *thing*. Just as a colour has its physiognomy, its 'concrete essence' which 'persists beneath appearances as the background persists beneath the figure' (*PP* 305/356), so too each thing has a 'concrete essence' which 'animates' it (*PP* 320/373), a 'unique accent' or 'unique manner of existing', and 'would not have this colour had it not also this shape, these tactile properties, this resonance, this odour' (*PP* 319/372). 'The lemon is extended throughout its qualities' (Sartre quoted in *WP* 48). This is, once again, apparent when such unity breaks down, as when one watches a badly dubbed film where the visible movements of the actors' mouths do not cohere with the spoken sounds they are making; one has the impression that '*something else* is being said', and has ears 'for nothing but those other soundless words that emanate from the screen' (*PP* 234/272).

The 'world of inter-acting senses' is 'achieve[d] with our whole body all at once' (*PP* 225/262, cf. 233/270). The term 'achieve' is key. We can begin by considering the absolutely mundane experience of focusing our eyes on a nearby object, and hence going from double to normal vision: my gaze 'must experience double vision as an unbalance or as an imperfect vision, and tend towards the single object as towards the release of tension'; we move to normal vision when the two eyes 'are used as a single organ by one single gaze'; thus the body, seeking once again the best 'hold' on the world, 'escapes' from this unbalanced and imperfect state. Again, this is *purposeful* activity on the part of the body: 'the sight of one single object is not a simple outcome of focusing the eyes' (*PP* 232/289); rather, it is what the body's focusing of the eyes is *aiming to achieve*: the body 'escapes from dispersion, pulls itself together and tends by all means in its power towards one single goal' (*PP* 232/270). 'On passing from double to normal vision, I am not simply aware of seeing with my two eyes *the same* object, I am aware of progressing towards the object *itself* and finally enjoying its concrete presence' (*PP* 233/271). Before the eyes were focused, there was *no* concretely present *object*.

The unity of the senses builds on this: 'the senses interact in perception as the two eyes collaborate in vision' (*PP* 234/271-2). My body, not as a 'collection of organs' but as a 'synergic system', strives for a unified object (*PP* 234/272). The body schema is not just the 'system of equivalent gestures' (*PP* 315/367) which we encountered in Ch. 3i; it is 'a ready-made system of equivalents and transpositions from one sense to another. The senses translate each other without any need of an interpreter' (*PP* 235/273). In the end, the unity of the intersensory thing is 'constituted in the hold which my body takes upon it' (*PP* 320/373); and this is just the reverse side of the unity of the body, since 'it is by taking things as our starting point that our hands, eyes and all our sense-organs appear to us as so many interchangeable instruments' (*PP* 322/375).

In the previous sections, we compared the work of the body with that of the painter, and here, above all, once again Cézanne is the painter *par excellence* in Merleau-Ponty's world: Cézanne, who said 'that one could see the velvetiness, the hardness, the softness, and even the odor of objects' (*SNS* 49-50), and who 'declared that a picture contains within itself even the smell of the landscape' (*PP* 318/371, cf. *SNS* 15). The painter must interrogate the intersensory object to discover, make explicit and incorporate into his painting the 'motives' of the woolliness in the visible red of the carpet, the odour of the landscape in the visible surfaces of the streets and the taste of the lemon in its colour. The body does this 'naturally'.

iv. ORIENTATION

As we have seen (Ch. 2), the most basic unit of perception is a figure or object on a background. The background constitutes the 'outer horizons' of the object, against which the object stands forth as a unified thing, with background and figure being internally related. Gestalt psychology deserves great credit for this recognition, yet it failed to ask the key question: how is 'a phenomenon in which the totality takes precedence over its parts' – that is, a Gestalt –*possible* (*PP* 100/114)? The answer is that 'one's own body is the third term, always tacitly understood, in the figure-background structure, and every figure stands out against the double horizon of external and bodily space' (*PP* 101/115). That is, we might say 'The lamp stands out as a figure against the background of the bookcase'; what we should strictly say is 'The lamp stands out as a figure against the background of the bookcase *from here*'. But that word 'here' refers to my *body,* 'a hither zone of corporeality from which to be seen' (*PP* 102/117). The same point applies to the 'inner horizons' of an object, that is, the fact that objects are always given perspectivally, so that at any given moment I 'genuinely see' only one *Abschattung* of the lamp. As with the outer horizons, there is an implicit 'from here', where the 'here' refers to my body: this particular profile of lamp is 'genuinely seen' *from here* (cf. *PP* 203/235).[17]

How exactly are we to understand this 'from here'? These words do not locate one's body 'in relation to other positions or to external co-ordinates'; rather, they 'lay down' *'the first co-ordinates'* (*PP* 100/115, italics added), in terms of which not just 'here' and 'there', but 'up' and 'down', 'nearer' and 'further', 'to the left' and 'to the right' are to be defined. In this section we will consider in more detail the body's role in up/down orientation. One way of seeing that my body is the source of 'the first co-ordinates' is to describe cases where spatiality is *disrupted*, where the body is literally 'disoriented' and 'doesn't know which way is up'.

Orientation, like depth, presents a particular problem for thinkers in the grip of the constancy hypothesis, since – given that the retinal image is *inverted* – that hypothesis entails that *what we strictly speaking see is 'upside down'*. It was this thought that was the inspiration for Stratton's famous experiments with so-called 'inverting spectacles' (1896, 1897), which he saw as 'correcting' the natural inversion. What happens over the course of a week is this: at first, objects appear inverted and unreal; the landscape then rights itself but the body is felt to be upside down or in an abnormal position; then the body gradually begins to occupy a normal position 'particularly when the subject is active', and objects gradually re-acquire 'a look of "reality"'. After about five days, 'actions which were at first liable to be misled . . . now go infallibly to their objective' (*PP* 244-5/285). Stratton took these experiments to show that 'upright vision' was simply a matter of learned correlations between visual and tactile data; after a week or so, these correlations could be unlearned and relearned, so that the world appeared again as upright. 'As soon as the tactile body links up with the visual one, that region of the visual field in which the subject's feet appeared stops being described as "the top"' (*PP* 246/387). Merleau-Ponty argues that this explanation is 'unintelligible' (*PP* 246-7/287); nor does it manage to explain the increasing look of *reality*. The intellectualist can do no better since he 'cannot even concede that the image of the world, after the glasses are put on, is inverted. For there is nothing, for a constituting mind, to distinguish the experience before from the experience after putting on the glasses' (*PP* 247/288). For Merleau-Ponty, 'there is an immediate equivalence between the orientation of the visual field and the awareness of one's own body as the potentiality of that field' (*PP* 206/239); both the increasing look of reality and the reversion of the landscape to its normal orientation depend on the body.

We can connect this to Merleau-Ponty's discussion of another experiment done by the Gestalt psychologist Wertheimer, wherein a subject is placed in a room, which he can see only through a mirror, which reflects it at an angle at 45° to the vertical. Here, 'the subject at first sees the room "slantwise". A man walking about in it seems to lean to one side . . . The general effect is "queer". After a few minutes, a sudden change occurs: the walls, the man walking about the room . . . become vertical' (*PP* 248/289), as 'the reflected room magically calls up a subject capable of living in it' (*PP* 250/291).

Merleau-Ponty's discussion of both of these experiments makes essential use of the language of 'gearing' or 'hold': 'my body is geared onto the world when my perception presents me with a spectacle as varied and as clearly articulated as possible , and when my motor intentions, as they unfold, receive the responses they expect from the world' (*PP* 250/292). It also adumbrates the notion of 'inhabiting': for one's body to be geared to a room, say, is to be at home in it, to live in it, to *inhabit* it, that is, for one's *habitual* modes of action to be called forth by the objects in the room and for those objects to respond in the way one expects. ('Habit! that skilful but slow-moving arranger who begins by letting our minds suffer for weeks on end in temporary quarters', but without which our minds 'would be powerless to make any room seem habitable', Proust, quoted in Weiss 2008: 223.) In Wertheimer's study, '[a]t first the mirror image presents the subject with a room differently canted, which means that the subject is not at home with the utensils it contains, he does not inhabit it' (*PP* 250/291). Similarly, at the beginning of Stratton's experiment, 'the visual field appears both inverted and *unreal* because the subject does not live in it and is not geared to it' (*PP* 251/293). A utensil like a cup or a pen does not call forth the habitual actions of lifting and drinking or of picking up and writing, and one's efforts to perform these actions result in spilled coffee and dropped pens. After several days, in the case of Stratton's experiment, or a few minutes in the case of Wertheimer's, I re-acquire 'a certain gearing of my body to the world' (*PP* 250/291). Thus, '[w]hat counts for the orientation of the spectacle is my body, but not my body 'as a thing in objective space, but as a system of possible actions . . . with its phenomenal "place" defined by its task and situations' (*PP* 249-50/291), my body as an 'agent' (*PP* 249/290).

Should we try to press the further question of *why* 'clear perception and assured action' are only possible in orientated space (*PP* 251/293), the answer is that 'being' is synonymous with being situated' (*PP* 251/294). The being of an object is 'a being-for the gaze which meets it at a certain angle, and otherwise fails to recognise it' (*PP* 253/295). And ultimately, 'my first perception and my first hold upon the world' are grounded in 'another subject beneath me, for whom a world exists before I am here': my body (*PP* 254/296).

*****

Gestalt psychology, in refusing to recognize 'motives' ('the silent language whereby perception communicates with us', *PP* 48/56) and the possibility of their being 'tacitly known' to perception in an obscure form' (*PP* 49/57), in making the figure-plus-background a determinate object and in treating the body as just one more such determinate object, deprived itself of the resources to account for its own most fundamental discoveries. If we reject its assumptions, we not only give a grounding to their discoveries which they themselves lacked, we 'reawaken our experience of the world' and 'rediscover' the body as our 'natural self' (*PP* 206/239).

It is manifestly the case that the exploration of the motives of perception and the concrete essences of colours and of things can enrich our experience of the perceived world, rather as a class in painting, in music appreciation or in the analysis of poetry may enrich our experience both of art and of the world.[18] (Indeed, even a culinary or a wine-tasting class might lead us to appreciate the motives of *taste* and its integration into the intersensory object. The taste of a Shiraz or a Pinot Grigio is in its colour, as is shown those well-known experiments by Brochet on dyed wine: 'in one tasting, he served a white wine and elicited all the usual descriptions: "fresh, dry, honeyed, lively." Later he served the same wine dyed red: Out came the red terms: "intense, spicy, supple, deep." '[19] The alteration in the colour changed the taste in a way that no chemical analysis could possibly explain. Modern chefs play with the unity of the intersensory object by offering us savoury ice cream.) Can anyone, having read Merleau-Ponty, *not* find themselves more attuned to the interplay between apparent size and distance, or the sombre power of a black fountain pen, or the sourness of the lemon's yellow?

It is also surely the case that we may come to appreciate not only the very birth of perception but also that which gives birth to it: the body as 'a natural self and, as it were, the subject of perception' (*PP* 206/239, cf. 225/261). There is temptation to read the body in Merleau-Ponty as a 'body-subject', where this is understood as the claim that Merleau-Ponty wants to attribute to the body 'the attributes that classical philosophy gives to the subject' (Flynn 2004: 10). So to read Merleau-Ponty would be exactly wrong. In the first place, to talk (for example) of the body's 'motor grasping of a motor significance' (as in Ch. 3) is to *distinguish* between 'motor grasping' and 'intellectual grasping' and between 'motor significance' and 'intellectual significance'; the body operates precisely at the level *between* a mechanism and the subject of 'classical philosophy'. In the second place, to make the body into a 'body-subject' in this sense would be to diminish, indeed entirely to undermine, its role in action and perception. Although this comparison is obviously tongue-in-cheek, it is as if each of us were a bumbling Bertie Wooster for whom the Jeeves who is our body so organizes the world that everything is always exactly as it should be – our dressing-gown cleaned and ready to don, the newspaper ironed and laid out ready for us to read, the hearty breakfast just waiting for our arrival – without any effort on our part, the Jeeves who keeps his own efforts invisible and whose efforts consequently go unappreciated.[20] 'I want to go over there, and here I am, without having entered into the inhuman secret of the bodily mechanism or having adjusted that mechanism to the givens of the problem ... I look at the goal, I am drawn by it, and the bodily apparatus does what must be done in order for me to be there' (*Signs* 66). 'Just my glance toward the goal already has its own miracles. . . . it is my glances themselves – their synergy, their exploration, and their prospecting – which bring the imminent object into focus' (*Signs* 66-7). I am my body, and yet I am not: there is 'another subject beneath me' which is my body (*PP* 254/296), and 'we never know whether the forces which bear on us' are those of this 'natural self' or ours: 'they are never entirely either its or ours' (*PP* 171/198). Let us, then, celebrate this 'captive or natural spirit' which is the body and which 'can, by its magic, confer its own spatial particularisations on the landscape without ever appearing itself' (*PP* 254/296).

v. CODA: CONCRETE ESSENCES AND THE LIFE-WORLD *A PRIORI*

There are a handful of broadly linked characteristically philosophical dichotomies which – like so many dichotomies – are challenged by Merleau-Ponty. I consider them here because these challenges emerge in connection with Merleau-Ponty's critique of Gestalt psychology; they are intertwined, of course, with his critical engagements with empiricist and intellectualist philosophers. The primary distinction I have in mind is that often drawn between necessary and contingent truths (those which in some sense *must* be true as opposed to those which just *happen* to be so). There are at least three other distinctions that, historically, have been linked to this distinction: *a priori* vs. *a posteriori* knowledge (that which is knowable in some sense 'prior' to experience and that which is knowable only 'posterior' to experience); essential vs. and accidental properties (attributes a thing must have if it is to be the kind of thing that it is, as against properties which a thing may have or lack and still remain the kind of thing that it is); and analytic vs. synthetic propositions (propositions in which the predicate-concept is, as opposed to those in which it is not, 'contained in' the subject-concept; or more loosely, between propositions which are and those which are not 'true solely in virtue of the meanings of the words').[21]

Debates about the status of these various dichotomies and about the relations between them define much of the history of philosophy. I focus here on two phenomenological concepts that set out to muddy these dichotomous waters: 'concrete (or material) essence' and 'the life-world *a priori*'.[22] (These two notions are themselves closely linked.) To understand the issues, we need a bit of background, both on traditional notions of essences and the *a priori/a posteriori* distinction, and on the logical positivist attacks on these notions (the latter because Merleau-Ponty begins his discussion of essence by attacking the positivists).[23]

- *The Scholastic conception of essence.* The term 'essence' has a long history. Scholastic conceptions of essences have three features that are directly echoed in Merleau-Ponty's conception: (i) the essence of something is that 'in virtue of which the thing is what it is', or without which it cannot be said to be what it is (thus they might say that the essence of human beings was rationality or that the essence of a triangle is three-sidedness). (ii) Essences were given in 'real definitions', as opposed to 'nominal definitions': that is, in 'definitions of things' as opposed to mere 'definitions of words'. (iii) Normativity: in asserting that the essence of human beings is rationality, they were not denying that some human beings were irrational; it was rather that irrational human beings were *deprived* of something which in some sense they *ought* to possess. In this sense, they spoke of blindness as a 'privation' in human beings (but not in, say, stones), since human beings (but not stones) 'ought' to be able to see.

- *A priori and a posteriori in Kant.* Kant's most famous doctrine in this area is that there is a category of synthetic *a priori* truths. These are, as *a priori*, knowable in some sense prior to experience; as synthetic, they are not such that the concept of the predicate is contained in the concept of the subject. This category of synthetic *a priori* truths is grounded in concepts like those of space, time and causality which cannot be *derived from* experience because they are *conditions for any possible* experience (this is what makes them *a priori*); they constitute the 'form' of experience. Thus, they would include (in Kant's view) truths such as that any event is preceded by another on which it follows according to a causal rule, that space conforms to Euclidean geometry and that time is linear, none of which is analytic.

- *The logical positivist attack on these conceptions.* Both of these conceptions came under heavy attack by the logical positivists or logical empiricists of the so-called Vienna Circle in the first half of the twentieth century. Their fundamental premise was that every meaningful sentence is either 'analytic' – that is, true in virtue of the meanings of the words, as for example 'All bachelors are unmarried' – or verifiable through 'experience' (which they understood in terms of 'sense-data'). Since analytic propositions ('tautologies') are knowable *a priori*, and since any proposition verifiable through experience is *a posteriori*, the Positivists thereby leave no room for synthetic *a priori* knowledge; so much for Kant. (They were bolstered in their rejection of Kant by the science of the day, which seemed to have demonstrated that Kant's alleged synthetic *a priori* truths about space, time and causality were not only not *a priori*, but not even true.) Much of their motivation was anti-metaphysical, and their main complaint against the Scholastic notion of essence was its metaphysical status. They preferred the much more down-to-earth notion of an analytic proposition whose truth was grounded in the meanings of words, themselves the product of 'conventions'. Thus, instead of saying 'The essence of human beings is rationality' or 'Man is [essentially] a rational animal', which is apt to be misunderstood as expressing a metaphysical insight deep into the nature of human beings, they wished us to say 'The sentence "Man is a rational animal" is analytic' or 'The word "man" means "rational animal"'. (This move they described as a shift from the 'material mode' to the 'formal mode' of speech.) They thereby rejected the very intelligibility of a 'real definition', a definition of the thing as opposed to the word; only words, not things, have meanings.[24]

- Merleau-Ponty expressly attacks the logical positivists in his discussion of the eidetic reduction in the Preface. He notes that for the positivists, seeking the essence of, say, man, or consciousness, or the world consists in developing the *Wortbedeutung* – the word-meaning – of the *word* 'man', 'consciousness' or 'world' (cf. *PP* xv/xvii). From Merleau-Ponty's point of view, their conception of experience – as consisting of atomized sense-data – has long since fallen by the board (see Ch. 2). Moreover, their shift to formal mode constitutes 'escaping from existence into the universe of things said'.[25] What one should be doing in seeking the essence of consciousness is 'rediscovering my actual presence to myself'; if seeking the essence of the world, we should not be 'looking for what it is as an idea once it has been reduced to a theme of discourse,' but 'looking at what it is as a fact for us, before any thematization'. Thus he reaffirms something like the Scholastic notion of a real definition: 'In the silence of primary consciousness can be seen appearing not only what words mean, but also what things mean' (*PP* xv/xvii).

- *'Concrete essences'*. What is perhaps Merleau-Ponty's most widely cited criticism of Gestalt psychology is this: that the figure-ground structure is not a contingent characteristic of perception (as, by implication the Gestalt psychologists presuppose), but a necessary feature, indeed part of the *essence* of perception (cf. *PP* 4/4).[26] 'It is not accidental [i.e., it is essential] for the object to be given to me in a "deformed" way, from the point of view which I occupy. That is the price of its being "real"', *PrP* 15-16.) The first two features of the Scholastic conception of essence highlighted earlier are again directly echoed in Merleau-Ponty's claim that the figure-ground structure 'is the very definition of the phenomenon of perception, that without which a phenomenon cannot be said to be perception at all' (*PP* 4/4). The third feature, normativity, also emerges in Merleau-Ponty's conception:[27] 'each object has its "top" and its "bottom" which indicate . . . its "natural" position, the one which it "should" occupy', in which its physiognomy, its concrete essence, is recognizable; these norms have as their correlative the 'best hold' of the body and its gaze on the world, as this chapter has brought out (*PP* 253/295). Thus, 'the attack on the constancy hypothesis carried to its logical conclusion' 'assumes' not only 'the value of a genuine "phenomenological reduction"' (*PP* 47/54, embedded quotation from Gurwitch), but also 'the value of a genuine "*eidetic* reduction"' (see Ch. 1), even if the Gestalt psychologists did not carry their critique to its logical conclusion.

- Despite embracing certain features of the Scholastic conception of essence, Merleau-Ponty's conception is hardly theirs.[28] First, the Scholastics considered existence as an *accidental* property (of everything with the possible exception of God); thus essences can be fully specified entirely without commitment to the existence 'in nature' of anything that possesses that essence. Phenomenology, by contrast, 'puts essences back into existence' (*PP* vii/vii). Secondly, essences – both for the Scholastics and for the positivists – were *abstract,* albeit in very different senses. Scholastics often thought of them as something like 'forms' in a Platonic realm, with actual individuals giving 'matter' or 'content' to these forms; the positivists thought of them as 'existing in a state of separation' from 'the ante-predicative life of consciousness' (*PP* xv/xvii) because of the sharp distinction they drew between analytic truths and experiential truths. Hence, when Merleau-Ponty introduces the notion of *concrete essence,* it should strike us with the same apparently oxymoronic force as many of his other novel concepts (e.g., 'bodily knowledge').

- The phrase 'concrete essence' (or 'material essence') appears only a handful of times in *PP*, although often when he uses 'essence' without the qualifier, he is evidently using it in this sense. He explains it most fully in Part III.1, in connection with the example of a triangle – striking because it picks up a typical Scholastic paradigm.[29] Here, Merleau-Ponty claims that the 'essence' of a triangle is 'its physiognomy, the concrete arrangement of its lines, in short its Gestalt' (*PP* 385/448); he goes on (*PP* 385-6/448-9) to characterize this essence as 'material' (as opposed to 'formal')

and as 'concrete': 'the concrete essence of the triangle . . . is not a collection of objective "characteristics", but the formula of an attitude, a certain modality of my hold on the world, a structure' (*PP* 386/449; cf. '[t]he Gestalt of a circle is not its mathematical law but its physiognomy', *PP* 61/70). (And it follows – since the body is the 'third term' in every perception of a Gestalt – that 'the subject of geometry is a motor subject', *PP* 387/450.) Merleau-Ponty's other uses of the phrase 'concrete essence' are consistent with this identification of concrete essence with physiognomy or Gestalt: for example, Schneider's procedures for working out that he is faced with a fountain pen contrasts with 'the spontane-ous method of normal perception, that kind of living system of meanings which makes the concrete essence of the object imme-diately recognisable' (*PP* 131/151; cf. *PP* 450/523).

- *The life-world a priori.* Husserl introduced the idea of the life-world *a priori* in terms that both echo and distance themselves from Kant's synthetic *a priori*: its propositions would specify the gen-eral structure of the life-world in terms of *lived* space, *lived* time and *lived* causality. Merleau-Ponty's discussion of the *a priori/a posteriori* distinction occurs in the context of his treatment of the unity of the senses (itself intertwined with his treatment of space, as we have seen), as a response to Kant's view that the unity of the senses was known *a priori*, their diversity only *a posteriori*. He argues that one could almost reverse this Kantian dictum and say that the unity of the senses is nothing but 'the formal expression of a fundamental contingency: the fact that we are in the world'; conversely, the diversity of the senses appears from the perspective of phenomenological reflection 'as necessary to this world, to the only world which we can think of consequentially' (*PP* 221/256).[30] That is, there is a fundamental contingent fact, namely that we are *in the world*; *a priori* truths spell out *what it is* to be-in-the-world. His examples of such life-world *a prioris* reveal the connections of this notion to what he calls concrete essences: 'we say *a priori* that no sensation is atomic, that all sensory experience presupposes a certain field . . . But these *a priori* truths amount to nothing other than the making explicit of a fact: the fact of sensory experience as the assumption of a form of existence' (*PP* 221/257). This is why we find Merleau-Ponty saying such things as '[t]he structure of actual perception alone can teach us what perception is' (*PP* 4/4).

CHAPTER 5

OTHERS

The main trajectory of Merleau-Ponty's argument as I have been presenting it is his identification and critique of the assumptions embodied in the Picture (Figures 2a–d). By the end of the previous chapter, the structure of this picture had been thoroughly dismantled. Nonetheless, one more presupposition has yet to be brought to light: we must consider the fact that the Picture apparently represents a *lone* perceiver; yet the world into which we are thrown is not one in which we find ourselves alone.

Anglo-American philosophers of mind will be familiar with the so-called 'problem of other minds', what more phenomenologically oriented philosophers will call 'the problem of others'. (The difference in labels is not merely superficial.) This 'problem' is typically expressed within Anglo-American philosophy as an epistemological problem: 'How do I know that other minds or other conscious subjects exist?' The conclusion is all too often a sceptical one: philosophers end up in *solipsism*, that is, scepticism about the existence of conscious subjects other than oneself. Merleau-Ponty argues that the very question is rooted in objective thought and vanishes when we reject it (see §i). This issue is intertwined with at least three others: first, the objectivist tradition takes for granted that there is a fundamental asymmetry between *I* and *the other*: that something like the Cartesian *cogito* delivers absolute certainty not only about one's own existence but about one's own thoughts and feelings, while leaving the other's existence and his thoughts and feelings in limbo. Merleau-Ponty requires us to re-examine this asymmetry and hence to rethink Cartesian *cogito* alongside rethinking others (see §ii). Secondly, Merleau-Ponty insists that the world is what *we* perceive; can he really justify that 'we'? Will the attempt to make sense of the idea that the world is a *shared* world not throw us back onto objective thought? (see §iii.) Thirdly, even if we can somehow convince ourselves that other conscious subjects *exist*, how do we *understand* others? How do we know what they are thinking and feeling? Objectivists cannot get beyond the idea that we understand others via some kind of argument from analogy with our own case or that the attempt to understand is futile and the best we can do is to try to predict their behaviour. Merleau-Ponty's approach to this introduces the arresting and suggestive notion of 'bodily recipro-city', a facet of the 'body schema'(see §iv).

In this chapter, I use Sartre's approach to the problem of others as an object of comparison and contrast for Merleau-Ponty's. *PP* Part II.4 ('Other selves and the human world') is one of the clearest loci of Merleau-Ponty's critical engagement with Sartre. Sartre made tremendous advances in avoiding what he termed 'the reef of solipsism' on which so many philosophical ships have foundered, and he and Merleau-Ponty coincide up to a point in their solutions (or dissolutions) of 'the problem of others'. They diverge signifi-cantly, however, on the other issues. I end with a Coda that high-lights those paradigmatic media of interpersonal communication, non-verbal gestures and speech.

i. THE PROBLEM OF OTHERS

'The existence of other people is a difficulty and an outrage for objective thought' (*PP* 349/406). Why? Sartre uses the labels 'realism' and 'idealism' rather than Merleau-Ponty's favoured 'empiricism' and 'intellectualism' as the dominant forms taken by objective thought, but there are clear parallels (e.g., Kant is a paradigm for both idealism and intellectualism, and most empiricists are realists). Sartre's 'realist' takes it that the other's soul 'is separated from mine by all the distance which separates first my soul from my body ['as a thing in the world'], then my body from the Other's body, and finally the Other's body from his soul' (*BN* 223, cf. *PP* 349/406, *PrP* 115, *CPP* 246). His term 'distance' indicates that on this picture, all these relationships are *external*; accordingly, the other's body (as well as my own) is simply a physical object that moves about, an object that may or may not contain a consciousness which is forever hidden from me. If one begins here, the best one can do to arrive at the other is via a *hypothesis*, and '[t]he hypothesis which gives the best account of its behaviour is that of a consciousness which is analogous to my own consciousness and whose various emotions the body reflects' (*BN* 224). But such a hypothesis is, at best, probable – indeed, rather less than that, as Sartre argues: it can barely count even as *conjectural*, since the existence of others for the realist is a hypothesis which is 'on principle such that no new instrument will ever be able to be conceived, that no new theory will come to validate or invalidate' it (*BN* 251).

Do idealism and intellectualism fare any better? At one level, as both Sartre and Merleau-Ponty note, there *is* no problem of the other for the transcendental idealist, since '[t]here is no difficulty in understanding how I can conceive the Other, because the I and consequently the Other are not conceived as part of the woven stuff of phenomena; they have validity rather than existence' (*PP* xii/xiii).[1] As Sartre puts it, for Kant, 'if certain "Others" exist and if they are similar to me, the question of their intelligible existence can be posed for them as that of my noumenal [intelligible] existence is posed for me; to be sure also, the same reply will be valid for them and for me'. But, as he goes on to note, this gets us nowhere with the other whom I encounter in 'my daily experience' (*BN* 225). And this is problematic for Kant, since for him 'the condition of possibility for all experience is that the subject organize his impressions into a connected system . . . The Other therefore can not without contradiction appear to us as organizing *our* experience' (*BN* 226, italics added). But this is precisely what the other who appears in my experience does, as we will see: that is what makes him *other*.

Thus, for realism, the other is the most speculative of all possible conjectures; for intellectualism and idealism, the other, insofar as he appears in my experience, cannot be *other*. However, once we have 'learned to shed doubt upon objective thought' (*PP* 350/407), the problem disappears. How exactly? I will begin by outlining Sartre's answer to this question; Merleau-Ponty will accept a large part of the core of Sartre's answer, while diverging significantly in respects that are more fully explored in §§ii–iv.

Sartre begins by distinguishing between the Other-as-object and the Other-as-subject, between the other at whom I am looking and the other who looks at me. Thus, his riposte to objectivism falls into two parts. (i) If the 'other' referred to in the question 'How do I know that other conscious subjects exist?' is the Other-as-*object*, the answer is that I *look and see*: it is only the objectivist assumption that what I see when I look at the other is the body understood as a mere *physical or physiological object* that prevents me from acknowledging that I can, for instance, see the other's *anger*, as opposed to seeing a red face and a clenched fist and inferring – by some argument from analogy with my own angry behaviour, say – the angry consciousness hidden behind them (*BN* 346). Thus, consciousness and body are internally, not externally, related.[2] (ii) If what is meant is the Other-as-*subject*, the first part of the answer is that 'certainty', not 'knowledge', is the relevant mode of apprehension – and this is certainty, not in the sense of mere subjective conviction, but in the sense that attached to Descartes' *cogito*: Sartre refers to our awareness of the other as 'a sort of *cogito*' (*BN* 251). The second part of the answer spells out how such certainty is manifest in our experience: Sartre's paradigm scenario is one in which I am aware – for example, through shame – of being looked at by another. To become aware of being seen is to become aware of undergoing certain transformations in one's very being, which can only be effected by another subject. I become the 'object' which the other sees (*BN* 261). Moreover, I am not the foundation of this object which I am: it 'preserves a certain indetermination, a certain unpredictability . . . like a shadow which is projected on a moving and unpredictable material' (*BN* 261-2). These characteristics stem from the fact that the other is *free*. Thus, the other's freedom, and hence his existence as a subject, 'is revealed to me across the uneasy indetermination of the being which I am for him' (*BN* 262).

There is real genius in Sartre's account, and much with which Merleau-Ponty will concur. First, the objectivist approach to the question seems to imagine us almost as scientists observing a hitherto unknown species, watching them moving about in the laboratory without actually interacting with them and asking in the abstract 'How do I know they are conscious subjects?'; whereas Sartre's paradigmatic example of shame involves interaction in some sense. (Cf. Wittgenstein: 'But can't I imagine that the people around me are automata, lack consciousness, even though they behave in the same way as usual? . . . just try to keep hold of this idea in the midst of your ordinary intercourse with others, in the street, say!', 1968: §420.) Secondly, whereas the objectivist presupposes that the other's body and his consciousness are externally related, and likewise my body and my consciousness, Sartre's account makes these relationships internal. As Merleau-Ponty puts it, '[i]f I experience this inhering of my consciousness in its body and its world, the perception of other people and the plurality of consciousnesses no longer present any difficulty . . . the antimonies of objective thought vanish' (*PP* 351/408-9).

However, Merleau-Ponty, as we might expect, rejects the sharp divide between the Other-as-object and the Other-as-subject. This has two consequences: (i) Sartre's most original move is his idea of the 'second *cogito*': my awareness of the other's existence is simply the reverse side of my awareness of an aspect of my *own* existence (what he calls my 'being-for-others'), and my certainty of the other's existence is equivalent to my certainty of my own. But to reject the sharp dichotomy between the Other-as-subject and the Other-as-object must be to reject the sharp dichotomy between *myself*-as-subject and *myself*-as-object; and to do that, Merleau-Ponty argues, requires us to rethink the *cogito*, i.e., our certainty of our own existence as subjects and of our own thoughts. (See §ii.) (ii) Secondly, Merleau-Ponty rejects Sartre's apparent implication that I and the other are in perpetual conflict. For Sartre, 'being-seen constitutes me as a defenseless being for a freedom which is not my freedom' (*BN* 267). This line of thought ultimately leads to Sartre's notorious claim – although he qualifies this by saying that he is referring to 'bad-faith' relationships – that '[c]onflict is the original meaning of being-for-others' (*BN* 364). I resist being 'objectified' by the other, so I objectify him in my turn, and our relationship degenerates into a battle of looks. As Merleau-Ponty caricatures this: 'The other transforms me into an object and denies me, I transform him into an object and deny him' (*PP* 360-1/420). Merleau-Ponty wants to say that 'the other's gaze is felt as unbearable only because it takes the place of possible communication' (*PP* 360-1/420); for the Sartrean struggle between subjectivities to begin, 'all must have some common ground and be mindful of their peaceful co-existence in the world of childhood' (*PP* 355/413-14).[3] In order to fully understand what lies behind this 'peaceful co-existence', we need to develop two notions that have no counterpart in Sartre: the notion of the *interworld*, and the notion of *bodily reciprocity*. These are developed in §§iii and iv respectively.

ii. *TACIT COGITO* AND 'SECOND *COGITO*'

We noted that traditional objectivism takes for granted that there is a fundamental asymmetry between *I* and *the other*: that something like the Cartesian *cogito* delivers absolute certainty not only about one's own existence but about one's own thoughts and feelings, while leaving the other's existence as well as his thoughts and feelings in the limbo of wild conjecture. Sartre's dissolution of 'the problem of the other' retains certain aspects of this picture: with respect to existence, the Cartesian *cogito* still delivers certainty of my own existence; however, through a 'second *cogito*' (this was Sartre's stroke of genius), I have equal certainty of the other's existence insofar as my awareness of the *other's* existence as a subject is internally related to my awareness of an aspect of my *own* existence, namely my being-for-others. With respect to what I and the other are actually thinking or feeling, my consciousness of my own thoughts and feelings is (at least through 'pure' reflection which excludes the possibility of bad faith) absolutely certain; as this point is often put, consciousness is 'transparent to itself'. I can however *know* what the other is thinking or feeling, and this knowledge is on the same level as my knowledge of the colour of this piece of paper (see §iv for this last point).

Merleau-Ponty contests the traditional picture yet more radically. He challenges the claim that the Cartesian *cogito* delivers absolute certainty about my own existence and he denies that consciousness is 'transparent to itself'. (The need for a new *cogito*, as a consequence of 'the recognition of phenomena', was recognized as far back as the Introduction: *PP* 50/58.) *His* stroke of genius is this: to suppose otherwise is to make the existence of *others* unreachable and understanding of *others* impossible.

The cogito. Descartes' project (in the *Meditations*) to provide an absolutely certain foundation for the sciences discovered its 'Archimedean point' in the reflection that even if he might be deceived about the existence of the 'external world', including his own body, his *own* existence was certain as long as he was thinking. Moreover, even if he might be deceived about the *truth* of some of his thoughts, e.g., the thought that he is seeing something (since that thought could only be true if there was indeed an 'external world'), he could not be mistaken that *he was thinking* that. His famous statement (actually from the *Discourse*) '*Cogito, ergo sum*' ('I think, therefore I am') sums this up, and the phrase 'the *cogito*' has come to encapsulate this whole movement of thought.

Anglo-American commentary on the *cogito* has tended to focus on its logic and epistemology. (Is it really an inference, as '*ergo*' appears to imply? Is Descartes really entitled, given his starting-point, to say 'I think', as opposed to 'There is thinking'? and so on.) Yet, most seem inclined to say that Descartes has nonetheless got at some fundamental universal truth. From this perspective, Merleau-Ponty's opening gambit will be a bit startling: 'The *cogito* is either this thought which took shape three centuries ago in the mind of Descartes, or the meaning of the books he has left for us, or else an eternal truth which emerges from them, but in any case is a cultural being of which it is true to say that my thought strains toward it rather than that it embraces it . . .' (*PP* 369/429). *PP* Part III.1 is the record of Merleau-Ponty's thoughts 'straining toward' this 'cultural being', in the light of the whole journey undertaken in the first two Parts of *PP*.

First, he reasons, there can be no question of separating 'I think' and 'I am'; this is *not* for the Cartesian reason that the sphere of my thought constrains the sphere of the certainty of my existence, so that all I can be absolutely certain of is my existence as an immaterial thinking thing. The *cogito* does not *narrow* my existence to the sphere of my thought as Descartes urges, but rather *widens* the sphere of my thought to my existence, i.e., to my *being-in-the-world* which it has been the task of *PP* to bring to light (cf. *PP* 383/446).

Secondly, Merleau-Ponty rejects the sharp separation on which Descartes relies between the truth of 'I see' and that of 'I think I see'. 'Perception and the perceived necessarily have the same existential modality, since perception is inseparable from the consciousness it has, or rather is, of reaching the thing itself' (*PP* 374/435-6). Seeing can 'be reduced to the mere presumption of seeing only if it is represented as the contemplation of a shifting and anchorless *quale*' (*PP* 374-5/436), and as *PP* has so pre-eminently demonstrated, this is not what seeing is. It follows that '[i]f I feel doubts about the presence of the thing, this doubt attaches to vision itself' (*PP* 375/436); '"thought about seeing" . . . is certain only so long as actual sight is equally so' (*PP* 376/437). So if Descartes is not entitled to say 'I see' then he is not entitled to say 'I think I see'.

Thirdly, the world to which perception 'throws me open' is a *world*, and there is 'absolute certainty of the world in general, but not of any one thing in particular' (*PP* 297/347), because those things 'outrun' both my perception and myself: it is 'absolutely necessarily the case that the thing, if it is to be a thing, should have sides of itself hidden from me', as well as its horizons of past and future; the world 'transcends' my perception, so that perception 'cannot present me with a "reality" otherwise than by running the risk of error' (*PP* 377/439; cf. *PP* 296/345-6). Truth and the possibility of error go hand in hand.

Finally, if 'I am' is inseparable from 'I think', if 'I think I perceive' is inseparable from 'I perceive', and if the world 'outruns' perception, which is as a consequence always open to error, then we 'cannot be transparent to ourselves . . . our contact with ourselves is necessarily achieved only in the sphere of ambiguity' (*PP* 381/444).[4] There is 'absolute certainty' of my own existence, correlative to that of the world in general ('[t]he consciousness of the world is not based on self-consciousness; they are strictly contemporary', *PP* 298/347), but my existence is never 'in full possession of itself' – although nor of course is it 'entirely estranged from itself' (*PP* 382/444). This is a profoundly anti-Cartesian as well as an anti-Sartrean conclusion; Sartre's idea of 'pure reflection' has no foothold here. It is expanded further in through a consideration of emotions as well as perception (*PP* 377ff./439ff.), and of the role of language and culture in 'mediating' my self-knowledge (*PP* 388 ff./451ff., cf. *WP* 86-7). It is in any case implied by the body's temporality (see Ch. 3v) and its 'anonymous' role in the basic sensibility in virtue of which the world is always intersubjective (see §iii below), which makes my body – my 'natural self' (see Ch. 4iii) – less than transparent to me. Cf.: 'My history is incarnated in a body that possesses a certain generality, a relationship with the world prior to myself, and that is why this body is [largely] opaque to reflection' (Beauvoir 2004: 163).

What if anything is left of the *cogito* after all this? The answer is: a 'tacit *cogito*' ('myself experienced by myself', *PP* 403/469) – the 'silent *cogito*' which Descartes sought but could only express through a 'spoken *cogito*' (*PP* 402/468), and which 'knows itself' explicitly 'only in those extreme situations when it is under threat, in the dread of death or of another's gaze upon me' (*PP* 404/470). Any attempt to speak this tacit *cogito* will inevitably sound vague: it is a 'single "living cohesion"' (*PP* 407/474, quotation from Heidegger; cf. *PrP* 22). And any attempt to use it as leverage for an absolutely certain foundation for science is a non-starter: the tacit *cogito* is an 'an open and indefinite unity of subjectivity' corresponding to the open and indefinite unity of the world (*PP* 406/473), and science is nothing more than the second-order expression of this open and indefinite unity.

The 'second cogito'. Sartre's 'second *cogito*' purported to show that the existence of the other was as certain as my own – that is, absolutely certain – precisely because the other is internally related to an aspect of myself, namely my being-for-others. At first sight, Merleau-Ponty may appear to be making the same point here: 'unless I have an exterior others have no interior' (*PP* 373/434). Now that we have seen Merleau-Ponty's treatment of the *cogito* (both 'spoken' and 'tacit'), we will be prepared to discover otherwise. Sartre had introduced a new *duality*, that between the Other-as-object and the Other-as-subject, and correspondingly between myself-as-object (i.e., my being-for-others) and myself-as-subject, or the Me and the I. (He insists that 'these are two species of phenomena which ... are radically distinct, and they exist on two incommunicable levels', *BN* 304.) 'Myself-as-subject' was supposed to be that whose existence the first (Descartes') *cogito* revealed and was supposed to be completely transparent to itself, at least in pure reflection. But 'myself-as-subject' proves to be intervolved with perception, the perceived world and the body with its legacy of sedimented habits, and hence neither completely transparent to itself nor distinct from 'myself-as-object'. Unless we recognize this intertwining of myself-as-object and myself-as-subject, Merleau-Ponty claims, 'none of these mechanisms called other bodies will ever come to life'; then follows the passage just quoted: 'unless I have an exterior others have no interior' (*PP* 373/434). Others too are 'both subjects and objects'; these aspects of the others are not only 'radically distinct and incommunicable', but are also intertwined.

In this connection, we might take note of one of the questions which Merleau-Ponty put to Ryle at the famous Royaumont conference. Ryle's lecture ended with his own reflections on the *cogito*. He spoke of what many Anglo-American philosophers have come to call 'first/third-person asymmetry'; this is their attempt to capture what they see as a profound Cartesian insight which nonetheless Descartes' epistemology and ontology distorts: 'present-tense, first-person declarations or "avowals" of mental states and acts', for example 'I am in pain' or 'I am depressed', 'seem to be exempt from any possibility of doubt or mistake' (as, allegedly, *instances* of 'I think'), by contrast with their third-person counterparts, and hence seem to be an ideal foundation for certainty; but Ryle and many other Anglo-American philosophers resist this epistemological spin. Ryle had, in *The Concept of Mind*, 'half-assimilated avowals to the yawns which manifest the sleepiness of which they are signs': 'an avowal of depression is not a report of depression but an ejaculation of depression' (Ryle 1971: 195). In the Royaumont lecture, he acknowledged that sometimes 'I am in pain' or 'I am depressed' could be a report, but it was still not like an ordinary report, since issues of 'finding out' or of being mistaken do not apply as they would with a third-person report. He ended by declaring such avowals to be a 'puzzle or trouble-spot in the philosophy of mind' (Ryle 1971: 196).

Merleau-Ponty's question concerned *second*-person propositions: 'When I listen to M Ryle, it is indeed certain that I consider him a first person who is not me. Does this transfer of the first person outside of us seem to him to pose a problem, to furnish the occasion for a philosophical elucidation?' (Merleau-Ponty 1962: 96). Ryle's response is simply to assert that the problem he was considering was different: namely 'why propositions in the first person of a certain type, a certain class, seem to us to occupy a privileged position in the order of knowledge – in the sense that they seem to present affirmations which their author could not in any way doubt, or think to be false'. That apparently 'privileged status' does not apply, he asserts, to either the second or the third person (Ryle 1962: 98-9).

And yet, had Ryle been more open to Merleau-Ponty's question, he might have seen that to focus on the first/second-person 'asymmetry' as opposed to first/ third-person asymmetry is to introduce interaction and the interworld (see the next section), and that from this perceptive the 'asymmetry' is far less pronounced: the first person looks less 'privileged' and the second person more so than Ryle was prepared to acknowledge.

iii. THE INTERWORLD

Consider Sartre's encounter with a man in a public park: I do not perceive him as a mere temporal-spatial 'thing', for example, as being 'two yards and twenty inches from the lawn, as exercising a certain pressure on the ground, etc.' Rather, I perceive him as a *man*, around whom 'the things in my universe' are now organized: 'To be sure, the lawn remains two yards and twenty inches away from him, but . . . [i]nstead of the two terms of the distance being indifferent, interchangeable, and in a reciprocal relation, the distance *is unfolded starting from* the man whom I see and *extending up to* the lawn'

(*BN* 254). Much of this description is insightful, and confirms that the 'Other-as-object' is not an *object* in the 'objective thought' sense (a mere 'temporal-spatial "thing"'); yet a certain note of hysteria creeps in: 'instead of a grouping toward me of the objects, there is now an orientation *which flees from me*', so that 'suddenly an object has appeared which has stolen the world from me' (*BN* 254-5). Merleau-Ponty is surely satirizing this here: 'The affirmation of an alien consciousness standing over against mine would immediately make my experience into a private spectacle, since it would no longer be co-extensive with being' (*PP* 353/411). How could another 'steal the world from me' unless I imagined that the world was only mine in the first place? Nevertheless, in some sense, this is evidently what Sartre does suppose. (It is part of what leads him to the idea that interpersonal relationships are almost inevitably conflictual.) Yet, surely the world is a *shared* world.

Here, there will be a great temptation to suppose that the only way to secure such a shared world is to insist that the world consists of (atomic, externally related, intrinsically meaningless) objects, to which human bodies, as mechanisms, causally respond in a regular way. This is not, however, the only way forward. In fact, Merleau-Ponty avers, the world is an 'interworld', part of what he refers to as 'the system "Self-others-things"' (*PP* 57/66). To make full sense of this, it is useful to identify two 'layers' of the interworld (themselves, of course, inextricably intertwined) which are presupposed by the 'personal' layer on which, arguably, Sartre focuses too much.

At the most basic level, the interworld is simply the obverse of the perspectivity of perceived objects: just as 'we have learned in individual perception not to conceive our perspective views as independent of each other; we know that they slip into each other and are brought together finally in the thing', likewise 'my perspective of the world . . . slips spontaneously into the other's' (*PP* 353/411). We know that the nonvisible sides of the object are given with its visible sides (*PrP* 14), but those very 'nonvisible sides' are visible to the other sitting opposite me, to whom the sides visible to me and nonvisible to him are also given. Others' (actual and possible) perceptions of objects form the horizon of my own, and *vice versa*.[5] If my friend Paul and I are looking at a landscape, we are looking at *the same landscape*; we 'point out to each other certain details of the landscape; and Paul's finger, which is pointing out the church tower, is not a finger-for-me that I think of as oriented towards a church-tower-for-me, it is Paul's finger which itself shows me the tower that Paul sees'. Conversely, 'my gestures invade Paul's world and guide his gaze' (*PP* 405/471-2; cf. *PrP* 17). Thus, '[i]n so far as I have sensory functions . . . I am already in communication with others' (*PP* 353/411).

There is also a social and cultural layer, mediated (in ways to be elucidated in the next section) by '[t]he very first of all cultural objects, and the one by which all the rest exist', namely 'the body of the other person as the vehicle of a form of behaviour' (*PP* 348/406). Recall from Ch. 3v that the acquisition of what Merleau-Ponty denominated 'motor habits' includes learning how to walk, learning how to perform activities such as dancing which are figurative variations on such 'primary actions', and learning how to use tools and other 'cultural objects'. The child finds himself surrounded by the bodies of others who sit and walk in particular ways, who gesture and gesticulate, who dance, and who utilize various objects. To learn how to walk, to gesture and to dance is to learn how these *others* do these things.[6] And to learn what a chair, a cup, or a rocking horse *is* is to learn how it *is used*, that is, how it is used by *others* (one's parents, teachers or peers): '[e]ach of these objects is moulded to the human action which it serves' (*PP* 347/405), such objects have an inherently interpersonal existence. ('Someone is making use of my familiar objects. But who can it be? I say that it is another, a second self', *PP* 353/412.) One cultural object in particular has a peculiarly central role in the perception of others: language (*PP* 354/413); and the meanings of words too are learned 'as I learn to use a tool, by seeing it used in the context of a certain situation' (*PP* 403/469). (There is more about language in the Coda to this chapter.) In virtue of this layer of shared existence, I am always already '*situated* in an intersubjective world' (*PP* 355/414).

The first layer of intersubjective existence is characterized by Merleau-Ponty as 'anonymous' and 'prepersonal'. 'Every perception takes place in an atmosphere of generality and is presented to us anonymously.' There is a sense in which 'I cannot say that *I* see the blue of the sky . . . I can see blue because I am *sensitive* to colours' (*PP* 215/250). The origin of this 'sensation' is 'anterior to myself, it arises from *sensibility* which has preceded it and will outlive it' (*PP* 216/250-1). Anybody – any *body* – sensitive to the same range of colours will also see the blue of the sky; my sensibility to blue is nothing to do with any conscious decision or any voluntary act on my part. Nor is the object's unity, its possession of inner and outer horizons: 'I am not myself wholly in these operations'. Thus, '[t]o say that I have a visual field is to say that by reason of my position I have access to and an opening upon a system of . . . visible beings . . . through a gift of nature, with no effort made on my part'; so 'vision is prepersonal' (*PP* 216/251). It is for this very reason that the world is intersubjective at this level: 'my' perspective 'slips spontaneously into the other's . . . because both are brought together in the one single world in which we all participate as anonymous subjects of perception' (*PP* 353/411). The second layer is characterized as 'impersonal' (*PP* 356/414) and as 'anonymous': 'Someone uses the pipe for smoking, the spoon for eating, the bell for summoning', so that '[i]n the cultural object, I feel the close presence of others beneath a veil of anonymity' (*PP* 348). (The scope of 'impersonality' and 'anonymity' in this case clearly implicitly extends in the first instance only to those who are members of one's culture or in 'one's own circle'.) There is, of course, a personal layer of existence as well: my conscious decision to be a writer or to 'devote my life to mathematics' (*PP* 215/250) is *my* decision.

It is this last, personal, layer of existence upon which Sartre appears to focus. The appearance of another subject in 'my' world is threatening because he has his own free projects which have the potential to come into conflict with mine. Of course, such projects need not *actually* conflict: cf. Merleau-Ponty's description of the experience of dialogue, where 'there is constituted between the other person and myself a common ground; my thought and his are woven into a single fabric . . . Our perspectives merge into each other, and we co-exist through a common world' (*PP* 354/413). Sartre however argues that such a 'we-experience' could not constitute a basic structure of human reality since it is 'experienced by a particular consciousness', i.e., me or you; all it takes to demonstrate this is the possibility of this experience of the 'we' being mistaken, as in this exchange between a couple in a café: ' "We are very dissatisfied." "But no, my dear, speak for yourself" ' (*BN* 414).

Merleau-Ponty does not deny the friability of the 'we'-experience: if we 'undertake some project in common, this common project is not one single project, it does not appear in the selfsame light to both of us, we are not both equally enthusiastic about it, or at any rate not quite in the same way, simply because Paul is Paul and I am myself' (*PP* 356/415).[7] Thus 'the difficulties inherent in the perception of others did not all stem from objective thought' (*PP* 356/415); there is 'a solipsism rooted in living experience'.[8] Yet, none of this threatens the impersonal and prepersonal facets of the interworld[9]: on the contrary, the personal layer of existence is *built upon* and *presupposes* them (cf. *PP* 357/416). Sartre's instance of misunderstanding presupposes that both people perceived the table, the wine glasses, the waiter; that both knew what the table was for and what to do with the glasses; that both knew what the word 'dissatisfied' meant. Thus, the world is fundamentally and inescapably an interworld, and if Sartre missed this, it was because he was overly preoccupied with the personal layer of existence.[10]

Why?

iv. BODILY RECIPROCITY

The objectivist's favoured method for arguing to the *existence* of the other is, as we have seen, the so-called 'argument from analogy'. It is also their favoured method for explaining how we *understand* others: that is, even if we put to one side the concerns about solipsism and take it for granted that other conscious subjects *exist*, there may seem to be a further question of how we actually understand *what* they are thinking and feeling. How do I know, for instance, that another is angry? The objectivist answer can only be that we see the other frown and shake his fist, we hear him hissing his words or shouting, and we reason that since our bodies do all these things when we are angry, most probably the other is angry.

Both Sartre and Merleau-Ponty reject this, and at first sight in remarkably similar terms, since for both of them the primary error resides in supposing that the other is an 'object' *à la* the prejudice of objective thought. Here Sartre: 'These frowns, this redness, this stammering, this slight trembling of the hands, these downcast looks which seem at once timid and threatening – these do not *express* anger, they *are* the anger'. (That is, there is an *internal* relation between the anger and its bodily manifestations.) Thus, there is no need to resort to reasoning by analogy 'in order to explain how we *understand* expressive conducts' (*BN* 346-7). And Merleau-Ponty: 'I do not see anger . . . as a psychic fact hidden behind the gesture . . . it is anger itself'. Hence, '[f]aced with an angry or threatening gesture, I have no need, in order to understand it, to recall the feelings which I myself experienced when I used these gestures on my own account' (*PP* 184/214; cf. *SNS* 52). Merleau-Ponty's diagnosis of the problems with the argument from analogy goes rather deeper. First, the analogy in question is supposed to be between two bodies seen '*from the outside*', i.e., from the second-person perspective: between my red face and clenched fist and the other's. Yet, 'I know very little, from inside, of the mime of anger', that is, what my own angry body looks like 'from the outside'; thus 'a decisive factor is missing' for any reasoning by analogy (*PP* 184/214; cf. *SNS* 52-3).[11] Secondly, I would need to be aware in my own case of the *connections* between what my body looks like when I am angry and my own anger, in order to be able to infer the other's anger from his body's looking like mine; because the objectivist disallows internal relations, he will have to insist on causal ones. So not only must I know what my angry body looks like from the outside but I must have grounds for inferring a *causal* relation between that appearance and my anger.

To reject the objectivist picture of the relationship between gestures and what they express is of course to reject this account of *how* we understand others' gestures; but what alternative account can the phenomenologists offer? Here, we see an apparently slight but ultimately important difference between Sartre and Merleau-Ponty. Although both can say that 'I perceive the grief or anger of the other in his conduct' (*PP* 356/415) and that 'the mental life of others becomes an immediate object, a whole charged with immanent meaning' (*PP* 58/67), Sartre claims that the other's expressive conduct 'is originally released to perception as understandable; its meaning is part of its being just as the colour of the paper is part of the being of the paper' (*BN* 347). This, Merleau-Ponty thinks, is not quite right.

It seems to me that Merleau-Ponty's reluctance to accept this stems from the fact that he is conscious, in a way that Sartre is not, that the less 'like us' another creature is, the less we understand it or him in this immediate way: 'I do not "understand" the sexual pantomime of the dog, still less of the cockchafer or the praying mantis' (*PP* 184/214). (He also suggests that the same thing applies to 'the expression of the emotions in primitive peoples or in circles too unlike the ones in which I move'.) And this suggests that there is an element of truth in the so-called argument from analogy, as long as we do not imagine it to be an *argument*, a process of intellectual *reasoning*; an entomologist can, after all, understand the sexual pantomime of the cockchafer or the praying mantis *intellectually*, but this is precisely not the way in which we understand the gestures of another human being.[12] 'The sense of the gestures is not given, but understood, that is, recaptured by an act on the spectator's part. The whole difficulty is to conceive this act clearly without confusing it with a cognitive operation' (*PP* 185/215). There gradually emerge two closely linked claims: first, that the understanding in question is *bodily*, not intellectual or cognitive: '[i]t is through my body that I understand other people' (*PP* 186/216).[13] Secondly, rather than 'analogy', we need a notion of *bodily reciprocity* to get at that whereby this understanding comes about.

I will, in good Merleau-Pontyan fashion even if Merleau-Ponty does not actually proceed this way on this occasion, try to illuminate these two claims about normal interpersonal understanding with examples of *abnormal* interpersonal understanding.

We can grasp the idea that the understanding in question is *bodily* by considering individuals with autistic spectrum disorders, including Asperger's syndrome (sometimes called 'high-functioning autism'), whose primary symptoms include what may almost seem like a blindness to others.[14] Sacks (1995: 269) makes mention of 'an intelligent autistic girl of twelve who . . . said, of another student, "Joanie is making a funny noise".' (In fact, Joanie was crying bitterly.) Most of his essay is devoted to a particular Asperger's sufferer, Temple Grandin, who has taught herself to cope, more or less, in a world of others; she describes herself as having built up a library of mental 'videotapes' 'of how people behaved in different circumstances. She would play these over and over again and learn, by degrees, to correlate what she saw, so that she could then predict how people in similar circumstances might act' (Sacks 1995: 260). Grandin has to '"compute" others' intentions and states of mind, to try to make algorithmic, explicit, what for the rest of us is second nature' (Sacks 1995: 270). Other children participated in 'an exchange of meanings, a negotiation, a swiftness of understanding so remarkable that she [as a child] sometimes wondered if they were all telepathic'. She can now 'infer' social signals, 'but she cannot perceive them, cannot participate in this magical communication directly, or conceive the many-leveled kaleidoscopic states of mind behind it' (Sacks 1995: 272). That she is 'abnormal' is beyond doubt; but what should we draw from her case about 'normal' understanding of others?[15]

Many philosophers and psychologists who write about autistic spectrum disorders assert that what such individuals lack is a 'theory of mind'[16]; but this description seems exactly wrong, at least with   regard to Grandin. First, she 'was already asocial at the age of six months and stiffened in her mother's arms at this time' – a common reaction in autism – yet 'theories of mind' are not expected to develop until age three or four (Sacks 1995: 291). And secondly, Grandin has *developed* a 'theory of mind' for herself – what else would we call that library of mental 'videotapes' 'of how people behaved in different circumstances'? – but still lacks that all-but-telepathic ability *just to understand* others: she is like those ento-mologists who understand the sexual pantomime of the praying mantis intellectually, but without understanding it, as we might say, viscerally. To borrow her own self-description, she is like 'an anthro-pologist on Mars' in her efforts to understand others.[17] The problem of those individuals with autistic spectrum disorders is not that they lack something intellectual or cognitive, a *theory* of mind, but some kind of *bodily* understanding. Those children's 'magical' ability to 'exchange meanings' was grounded in their bodies, not their intellects.

The notion of bodily *reciprocity* builds on this. Merleau-Ponty develops this notion in the first instance by reference to infants, especially in his oft-quoted example of the 15-month-old baby which 'opens its mouth if I playfully take one of its fingers between my teeth and pretend to bite it . . . "Biting" has immediately, for it, an intersubjective significance' (*PP* 352/410). Merleau-Ponty dis-cusses this example in connection, once again, with rebutting the idea that we understand others via a kind of argument from analogy, and infants have a certain polemical advantage in making this case. A young baby lacks the conceptual and intellectual repertoire to elaborate an *argument* about what the other's intentions might be, thus reinforcing the bodily nature of the reciprocity in question. (Cf. *PrP* 115; *CPP* 246.) In any case, the infant has no idea what its own mouth and teeth look like ('it has scarcely looked at its face in a glass'), so lacks access to the premise that would be essential to any argument from an analogy between its mouth and mine (cf. *PP* 184/214). Rather, the body schema as a 'system of equivalents' between (*inter alia*) the other's body and one's own (cf. Ch. 3i) means that the baby's 'own mouth and teeth, as it feels them from the inside, are immediately, for it, an apparatus to bite with, and my jaw, as the baby sees it from the outside, it immediately, for it, capable of the same intentions' (*PP* 352/410). This internal relation between my body and that of the other is bodily reciprocity. It is not simply that the infant perceives the other's intentions immediately in perceiving his gestures (as Sartre appeared to suggest) but that it 'perceives its intentions in its body, and my body with its own, and *thereby my intentions in its own body*' (*PP* 352/410, italics added).[18] Thus, we understand the other through 'the reciprocity of my intentions and the gestures of others, of my intentions and gestures discernable in the conduct of other people. It is as if the other person's intention inhabited my body and mine his' (*PP* 185/215; cf. *PP* 352/410).

Thus, although mimicry (of a biting gesture or of a smile) may seem an utterly mundane capacity, objective thought makes mimicry *inconceivable*: the child would have to 'translate its visual image of the other's smile into a motor language. The child would have to set his facial muscles in motion in such a way as to reproduce the visible expression that is called "the smile" in another. But how could he do it? . . . [T]he problem comes close to being resolved only on condition that certain classical prejudices are renounced' (*PrP* 116): 'imitation cannot be this effort at double translation' (*CAL* 32, *CPP* 21). Note that this is an account of the *possibility* of imitation; it does not by itself explain why infants *in fact* imitate others, which they evidently do. Some would no doubt posit an 'instinct for mimicry'; Merleau-Ponty prefers a different route. According to him (who, we must remember, held the Chair of Child Psychology and Pedagogy at the Sorbonne for three years), the young child, up to around age three, 'has no awareness of himself or of others as private subjectivities' (*PP* 355/413).[19] From this perspective, when the infant perceives 'my' biting intention in 'its' body, it does not distinguish this from its own biting intention – so it opens its mouth and makes as if to bite. We gradually become individuals; however, the process of 'segregation', of individuation, 'is never completely finished' (*PrP* 119; cf. *CPP* 260): 'the unsophisticated thinking of our earliest years remains as an indispensable acquisition underlying that of maturity' (*PP* 355/414).[20]

It is in virtue of this bodily reciprocity that the infant comes to inhabit the cultural interworld; it is this which justifies the claim that '[t]he very first of all cultural objects, and the one by which all the rest exist, is the body of the other person as the vehicle of a form of behaviour' (*PP* 348/406). We saw in the previous section that to learn how to walk is to learn how 'one' walks, i.e., how those 'in one's own circle' walk, and to learn what a chair, a cup, or a rocking horse *is* is to learn how it is used (in that circle). This learning is in the first instance a *bodily* learning, and could not even begin unless *the other's conduct* spoke to the child as a *mobile* subject; its bodily understanding is 'ensured' by the body schema as a system of equivalents (*PP* 354/412).[21] As 'a consciousness turned toward things, I can meet in things the actions of another and find in them a meaning, because they are themes of possible activity for my own body' (*PrP* 117), there is a kind of 'postural impregnation' of my own body by the conducts I witness (*PrP* 118). The child witnesses the parent picking up a fork and spearing a potato with it, or watches a playmate clamber up on the rocking horse and begin to rock; unless his *body* in effect says 'I can do that too' (even if it cannot yet quite manage to do the thing), his even making the attempt to 'do that too' would be incomprehensible.

This notion can once again be illuminated through a consideration of abnormal cases. One of the epigrams to the neurologist Jonathan Cole's book *About Face* is a quotation from Merleau-Ponty which clearly expresses bodily reciprocity: 'I live in the facial expression of the other, as I feel him living in mine'. Cole records (*inter alia*) the experience of a number of individuals with Möbius' syndrome, a congenital neurological condition in which the facial muscles are paralyzed: one wrote that 'I am unable to raise my eyebrows, close my eyes tightly, move my eyes to the side, smile or move my lips . . . my face has a mask-like appearance' (quoted in Cole 1999: 118).[22] One obvious consequence is that such individuals have a reduced repertoire of nonverbal communication. Thus, their emotions, thoughts and wishes are not 'automatically' reflected in their faces, nor can they voluntarily signal them with smiles, frowns or quirked eyebrows.

What might we expect from the perspective of Merleau-Ponty's notion of bodily reciprocity? First, that they would have difficulty 'reading' *others'* emotions and intentions from their faces, and this is indeed what tends to be found. James said that he had only recently 'latched onto' the signals that indicated whether someone coming toward him was going to speak to him (quoted in Cole 1999: 119).[23] Secondly, that even though adults may acquire 'compensatory strategies' (Goldman & Sripada 2005) and learn consciously to scan for the nonverbal signals that indicate others' emotions and intentions (much as Temple Grandin learned to use her intellect to compensate for her lack of the bodily 'telepathy' that others possessed), these will at best enable these patients to understand others intellectually, not bodily. So we might expect that they will have difficulty responding to the perception of happiness or sadness in their interlocutor with a *felt* pleasure or *felt* sympathy; and indeed when someone confides their grief in James, 'I tell the person that I feel very sorry for you but I'm thinking that rather than feeling it' (quoted in Cole 1999: 127). Thirdly, that they would themselves feel emotions more intellectually than bodily, and again, this is what tends to be found: 'I sort of *think* happy or I *think* sad, not really saying or recognizing actually feeling happy or feeling sad . . . I have to say this thought is a happy thought, and therefore I am happy' (quoted in Cole 1999: 127).

We might also take note of certain research done from the perspective of embodied cognition; bodily reciprocity is recognizable in the 'facial feedback hypothesis' (e.g., Goldman & Sripada 2005; Niedenthal et al. 2010).[24] A recent study (Neal & Chartrand 2011) grounded in this model offered evidence that individuals who have been injected with BOTOX® (a widely used cosmetic product which reduces the appearance of wrinkles by paralyzing the expressive muscles of the face with injected botulinum toxin) are worse than controls in recognizing which emotion was being expressed in photographs of faces.[25] The suggestion is that because the BOTOX® subjects cannot mimic the facial expressions, they are less good at recognizing them: as Neal commented, ' "When we mimic, we get a window into another person's inner world." And conversely, "When we can't mimic, that window is a little darker" '.[26]

Bodily reciprocity clearly makes such phenomena intelligible in a way that Sartre's claim that we simply *perceive* others' intentions and emotions does not. Yet, is there not a problem here? Does bodily reciprocity not obliterate the distinction between I and the other? Not at all: 'first/second -person asymmetry' remains, even at the basic level of the distinction between the visual smile of the other – emotional conduct seen from the outside – and one's own motor smile – emotional conduct felt from the inside. 'The grief and the anger of another have never quite the same significance for him as they have for me. For him, these situations are lived through, for me they are displayed . . . Paul suffers because he has lost his wife . . . whereas I suffer because Paul is grieved' (*PP* 356/415). Just because 'my body and the other's are one whole, two sides of one and the same phenomenon' (*PP* 354/412), it does not follow that there are not *two* bodies. Moreover, the 'miraculous prolongation of my own intentions' (*PP* 354/412) that my body discovers in the other's is not my actual intention but a *possible* intention of mine, and, very importantly, 'miracles' can be unwelcome. My body may discover in yours the intention to punch me in the nose: in boxing, 'each move triggers off a counter-move, every stance of the body becomes a sign pregnant with a meaning that the opponent has to grasp while it is still incipient, reading in the beginnings of a stroke or a sidestep the imminent future' (Bourdieu 1977: 11; cf. 18).[28]

Finally, the *possibility* of misunderstanding is inevitable. The other outruns me, just as the perceived world in general does: 'when I say that I know and like someone, I aim, beyond his qualities, at an inexhaustible ground which may one day shatter the image I have formed of him. This is the price for there being . . . "other people"' (*PP* 361/421, cf. 359/419), just as the price for perceiving is the possibility of illusion and error.

v. CODA: GESTURES AND SPEECH

Once we have dispensed with the 'the problem of the other', it seems anodyne to say that we understand each other through understanding the meanings of our words and gestures. However, objective thought has great difficulty in making sense of what it is for words and gestures to 'have' meanings.[29] The issue of word-meaning is a standard topic within Anglophone philosophy of language (as is the connected issue of the relationship between thought and language); the issue of gesture-meaning (more broadly, what today is colloquially referred to as 'body language') is seldom considered in its own right: it tends to be presupposed that the phrases 'word-meaning' and 'gesture-meaning' use the word 'meaning' in radically different ways, and that 'gesture-meaning' is not particularly philosophically significant (cf. Ch. 2i on so-called 'natural meaning'). Here, I can do more than gesture at some of the issues and at Merleau-Ponty's alternative way of looking at things.[30]

- *Word-meanings.* Objectivist accounts find it impossible to admit what appears undeniable: that *words have meanings* (*PP* 177/206). The empiricist will say that what we call 'word-meaning' is simply a matter of the association of a certain sound with a certain stimulus, and that 'understanding' the word is a matter of the revival of 'verbal images': traces left in our brains or our unconscious mind by hearing the words spoken (cf. *PP* 174-5/203). The intellectualist will say that *words* do not have meanings; rather, *thought* does: the word is nothing but a container for the thought which is the true vehicle of meaning (cf. *PP* 176-7/204). One strategy Merleau-Ponty uses to undermine these accounts is a particular type of aphasia, i.e., a neurological difficulty with language. The patient he describes is capable of 'concrete' but not 'abstract' language, much as Schneider was capable of concrete but not abstract movement (Ch. 3iii): he can find the word 'no' 'when he intends to furnish a denial arising from his present experience', but not 'when it is a question of an exercise having no emotional and vital bearing' (*PP* 175/203-4). Has he lost the word 'no' or not? This 'paradox', like Schneider's paradox of knowing and not knowing where his nose is, is insoluble from an objectivist perspective.

- The intellectualist account of linguistic meaning presupposes that *thought and language* are externally related, just as it presupposes that consciousness and body are: speech is the clothing of thought or the container for thought just as the body is the clothing of consciousness. Merleau-Ponty expends considerable effort on undermining this conception: it would render incomprehensible 'why thought tends toward expression as toward its completion, why the most familiar thing appears indeterminate as long as we have not recalled its name, why the thinking subject himself is in a kind of ignorance of his thoughts so long as he has not formulated them for himself' in language (*PP* 177/206). In fact, speech 'does not translate ready-made thought, but accomplishes it' (*PP* 178/207); 'speech is not the "sign" of thought' as smoke is a sign of fire, i.e. speech and thought are not externally related (*PP* 181-2/211).[31] Rather, speech 'is the presence of thought in the phenomenal world' (*PP* 182/211); '[t]hought is no "internal" thing, and does not exist independently of the world and of words' (*PP* 183/213).

- *Verbal vs. non-verbal gestures.* At first glance, speech and non-verbal gestures may seem rather similar: 'I'm happy' and a smile both express my happiness, 'Look over there' and pointing both call my interlocutor's attention to something in our shared perceptual field. At second glance, they are very different: the verbal gestures will only be understood by someone who speaks English, whose '[a]vailable meanings . . . establish between speaking subjects a common world' (*PP* 186/216-17), whereas non-verbal gestures, we are inclined to say, are a universally understood mode of expression. The temptation is thus to say that non-verbal gestures are 'natural', verbal gestures 'conventional' or 'arbitrary' (*PP* 186-7/217). Merleau-Ponty however argues that the former are less 'natural' and the latter more so than we tend to suppose. Thus, *'natural' vs. 'conventional'* is yet another duality in need of breaking down. On the one hand, the phrase 'natural gesture' or 'natural sign' suggests that 'the anatomical organization of our body' produces a one-to-one correspondence 'between specific gestures and given "states of mind"'. But this is less true than we might suppose: 'the behaviour associated with anger or love is not the same in a Japanese and an Occidental. Or, to be more precise, the difference of behaviour corresponds to a difference in the emotions themselves' (*PP* 188-9/219). Hence, '[i]t is no more natural and no less conventional, to shout in anger or to kiss in love than to call a table "a table"' (*PP* 189/220). On the other hand, verbal gestures are not arbitrary if we take into account 'the emotional content of the word', its "gestural" sense'.[32] 'The predominance of vowels in one language, or of consonants in another . . . do not represent so many arbitrary conventions for expressions of one and the same idea, but several ways for the human body to sing the world's praises and in the last resort to live it' (*PP* 187/218). Thus, 'there are no conventional signs, standing as the notation of a thought pure and clear in itself, there are only words in which the whole history of a language has been compressed' (*PP* 188/218).

- This has implications for the *translatability* of languages: 'the *full* meaning of a language is never translatable into another' (*PP* 187/218). Striking confirmation of this conclusion is given by the linguist Anna Wierzbicka: to take a particularly relevant example, '*friend* and *friendship* are English words, embodying concepts which are cultural artifacts of the society which created them' (1997: 33). She notes that even the meaning of the English word 'friend' has changed 'in ways which are revealing of underlying changes in human relations' (Wierzbicka 1997: 35; and she was writing this well before the phenomenon of Facebook). And when one examines the use of those words in other languages that may look at first sight like exact equivalents of 'friend' or 'friendship', it proves to be both more complicated and more culturally illuminating than we might naively imagine. E.g., in Russian, there are several words – *drug, tovarišč, prijatel'* and so on – all of which might be translated as 'friend'. Yet, none has an exact equivalent in English. E.g., *drug* (plural *druz'ja*) is hugely important in Russian life: one's *druz'ja* help one out in times of need, are invited to stay, spend holidays with one; they are people in whom one has complete trust, to whom one 'pours out one's soul', and so on (Wierzbicka 1997: 60-1). To translate *'drug'* as, say, 'close friend' would be unbearably crude.

- All these observations apply to speech, which has 'settle[d] into a sediment' (*PP* 190/220), in which 'the meaning of speech is nothing other than the way in which it handles this linguistic world or in which it plays modulations on the keyboard of acquired meanings' (*PP* 186/217); here we have 'a kind of habituation, a use of language as a tool or instrument' (*PrP* 99; cf. *CPP* 242). And yet, 'significances now acquired must necessarily have been new once' (*PP* 194/226). This leads us to what is perhaps Merleau-Ponty's best-known contribution to the subject: **the distinction between the *speaking word* and the *spoken word*** (*PP* 197/229) or between 'first-hand' and 'second-hand' speech (cf. *PP* 179 n.1/208 n.5). In the first, 'the significant intention is at the stage of coming into being'; the second 'enjoys available significances as one might enjoy an acquired fortune' (*PP* 197/229).

- This distinction is not exactly well-drawn in *PP*. Paradigms of 'speaking speech' or 'authentic expression' include the speech of the writer, artist or philosopher (*PP* 197/229) or 'that of the child uttering its first words, of the lover revealing his feelings, of the "first man who spoke"' (*PP* 179 n.1/208 n.5). These are *very* different examples. As Baldwin points out, Merleau-Ponty's use of the term 'authentic' here seems to echo Heidegger (and to suggest that 'spoken speech' is mere 'idle talk'); his artist or writer might issue 'authentic speech' by creative imagery and metaphor, yet the philosopher – even one who 'reawaken[s] primordial experience anterior to all traditions' (*PP* 179 n. 1/208 n.5) – may not be inventing new language but merely seeking to make himself as clear as possible 'by sticking closely to established meanings'; such a philosopher is hardly engaging in idle talk (Baldwin 2007: 94). Again, lovers revealing their feelings 'do not need to create new idioms, but only to express themselves in ways that are new to their relationship' (Baldwin 2007: 90).[33]

- Despite these weaknesses, there are two valuable points that issue from this distinction. (i) One is the *continuity between non-verbal gestures and speech*, particularly evident in 'the "first man who spoke"' and 'the child uttering its first words' – a continuity which, like bodily reciprocity, still casts a shadow in adulthood: 'the words take up the gesture and the gesture the words, and they inter-communicate through the medium of my body' (*PP* 234-5/273). (ii) The second is *the 'paradoxical' nature of expression* (cf. *PP* 389/452): the dialectical interplay between 'spoken speech' and 'speaking speech'. The 'acquired fortune' of 'spoken words' required 'speaking words' in order to be acquired in the first place, but is also what makes new 'speaking words' possible (*PP* 197/229); 'I express when, utilizing all these already speaking instruments, I make them say something they have never said' (*PrP* 91). Thus 'to give expression' is 'to ensure, by the use of words already used, that the new intention carries on the heritage of the past . . . to incorporate the past into the present, and weld that present into a future' (*PP* 392/456). Like the sedimentation of habit in the body, the sedimentation of language provides both inertia and momentum; it reveals, we might say, that the ambiguity of being-in-the-world is translated by that of speech as well as that of the body, and that both (as well as that of the world, the thing, and others) are to be understood through that of time (cf. *PP* 365/425).[34] Some speech is almost entirely 'spoken': for Schneider, 'the "life" of language is impaired', and 'meaning is, as it were, ossified' (*PP* 196/228). Other speech is almost entirely 'speaking': cf. the anthropologist Thomas Csordas' compelling analysis of the glossolalia ('speaking in tongues') that occurs in certain Charismatic Catholic ritual healing sessions as a way of maximizing a 'pure act of expression', 'never subject to codification' (2002: 77).[35] Each extreme eloquently demonstrates the limits of the other.

CHAPTER 6

MERLEAU-PONTY *VIVANT*

Even as I was putting the finishing touches on the manuscript for this book, new writings were appearing which bore out the assertion that Merleau-Ponty's spirit lives on. So too was a constant stream of new evidence of the continued vigour, in modern dress, of 'the prejudice of objective thought'. I cannot help thinking that the two are connected.

Merleau-Ponty is gradually infiltrating the strongholds of Anglophone psychology and philosophy of perception, if only around the edges. There is the protracted exchange between Dreyfus (e.g., 2007a and b) and McDowell (e.g., 2007a and c), which continues to generate lively discussion; it concerns the issue of whether, and how, rationality informs perception and action (in particular, what Dreyfus refers to as 'absorbed coping'; see Ch. 3).[1] There are also a couple of trends in Anglophone philosophy and psychology, which I will mention more generally without developing them. One is a corner of 'cognitive science' whose buzzwords are signalled in the title of one section in Carman 2008: 'Embodied cognition, extended mind, enactivism'; Carman expresses a scepticism which I am minded to share about the Merleau-Pontyan-ness of these endeavours.[2] Another may not be recognized as Merleau-Pontyan even by some of its practitioners, since it has largely been mediated via the psychologist J. J. Gibson, who was himself influenced by both the Gestalt psychologists and Merleau-Ponty.[3] (Eagle-eyed readers might spot Gibson's name in several footnotes in this book; Gibson's language of 'affordances' also infuses the McDowell-Dreyfus exchange.) Its key terms are 'ecological perception' (the term 'ecological' stressing, as of course Merleau-Ponty does, the interrelatedness of perceiver and environment), 'direct perception' (in contrast to the notion that perception is sensation embellished by learning and inference; see Ch. 2) and the 'co-perception of self and environment' (see Ch. 4).[4]

Outside analytic philosophy and psychology, Merleau-Ponty's influence has reached a wide variety of disciplines. This in part reflects the range of disciplines on which he explicitly touches in *PP*, some of which he developed further in essays and lectures. He has inspired thinking in fields ranging from aesthetics and art history (e.g., Crowther 2001) through environmental studies (e.g., Cataldi & Hamrick 2007, Toadvine 2009) to geography (e.g., Ingold 2000)[5] and architecture (McCann 2008), not to mention the healthcare professions (see §i), and sociology and anthropology (see §iii). He has also had a real impact on feminism (see §ii), a set of theoretical orientations which is interdisciplinary; he is just beginning to have an impact on the ways in which animals are conceptualized (see §iv) which, it is to be hoped, will eventually trickle over into other disciplines.

It would clearly be impossible to survey all of these developments in the short space available. In order to provide a sense of the continued fertility of Merleau-Ponty's thought, my strategy in this final chapter will be to focus on studies of 'different' ways of being in the world.[6] Merleau-Ponty comments that 'classical thought has little time for animals, children, primitive people and madmen' (*WP* 54), a moment later adding 'the sick' to this strange list, and elsewhere women (*CPP* 373, cf. Baldwin's introduction to *WP*, 19).[7] And he indicates that 'modern thought' (i.e., phenomenology and its allies) can offer a way into these other ways of being in the world, by 'bring[ing] to light the movement by which all living things, ourselves included, endeavour to give shape to a world that has not been preordained to accommodate our attempts to think it and act upon it' (*WP* 57). This sounds like an invitation to explore other ways of being in the world; there is a vast and growing literature which has in effect taken up this invitation, both drawing inspiration from *PP* and indicating its limitations, so as to mark this work out as a true 'classic'.[8]

In the main body of this chapter, I attempt to give a feel for this literature in just four areas (the choice is unashamedly personal): illness, women, culture and animals.[9] The first three have undergone a good deal of cross-fertilization in recent decades: anthropologists (including feminist anthropologists) may study the experience of women in our/their own or other cultures, or the experience of illness in our/their own and other cultures; feminist theorists often thematize what has been called 'the grip of culture on the body' and may offer social critiques of largely 'gendered' illnesses such as anorexia nervosa, etc.; and medics and health-care workers are becoming more attuned to the 'patient voice' and to gender issues and now recognize the need for 'cultural competence'. Anglophone investigation of 'the phenomenology of animal life', by contrast, has on the whole not been involved in this cross-fertilization;[10] this may suggest a sharp Anglophone division between the 'social sciences' and the 'life sciences' which Merleau-Ponty himself tried to bridge. The brief summaries and vignettes which follow should give a sense both of what has been done so far and of areas for possible future exploration. The Coda to this chapter finally thematizes the notion of an intellectual prejudice: a leitmotif both in this book and in *PP*.

i. ILLNESS

It is noteworthy that *pain* figures only very briefly in *PP* (93/107),[11] where it simply serves to exemplify the idea of the body as affective and thus to put pressure on the idea that the body is an object.[12] Moreover, although descriptions of particular illnesses (e.g., of Schneider's difficulties) are far more detailed, they figure in *PP* largely instrumentally (see Ch. 3): either to subserve polemical purposes, or to shed light on 'normal' experience (directly or through contrast). That is, Merleau-Ponty's aim in *PP* is not really to describe the world of the ill *for its own sake*.

Many other writers have seen enormous value in doing so. In some cases, this may be said to be for the sheer fascination of travel, be it to distant and unimaginable lands (cf. Sacks 1985) or to one's own village. In others, it stems from a deep-rooted *cultural* concern: '[t]he traditional biomedical paradigm focuses exclusively along "Cartesian" lines on the body-as-machine, with a concurrent de-emphasis on the personhood of the patient and the reality and importance of the human experience of illness' (Toombs 1988: 201);[13] she aims to shift that focus: illness, she urges, 'is experienced by the patient not so much as a specific breakdown in the mechanical functioning of the biological body, but more fundamentally as a disintegration of his "world"' (1988: 207). In yet others, it stems from a dissatisfaction with a tendency to stress ways in which the ill person *falls short* of 'normality': it may be suggested that 'what is interesting is not where [the patient] fails, but how he still succeeds in restoring coherence and repairing breakdowns' (Widdershoven 1998: 30). Many of these explorations make use of Merleau-Ponty's vocabulary, in some cases supplementing it in ways that indicate limitations in Merleau-Ponty's descriptions.[14]

There are two seminal works to which I will call attention: S. Kay Toombs' 1988 article and Drew Leder's 1990 book; both draw on Zaner (e.g., 1964 and 1981) and Sartre as well as Merleau-Ponty.[15] (See also Toombs 1993.) There are many similarities in their descriptions of the experience of pain and illness, as we will see, but different contexts for those descriptions. Toombs' motivation is the cultural concern sketched above. Leder locates his discussion in the context of a fuller phenomenology of the body, together with a wider cultural critique. He first develops the basic thought that the body in everyday experience is 'absent' or 'recessive', precisely because it is normally 'ec-static', i.e. oriented toward the world. (Cf. Ch. 3.) Leder elaborates on various modes of bodily 'disappearance', but his best-known contribution to phenomenology is his description of the ways in which the body emerges from its normal 'recessive' existence, most notably in pain and illness. Thus he refers to the body's 'dys-appearance', 'a heightening of body-focus at times of suffering or disruption' (Leder 1990: 92). A sudden pain immediately disrupts the structure of everyday action and forces the painful body-part to the fore; this region of the body 'suddenly speaks up' (Leder 1990: 71); the pain effects an 'intentional disruption' by making it difficult for the sufferer to continue to focus on what he was doing and even by immobilizing him (Leder 1990: 74), and 'exerts a telic demand upon us', 'crying out' for its removal (Leder 1990: 77). At the same time, he argues that a 'focus on dys-appearance has helped skew our cultural reading of the body toward the negative' (Leder 1990: 92).

Illness transforms our experience of the body, of objects and of lived space and time. 'First and foremost', Toombs tells us, 'illness represents dis-ability, the "inability to" engage the world in habitual ways' (1988: 207). If for Merleau-Ponty '[c]onsciousness is in the first place not a matter of "I think that" but of "I can"' (*PP* 137/159), in illness it becomes an 'I cannot' – or perhaps better, an 'I no longer can' (Leder 1990: 81; cf. Toombs 1988: 208).[16] Again, whereas ordinarily our body remains in the background, in pain and illness it becomes the figure 'against which all else is merely background'

(Toombs 1988: 208, quoting Rawlinson; cf. Leder 1990: 71; for whom this foregrounding is an aspect of dys-appearance.) Habitual actions, 'hitherto performed unthinkingly, now become effortful and must be attended to' (Toombs 1988: 208; cf. Leder 1990: 82). More generally, 'the body can no longer be taken-for-granted or ignored' (Toombs 1988: 214).

Changes in the lived body are correlative with alterations in the life-world. Leder identifies the interesting category of simply 'feeling poorly', which may be experienced 'as a change primarily in their outer world', such that it 'takes on an unappetising and resistant demeanor' (1990: 82). In illness, objects formerly presented as utilizable 'are now obstacles "to be circumvented", "avoided", or even "feared"' (Toombs 1988: 208); 'for the person with a tremor the mug is no longer simply there "to be grasped" but, rather, presents itself as a problem to be solved' (Toombs 1988: 211). Illness also effects a 'spatiotemporal constriction': '[s]pace loses its normal directionality as the world ceases to be the locus of purposeful action', and 'pulls us back' both to the here and to the now (Leder 1990: 75, 80; cf. Toombs 1988: 211). The significance of past, present and future changes: 'the primordial causality of the body, is interrupted'; future goals 'suddenly appear irrelevant or out of reach' (Toombs 1988: 212). The rhythms of bodily temporality are disrupted (Toombs 1988: 213), and '[t]he diseased body introduces its own episodic temporality of rally and relapse, which makes it stand out from the amorphous time of health' (Leder 1990: 81).

These descriptions of the transformations undergone by the body and the life-world in illness are insightful and fruitful;[17] they are beginning to have an impact on health-care practitioners.[18] Taken together, these studies reveal shortcomings of Merleau-Ponty's description of the body: his relative neglect of 'dys-appearance' by virtue of his stress on its 'disappearance', and his relative neglect of the vulnerability and passivity of the body by virtue of his stress on its activity. Moreover, as we have noted, Merleau-Ponty's use of ill individuals in *PP* is almost entirely instrumental to his philosophical purposes, as has been my own: e.g., treating individuals with Asperger's or Möbius' syndrome as 'refutations' of objective thought about interpersonal understanding. Yet, he offers the materials for something very different (cf. Rothfield 2008): 'For many years, our knowledge of children and the sick was held back' because '[l]ittle attempt was made to understand the way that they themselves lived; instead, the emphasis fell on trying to measure how far their efforts fell short of what the average adult or healthy person was capable of accomplishing' (*WP* 54-6; cf. *PP* 107/123). In something like this spirit, the authors from whom I have drawn 'cases' place the emphasis on what may be called a *healthy* response to illness. (Such a notion inevitably complicates the notion of normality sketched in the Coda to Ch. 3). Luria's 'romantic science' strove to understand individuals as 'human beings coping or failing to cope with the human condition rather than simply having "a medical problem"' (Foreword to Luria 1987: xii). For Sacks, 'a disease is never a mere loss or excess . . . there is always a reaction, on the part of the affected organism or individual, to restore, to replace, to compensate for and to preserve its identity' (1985: 4). Equally, Cole's book *Pride and a Daily Marathon* (1995, about the patient Ian mentioned in Ch. 3) shows, as Sacks says in the Foreword, 'how a human being can be thrown into a neurological hell and yet fight his way out of it to a new self-creation and life' (Cole 1995: xiii). Pain and illness may 'unmake the world', but 'the dissolution of the lifeworld is countered by a human response to find or fashion meaning' (Good 1994: 128; cf. Toombs 1988: 221f.; Leder 1990: 78).

ii. WOMEN

There is only one place to begin to elucidate the feminist reception of Merleau-Ponty, and that is with his friend and contemporary Simone de Beauvoir. We should mention her 1943 novel *L'Invitée* (*She Came to Stay*), and Merleau-Ponty's 1945 essay 'Metaphysics and the novel' (*SNS* 26-40), which treats *L'Invitée* as a herald of a new kind of literature, the metaphysical novel, seeing it as a concrete expression of the ambiguities of embodied interpersonal relations (see Ch. 5) which 'laid the foundations for existential phenomenology' (Olkowski 2006: 4). We should also mention Beauvoir's review of *PP* (1945); *PP* aims, she says, to 'give back to man this childish audacity . . . to say "I am here"'; as such, 'the whole human condition is at stake in this book' (2004 [1945]: 160).[19] Of most importance for present purposes, however, is Beauvoir's classic *The Second Sex* (1949; later hailed as a seminal feminist text, even amongst those who recognized its weaknesses), whose ontology is at least as much Merleau-Pontyan as Sartrean.[20] Also of great interest are Merleau-Ponty's lectures at the Sorbonne (*CPP*) which include extended discussion of the development of girls and women, in which one can hear many echoes of *The Second Sex*. These have not yet been much discussed in the Anglophone feminist literature, no doubt because they have only very recently been made available in an English translation. (See Welsh 2008, by the translator of these lectures).

The Second Sex (itself until very recently only available to English readers in a bowdlerized and inadequate translation) consists of two volumes bound together, entitled 'Facts and Myths' and 'Lived Experience' respectively. The Introduction argues that 'what singularly defines the situation of woman is that being, like all humans, an autonomous freedom, she discovers and chooses herself in a world where men force her to assume herself as Other' (Beauvoir 2011: 17), that is, the 'second sex', 'doomed to immanence'. The opening sentence of Volume II is perhaps the most famous in the book: 'One is not born, but rather becomes, a woman' (Beauvoir 2011: 293). This can be understood as affirming, on the one hand, that '[n]o biological, psychical, or economic destiny defines the figure that the human female takes on in society' (demonstrating this is the burden of Volume I.i) and, on the other hand, that 'it is civilisation as a whole that elaborates this intermediary product between the male and the eunuch that is called feminine' (Beauvoir 2011: 293; demonstrating this is the burden of the considerations from history and anthropology in Volume I.ii and the exploration of prevalent myths about women, e.g., that of the 'eternal feminine', in Volume I.iii). Thus, while not denying that there are biological differences between men and women, she seeks to show that these differences do not destine women to be relegated to the status of 'Other'. Volume II aims to describe 'the world from the woman's point of view such as it is offered to her' (a description which 'has shocked later writers by its unrelenting negativity', Lennon 2010: 4), and to 'see the difficulties women are up against just when, trying to escape the sphere they have been assigned until now, they seek to be part of the human *Mitsein* ["being-with"]' (Beauvoir 2011: 17). In particular, it explores 'how woman is taught to assume her condition, how she experiences this, what universe she finds herself enclosed in and what escape mechanisms are permitted her' (Beauvoir 2011: 289).

Merleau-Ponty's Sorbonne lectures contain many echoes of *The Second Sex*. Merleau-Ponty calls for a methodological eschewal of the notions of 'feminine nature' as well as 'masculine nature' (*CPP* 377); he sees 'the traits of the "feminine nature"' as 'the result of the history and the style of education under which women have been subjected': 'at ten, a girl is much more lively than a boy'; by twenty, thanks to that education, she is 'a "great timid idiot who is afraid of spiders"' (*CPP* 378, quotation from Stendhal). Alluding to the Gestalt idea of a 'field of force' (see Ch. 2), Merleau-Ponty notes that the very words 'boy' and 'girl' represent the child's situatedness 'in a force field which at every moment represents a particular nuance of masculinity or femininity' (*CPP* 381; cf. *SB* 157). And following an extended discussion of the anthropologist Margaret Mead's studies of sex and gender in a variety of cultures, he concludes that '[w]e have no grounds for speaking of "the" masculine or "the" feminine since each civilisation, according to its mode of existence, elaborates a certain type of masculinity in correlation to a certain type of femininity' (*CPP* 398).[21]

Beauvoir has been hugely influential, in ways that cannot possibly be indicated in the present context. (See, e.g., Moi 1990; Fallaize ed. 1998; Grosholz ed. 2004.) She has also been much criticized by later feminists. One group of criticisms is nicely summed up by Okely when she characterizes Beauvoir as having done 'an anthropological village study of specific women, but without the anthropological theory and focus. Her village is largely mid-century Paris and the women studied, including herself, are mainly middle-class' (Okely 1986: 71; see also §iii below).[22] Another is summed up by Bordo: 'Subsuming patriarchal institutions and practices under an oppressor/oppressed model which theorises men as possessing and wielding power of women . . . proved inadequate to the social and historical complexities' (Bordo 1993: 12). Many feminists have in consequence turned to Foucault (see the Coda to Ch. 3) as an important ally in developing a more nuanced conception of power than is visible in Beauvoir, and in theorizing the subtle and multifarious mechanisms by which power is exercised directly on bodies. (Bordo herself is one prominent example.) Merleau-Ponty too has been charged with lacking 'a "body politics"' (Hass 2008a: 94; but see Crossley 1996, which argues that Merleau-Ponty and Foucault are mutually supportive: they fill in gaps in each other's accounts). Some have found it possible to combine Foucault and phenomenology (e.g., Bartky 1990, Dolezal 2010).

Merleau-Ponty is similarly ambivalently treated by feminists.[23] Some (Butler 1989) argue that his descriptions of sexuality (in *PP* Part I.5) implicitly presuppose heterosexuality and thereby simply reproduce culturally constructed norms of sexuality. (See Oksala

2006 for a carefully considered defence; see Hass 2008a: 97-8 for further critiques of Merleau-Ponty's account of sexual desire.) Others claim that 'his theory of embodied subjectivity . . . presupposes a generic body that is male' (Kruks 2006: 27, although she robustly defends the usefulness of his account for feminist theory). Yet, others have accused him of privileging sight over touch and sound; e.g., his account of the infant's bodily reciprocity (see Ch. 5iii) is entirely visual, thus effacing intrauterine tactile and auditory experience (Irigaray: 1987; see also Olkowski 2006, Andrews 2006).[24] Indeed, some have argued that '[a]n epistemology spoken from a feminist subjectivity might privilege touch rather than sight' (Young 1990: 193).

Despite this, Merleau-Ponty has also been influential in feminism. First, his general instinct for and strategy of challenging dichotomies (mind/body, subject/object, ego/alter ego, nature/culture, essence/existence, etc.) resonates with similar (and further) feminist challenges to various 'dualisms'. One major feminist concern is that women have tended culturally to be associated with one half of many such dichotomies, e.g., the body, or nature, and at the same time, that half has been culturally *disvalued* (e.g., Bordo 1993: Introduction; see e.g. Moore 1988 Ch. 2 for a more anthropologically nuanced statement); they may respond either by attempting a revaluation of those values, or by attempting to break down the dichotomy, or (more often) both. More generally, Beauvoir has, rightly or wrongly, been read as foreshadowing a distinction between 'biological' sex and 'socially constructed' gender, together with a conviction that there are two and only two sexes; the idea that sex is purely biological, as well as the idea that there are two and only two sexes, have been challenged by post-Foucauldian feminists (e.g., Butler 1990) and historians (see the articles in Schiebinger ed. 2000, Part I), thereby problematizing the sex/gender dichotomy. (Merleau-Ponty's contestation of the nature/culture dichotomy will allow him likewise to challenge at least the first.)

And secondly, the theoretical approach within feminism which is known as 'corporeal feminism' clearly owes a great deal to Merleau-Ponty.[25] Grosz (1994) and Weiss (1999) are key figures in this approach; I want to present a seminal instance, which draws on both Beauvoir and Merleau-Ponty: Iris Marion Young's 'Throwing like a girl'. She begins with a description of the differences in the ball-throwing styles of boys and girls; 'The girl of five does not make any use of lateral space. She does not stretch her arm sideward; she does not twist her trunk; she does not move her legs, which remain side by side'. By contrast, '[a] boy of the same age, when preparing to throw, stretches his right arm sideward and backward; supinates the forearm; twists, turns and bends his trunk; and moves his right foot backwards' (Straus quoted in Young 1990: 141). This leads her to explore from a phenomenological standpoint the modalities of feminine motility and bodily comportment (in 'women situated in contemporary advanced industrial, urban, and commercial society', Young 1990: 143), of which she identified three: first, '*inhibited [motor] intentionality*, which simultaneously reaches toward a projected end with an "I can" and withholds its full bodily commitment to that end in a self-imposed "I cannot"' (Young 1990: 148); secondly, '*ambiguous transcendence*', so that rather than the lived body being 'pure fluid action, the continuous calling-forth of capacities that are applied to the world', feminine bodily existence remains '*overlaid* with immanence' (Young 1990: 148); and '*discontinuous unity*' : since 'women tend to locate their motion in part of the body only, leaving the rest of the body relatively immobile', the body's 'synthesizing' itself as well as its surroundings is disrupted (Young 1990: 149-50). She sums up by saying that '[w]omen in sexist society are physically handicapped' (1990: 153).[26]

This is a remarkable and influential piece in its own right; it has also been the occasion for criticism. Young has been read as presenting masculine embodiment as the ideal, via the thought that Merleau-Ponty's descriptions in *PP* are covertly descriptions of *masculine* motility and comportment (see, e.g., Grimshaw 1999; see Oksala 2006 for a defence of both Young and Merleau-Ponty). She actually makes it clear that that is not her intention: her term 'modalities' indicates that she takes *PP*'s descriptions as *general*, with feminine embodiment as one modality or specification, and masculine embodiment as another (Young 1990: 144 and 157n.8). Chisholm's 'Climbing like a girl' reiterates the claim that Young 'idealises' masculine embodiment and misreads her as claiming that her description applies to 'all women at all times' (Chisholm 2008: 3). Yet she rightly identifies the negativity of Young's analysis and offers a phenomenological analysis of the mountain climber Lynn Hill's experiences via 'the positive modalities of "reach", "crux coordination", "flow", "freedom" and "synaesthesia"' (Chisholm 2008: 12), even contrasting the positivity of Hill's experience with the 'alienated', instrumentalized bodily experience of a male climber (Chisholm 2008: 31; see also Young's reflections on 'Throwing like a girl' 25 years on, 2005: Introduction).

iii. CULTURE

Merleau-Ponty clearly had some knowledge of the sociology and anthropology of his day, as we might expect, with Lévi-Strauss as a close friend and with disciplinary boundaries in any case more fluid in France than in Anglophone countries.[27] In *PP*, Merleau-Ponty invokes a few anthropological facts (e.g., 'The angry Japanese smiles, the westerner goes red and stamps his foot or else goes pale and hisses his words', *PP* 189) which may strike today's anthropologists as crude (cf.: Beauvoir's claims about the taboos of 'primitive peoples' around menstruation and childbirth are 'clichéd' and treat such people as 'an undifferentiated lump', Okely 1986: 77).[28] In similar vein, Merleau-Ponty's adjectives 'primitive' and 'barbaric' (also visible in Beauvoir) may ring offensive to modern sensibilities, but they were common currency of the contemporary social theorists, e.g., Lévy-Bruhl's *Primitive Mythology* (see the Coda to Ch. 2) and Lévi-Strauss' *The Savage Mind*, dedicated to Merleau-Ponty's memory.

We should also, however, take note of Merleau-Ponty's dismissal of a sharp 'nature'/ 'culture' dichotomy (*PP* 189; see the Coda to Ch. 5 and *Signs* 122ff.), of a piece with his refusal of dichotomous thinking elsewhere. This is now orthodoxy among anthropologists, but it was not in his time. Moreover, he would surely be open to the modern anthropological refusal to reify 'cultures' as relatively permanent, stable, unified and impermeable 'objects', even if it does not seem to have occurred to him (Pandya 2008). As we will also see, his identification of bodily sensitivity and bodily reciprocity as at the heart of the perceptual and cultural interworld (see Ch. 5ii and iii) gives him resources to begin to theorize the bodily 'mechanism' of the intertwining of 'culture' and 'nature' and of 'culture' and 'individual'.[29]

We have seen Merleau-Ponty's views on the relationships between philosophy and science (see the Coda to Ch. 2): philosophy can both learn from and criticize the 'social sciences', just as it can both learn from and criticize psychology.[30] This is what gives Merleau-Ponty the right to 'reinterpret' the facts about magic, kinship, myth and so on which social theorists such as Lévi-Strauss had observed.

Lévi-Strauss was the founder of an influential anthropological approach called 'structuralism'.[31] We have of course already met with a notion of structure, meaning 'the way in which a Gestalt is organized' (see Ch. 2). Lévi-Strauss's use of the term was (at least initially) directly influenced by Gestalt theory; later it drew more heavily on its use in the 'structural linguistics' of Saussure and Jakobson.[32] Merleau-Ponty sees a continuity throughout: if 'structure' in Gestalt theory points us toward 'the configurations of the perceptual field, those wholes articulated by lines of force and giving every phenomenon its local value', structural linguistics makes us 'see the unity which lies behind a language's explicit signification, a systemization which is achieved in a language before its conceptual principle is known'; and for structural anthropology, 'society is composed of systems of this type', e.g. of kinship, myth, and ritual (*Signs* 117).[33] Indeed, society itself is a 'structure of structures', so that there is some kind of *internal relation* between a society's various structures (*Signs* 118). Now comes the critique: one might dream (with Lévi-Strauss) 'of a periodic table of [e.g.] kinship structures comparable to Mendeleev's periodic table of chemical elements' (*Signs* 118), as long one does not mistake this table for objective reality (even the objective reality of unconscious mental structures or indeed brain structures), as Lévi-Strauss did (1977: 29).[34] Like science in general, such a formal structure would be nothing but a second-order expression of the 'basic experience of the world' (*PP* viii/ix). If we are to be justified in talking about such structures, 'there ought to be a sort of lived equivalent of that structure'. (This is far closer to Bourdieu's notion of 'practice' than Bourdieu himself perhaps recognizes; see below.) By implication, Merleau-Ponty suggests that Lévi-Strauss suffers from the prejudice of objective thought, and that he is thus in danger of losing sight of his proper task *qua* anthropologist, which is, Merleau-Ponty urges, the process 'of joining objective analysis to lived experience' (*Signs* 119).

Structural anthropology has fallen out of favour, and for reasons that Merleau-Ponty would recognize. Although its demise did not come about through Merleau-Ponty's direct influence, one of his most famous students, Pierre Bourdieu, can be credited with contributing to it directly.[35] Bourdieu's *Outline of a Theory of Practice* (later elaborated into *The Logic of Practice*, 1990) put forward a powerful critique of structuralism. His twin targets – in terms which echo Merleau-Ponty – are 'subjectivism' and 'objectivism' (of which structuralism is one manifestation, as Merleau-Ponty had already hinted), in particular the latter's inherent 'intellectualist tendencies' (Bourdieu 1977: 19), which inevitably distort the phenomena on which Bourdieu's own 'theory of practice' puts emphasis: 'practical knowledge' and 'practical mastery'. Bourdieu notes that his 'questioning of objectivism is liable to be understood at first as a rehabilitation of subjectivism', when what he is after is to 'escape from the ritual either/or choice between objectivism and subjectivism in which the social sciences have so far allowed themselves to be trapped', and to see them as 'dialectically' related (Bourdieu 1977: 3-4). (Unfortunately, he locates the notion of 'lived experience' as a *subjectivist* notion, and thereby effaces – at least for some subsequent social theorists – what is in fact a deep affinity between his enterprise and Merleau-Ponty's.)[36]

Lévi-Strauss was right to see an analogy between language and culture; in both cases we see the kinds of regularities in behaviour that led some to want to talk about 'rules' or 'structures'.[37] Lévi-Strauss' problem, Bourdieu urges, is that in adopting Saussurean linguistics as his theory of language, he inherited the problems that Saussure had in making sense of the language-speech (*langue-parole*) relationship in his own understanding of the analogous culture-conduct relationship (cf. Bourdieu 1977: 23). Bourdieu highlights two linked problems: the first is that Saussure 'privileges the *structure* of signs, that is, the relations between them, at the expense of their *practical functions*' (Bourdieu 1977: 24). Saussure sees his approach as having solved the problem of how it is possible for people to understand and generate a potentially infinite number of sentences; but the real problem, Bourdieu urges, is 'the power of adaptation that is required in order to make relevant use of these sentences in constantly changing situations' (Bourdieu 1977: 25). And 'rules' and 'structures' are just too rigid to capture the 'practical mastery' required for such adaptation; instead one needs notions like 'tact', 'dexterity' and '*savoir faire*' (Bourdieu 1977: 10): in anthropology, we find more 'a sense of honour' than 'rules of honour'. Secondly, although up to a point Saussure's or Lévi-Strauss' structures *model* many of the regularities in linguistic and social conduct, they make the mistake of slipping 'from the model of reality to the reality of the model' (1977: 29). (This point clearly parallels Merleau-Ponty's from above.) Rather as those who attempt to explain interpersonal understanding may invoke 'theories of mind' (see Ch. 5iii), these theorists make the basic intellectualist error of imagining that the natives themselves have this model in their unconscious minds or brains, and that this internal model is what explains the regularity in their behaviour. What is needed instead is a way of understanding how practices can be 'regulated without any express regulation' (Bourdieu 1977: 17), an account 'of the mechanisms producing this conformity in the absence of the intention to conform' (Bourdieu 1977: 29).

Bourdieu's notion of habitus is the central notion in this account;[38] we met this notion briefly already in Ch. 3. At a basic level, we may see habitus ('systems of durable, transposable *dispositions'*, Bourdieu 1977: 78) as Merleau-Ponty's habit-body with a sociological twist, and with a scope that explicitly goes beyond (socially informed) motor skills and competences to social and cultural competences. As Crossley puts it, the social 'is no more separate from us than our bodies. It is what we "do"', indeed 'what we do *collectively* in the context of social relations . . . our habits are the *collective* habits of a shared culture or subculture' (2000: 34, italics added). As the habit-body embodies the past, which thereby becomes in a certain sense 'unconscious', so habitus is 'history turned into nature, i.e. denied as such' (Bourdieu 1977: 78). In Bourdieu's infamous words, habituses are 'structured structures predisposed to function as structuring structures' (Bourdieu 1977: 72). Like the body schema, they are 'structures'; *what* 'structures' these 'structures' (for both Merleau-Ponty and Bourdieu) is repeated experience: I learn how to type through practice, and this past experience becomes sedimented in my body as bodily knowledge, 'inscribed in the body schema' (cf. Bourdieu 1977: 15; hence the body is condition of possibility of 'all expressive operations and all acquired views which constitute the cultural world', *PP* 388/451). Bourdieu's emphasis is on the fact that this repeated experience is largely *common* to everyone within a particular group, class or tribe. Thus, the habit-body becomes a 'tribe habitus' or a 'class habitus', with individual habituses being but 'structural variants' on this group habitus (Bourdieu 1977: 86, cf. Bourdieu 1990: 60).[39] This is how practices can be regulated 'without in any way being the product of obedience to rules' (Bourdieu 1977: 72), hence how Bourdieu can account in a non-intellectualist way for the regularity which so gripped Saussure and Lévi-Strauss. These 'structured structures' are at the same time 'structuring structures' (cf. *Signs* 101: 'the body is a "structuring" principle'): they give shape to the environment. Just as, for Merleau-Ponty, the 'physiognomies' of things, their demand and functional characters, are correlative to an individual's motor skills (so that for someone who has learned how to type, when sat before a typewriter a space opens up beneath the hands and the keys 'solicit' the hands to move in particular ways), so too a group habitus will 'give a social environment its *physiognomy*, with its "closed doors", "dead ends" and limited "prospects"' (Bourdieu 1977: 86). The social environment itself is a *field* (cf. Merleau-Ponty: 'the social world' is not an object or a collection of objects but 'a permanent field or dimension of existence', *PP* 362/421), a notion which ultimately goes back to the Gestalt psychologists (see Ch. 2). Thus, we might say: habitus is social-being-in-a-social-world.

Bourdieu provides a convincing way of supplementing Merleau-Ponty's account of the habit-body in its social and cultural dimensions, and of giving more concrete meaning to Merleau-Ponty's claim that 'Our relationship to the social is like our relationship to the world, deeper than any express perception or judgement' (*PP* 362/421). At the same time, Merleau-Ponty has something to teach Bourdieu (see also Ostrow 1990; Weiss 2008).[40] It has been commented that habitus, despite Bourdieu's explicit statements that it is 'incorporated in the form of bodily schemes' (Bourdieu 1977: 15), seems somehow *disembodied*. Perhaps we can see why. First, there is no hint in Bourdieu of that 'anonymous' and 'prepersonal' layer of intersubjective existence which arises from the body's basic *sensibility*, e.g., to colours (e.g., *PP* 216/251; see Ch. 5ii); one can make this point without thereby implying that perception is pre-cultural. And secondly, Bourdieu has no equivalent of Merleau-Ponty's notion of *bodily reciprocity* (Ch. 5iii).[41] Since Bourdieu's concern is to make the understanding of others' actions 'automatic' and 'impersonal' as opposed to explicitly thetically conscious, one might think he could easily embrace this notion. As it is, Bourdieu leaves himself unable to account for the imitation which is surely a *pre-requisite* of the acquisition of habitus: the child who is surrounded by others speaking a particular language, articulating that language in a particular way, using implements to eat, eating particular kinds of things in particular ways, will not learn to do these things in these ways without *imitating* them, and as Merleau-Ponty has argued, bodily reciprocity is the only way to make sense of the capacity for imitation.

Bourdieu continues to be hugely influential in social theory. (In sociology this is under the banner of 'structuration theory', in anthropology under the banner of 'practice theory'.) I want to end by providing a glimpse at the work of a couple of contemporary social theorists who explicitly see value in combining Merleau-Ponty and Bourdieu.

One is the sociologist Nick Crossley. In one study, he investigated what he calls 'reflexive body techniques', i.e., body techniques (he takes the term from Mauss) 'whose primary purpose is to work back upon the body, so as to modify, maintain or thematize it' (Crossley 2005: 9, in italics in original); such techniques by their very nature exhibit the ambiguity of the body as 'subject' and 'object' (one of the main lessons he draws from Merleau-Ponty). Each society including our own has a repertoire of such techniques which are 'collectively shared but individually rooted in the corporeal schemas of agents' (Crossley 2005: 31). Many are utterly mundane maintenance routines which 'everyone' performs in a taken-for-granted way, e.g., showering or cleaning one's teeth; others are both statistically and socially normal (see the Coda to Ch. 3) for members of a particular category (e.g., shaving one's legs for women, shaving one's face for men); yet others are both statistically and socially deviant (body piercings, using steroids for bodybuilding). His study of such techniques, a contribution to what he calls 'carnal sociology', highlights a pervasive and seldom thematized aspect of the socially informed body schema which also, we may note, has a clear bearing on feminist issues.

Another is the medical anthropologist Thomas Csordas, best known for his work on the ritual healing practices of various Charismatic Catholic communities in the United States. He describes one incident at a 'healing conference'; following a period of healing prayer at which the leader had highlighted certain themes such as 'rejection' and 'passivity' as calling for healing, one man being prayed over suddenly burst out laughing and continued for some minutes. He explained that the themes had provoked an image of 'a stream flowing over rocks through a broken wall', and immediately felt joy, expressed through laughter (Csordas 2002: 71). Csordas stresses both the indeterminacy and the cultural specificity of the themes 'rejection' and 'passivity' ('indeterminacy' is one of Csordas' primary acquisitions from Merleau-Ponty), and calls attention the complex multi-sensory nature of the man's experience (visual, kinaesthetic and affective), the elements of which are 'spontaneously coordinated within the North American habitus . . . and constitute an embodied healing'. Indeed, he suggests, it is a specifically *male* variant of that habitus: the expression of release from rejection takes a notably *active* form in laughter (Csordas 2002: 72). Csordas' 'embodiment paradigm', whose central premise is that the body is 'the existential ground of culture', allows us to make intelligible Merleau-Ponty's claim that '[i]t is impossible to superimpose on man a lower layer of behaviour which one chooses to call "natural", followed by a manufactured cultural or spiritual world' (*PP* 189/220): culture permeates even the level of the indeterminate and the pre-objective.

iv. ANIMALS

Until recently, most Anglophone philosophers writing about animals wrote about animal *ethics*. It is beginning to be recognized that before we can ask such questions – Do animals have rights? Is there anything wrong with eating or experimenting on animals? What virtues or vices are exhibited in our treatment of animals? – we must ask first what animals *are*. Descartes had a clear answer to this question: animals are machines. That is, animals are exactly comparable to the human *body*, which, considering it independently of its union with the soul or mind, is (according to Descartes) also a machine: its operations, and theirs, are wholly explicable by the principles of mechanics. Given that Merleau-Ponty has so thoroughly dismantled the Cartesian conception of the human body (see Ch. 3), we should not be surprised to learn that he also dismantles the Cartesian conception of animals. Objective thought is no more capable of understanding the nature of animals than it is of understanding the nature of the human body.

Attentive readers of *PP* will have noted a few references to animals: there is the dog whose gaze 'directed toward me causes me no embarrassment', unlike a human gaze (*PP* 361/420); there are the dog, the cockchafer and the praying mantis whose 'sexual pantomimes' I do not understand (*PP* 184/214); there is the insect which, 'in the performance of an instinctive act, substitutes a sound leg for one cut off' (*PP* 78/90; see *SB* 38f. for further discussion of this case). *PP* largely presupposes the analyses of animal behaviour from Merleau-Ponty's earlier book *SB*, which until the publication of his lecture notes entitled *Nature* was the principal place to look for his treatment of animals. I will begin, however, by mentioning two further bits of background, which already begin to put pressure on the *bête-machine* doctrine.

First, Jacob von Uexküll, a Swiss biologist (1864–1944), is sometimes called 'the father of ethology', although more often this accolade is bestowed on the younger (and now much better known) Nobel Prize winners Konrad Lorenz and Nikolaas Tinbergen. Ethology is the study of animals in the environment to which they are adapted (as opposed to in the laboratory).[42] Uexküll's great contribution was to develop the notion of environment (*Umwelt*), which he described as the sum of the 'perception world' (*Merkwelt*) and the 'effect world' (*Wirkwelt* – i.e. the world of acting or doing) and which varied from species to species, so that each type of animal has its own 'world'. He explicitly set himself against those who 'hold onto the conviction that all living things are machines' (2010 [1934]: 41). His most famous study was of the world of the tick (1921); the tick's 'perception world' is fixed by its receptors (its skin is photosensitive; it can detect the smell of butyric acid; and it can sense warmth), its 'effect world' by what it does in the service of life (climb branches, drop onto passing warm-blooded animals, drink their blood).[43] Even such simple and humble animals could be addressed 'not merely as objects but also as subjects, whose essential activities consist in perception and the production of effects [i.e., acting]' (2010 [1934]: 42). His later (1934) work, a 'picture book' whose title is variously translated as 'A Stroll through . . .' or 'A Foray into the Worlds of Animals and Men', is enlivened by drawings of the 'bubbles' around the animals in a meadow, the bubbles representing 'each animal's environment' and containing 'all the features accessible to the subject' (2010: 43). There is one (second-hand) quotation from Uexküll in *SB*, where Merleau-Ponty quotes approvingly 'Every organism is a melody which sings itself' (*SB* 159); later Merleau-Ponty (in *Nature*) engaged with Uexküll in much more detail.

Secondly, the Gestalt psychologists, particularly Köhler and particularly as recorded in his 1921 book *The Mentality of Apes*, did experiments with animals on which Merleau-Ponty picked up in *SB*. For instance, Köhler found that monkeys were able to (in modern jargon) 'transfer' skills – e.g., using a stick to reach a piece of fruit on the other side of a grill – to new situations – e.g., using the stick to reach a box containing a piece of fruit, the fruit itself being out of reach of the stick. Both Köhler and Merleau-Ponty see such experiments as undermining a modern version of the *bête-machine* doctrine, namely behaviourism.

Merleau-Ponty argued that the behaviourist notion of the conditioned reflex could not account for such behaviour: it is a *new stimulus*, but the monkey *treats* what it encounters as 'a new form of already "known" problems' (*SB* 98). Thus, what it 'responds' to is not a *stimulus* with particular material properties which then *causes* (and is thus externally related to) a response, but a *situation* which is *meaningfully* (and thus internally) related to the response (*SB* 103; *CPP* 345). In *CPP*, Merleau-Ponty invokes the Gestalt psychologists' distinction between a 'behavioural' and a 'geographical' setting (although not without reservations). Two chimpanzees may be in the same geographical setting – say, in a room with a stool and some bananas suspending from a ceiling – but in different behavioural settings, as revealed in their behaviour: one sits on the stool, the other uses it to reach the bananas (*CPP* 343-4), so that 'immanent in their behaviour' are two different 'valuations of the stool-object' (*CPP* 344). Thus, '[i]t is necessary to interpose, between the stimulus and the reaction, the behavioural context that defines an individual and that distinguishes what may be obscured or confused in the geographical setting' (*CPP* 344). Although the stress here is on individuals, generally speaking members of a species in the same geographical setting share much of their behavioural setting: 'The gestures of behaviour, the intentions which it traces in the space around the animal, are not directed to the true world or pure being, but to being-for-the-animal, that is, to a certain milieu characteristic of the species' (*SB* 125); thus he often uses the phrase 'the *a priori* of the species'. 'The mouse in The Metropolitan Museum of Art is affected by the crumbs of cookies on the floor, but not by the Velázquez painting on the wall. In the milieu that the mouse constitutes, the crumb is desirable and the painting does not exist' (Flynn 2004: 3). 'Behavioural setting' (situation, milieu) is thus a philosophically elaborated cousin of Uexküll's *Umwelt*.

Merleau-Ponty's consideration of Gestalt psychologists' experiments with animals thus reveals that animals are not machines (they belong to the 'vital order', not the 'physical order'),[44] but that they, like us, are 'being-in-the-world' (*SB* 125-6). Yet, he still differentiates between human beings and non-human animals. He distinguishes between three 'forms' of behaviour, which he labels 'syncretic', 'amovable' and 'symbolic'. In the first, behaviour is 'imprisoned in the framework of its natural conditions' which 'release' 'instinctive' behaviour (*SB* 104). The distinction between amovable and symbolic forms is of particular interest: it closely parallels the distinction between 'concrete' and 'abstract' movement which we met in Schneider (Ch. 4iii; Merleau-Ponty refers to the Schneider case in his description of the amovable forms, *SB* 117).[45] Amovable forms of behaviour allow the appearance of '*signals* which are not determined by the instinctual equipment of the species' (SB 105); to the animal capable only of amovable behaviour, 'the object appears clothed with a "vector", invested with a "functional value" which depends on the effective composition of the field' (*SB* 116-17), and – this is the crucial point – the animal cannot choose to adopt a different point of view to invest the object with a *different* functional character. In symbolic forms of behaviour, by contrast, we have *symbols* rather than *signals*. A subject who knows how to type or play the organ (cf. Ch. 3v), that is, for whom such behaviour is symbolic, 'is capable of improvising', as well as switching to an unfamiliar instrument (*SB* 121), whereas a dog trained to jump up on one chair and then another on command is not thereby trained to perform the parallel actions with two stools (*SB* 120). Thus, in symbolic forms of behaviour, 'stimuli' are 'liberated' from 'the here-and-now relations . . . and from the functional values which the needs of the species . . . assign to them' (*SB* 122). Even if every organism is 'a melody which sings itself', as Uexküll said, '[t]his is not to say that it knows this melody and attempts to realise it' (*SB* 159). Although these categories 'do not correspond to three groups of animals: there is no species whose behaviour *never* goes beyond the syncretic level nor any whose behaviour *never* descends below the symbolic forms', nonetheless only human beings exhibit the symbolic forms and bring about space and time as an 'unlimited milieu' (*SB* 104).

We have noted already that Heidegger got his own term '*Umwelt*' or 'environing world' from Uexküll; and, not in *BT* but in his lectures on 'The Fundamental Concepts of Metaphysics', he began to consider animals. He concluded that whereas stones had no 'worlds', animals did, but animals were 'world-poor' compared to human beings. It seems in the end that *SB*'s conclusion is not dissimilar. Depending on whether we emphasize Merleau-Ponty's insistence that animals do after all have worlds and are 'being-in-the-world', or whether we emphasize his insistence that they lack symbolic forms of behaviour and thus have 'merely as a privative mode of existence' (Toadvine 2007: 17), we might read *SB* as either good news or bad news for animals. In either case, his reflections are further developed in *Nature*, although I will not expand on that here.

It seems to be only fairly recently that 'the question of the animal' has been raised again in its own right. We are suddenly getting 'zoontologies' (e.g., Wolfe 2003) and 'zoographies' (e.g., Calarco 2008), although neither of these makes use of Merleau-Ponty. We are also (following the publication of an English translation of *Nature*) seeing Merleau-Ponty's reconceptualization of animals being taken up in Anglophone phenomenology, e.g., in the ideas of 'animal others' (Steeves 1999) and 'onto-ethologies' (Buchanan 2008). Both Buchanan and Toadvine (2007) look at Merleau-Ponty's analysis of animal life in conjunction with Uexküll and Heidegger, as well as with the later philosophers Deleuze and Guattari.[46] See also Dillard-Wright's (2009a and b) invitations to 'think across species boundaries' à la Merleau-Ponty. For my part, I will only say that it is manifestly obvious that my cats transcend the *a priori* of their species.

v. CODA: INTELLECTUAL PREJUDICES

At the end of this book, Anglophone philosophers will be wont to ask: has Merleau-Ponty *demonstrated the correctness* of his vision of perception and the perceived world? This question is out of place: this was never his aim. His purpose was, rather, to help his readers 're-learn to look at the world', to 'rediscover the world in which we live, yet which we are always prone to forget' (*WP* 32). His strategy is multi-pronged. We have drawn attention to some prongs of this strategy already (esp. in Ch. 3): e.g., he draws our attention to aspects of the phenomena that we may never have hitherto explicitly focused upon, sometimes by direct description, sometimes via 'abnormal' cases, and he develops a theoretical vocabulary which aims to capture the phenomena better than that of his predecessors. (If some of his vocabulary is unclear or underspecified, that is no more than an invitation to do it better.) I submit that there is a further prong to his overall strategy: he is endeavouring to free us, his readers, from the preconceptions or prejudices which may *interfere* with our seeing the life-world aright; success in this part of his strategy is a *prerequisite* of success in the other parts. Here, however, those same Anglophone philosophers will be wont to ask: has Merleau-Ponty *refuted* the prejudice of objective thought? This question too is out of place; the purpose of this Coda is make it clear why, by exploring the notion of an intellectual prejudice. This term is seldom taken fully seriously by Merleau-Ponty commentators; I think this a mistake.

In urging that we take the term 'prejudice' seriously, I do not mean that we ought to be fixated on the particular *word*; Merleau-Ponty uses others (e.g., 'dogma'), and he is capable of indicating that he sees an intellectual prejudice or dogma in operation without actually using either term. Rather, I want to indicate, that 'the prejudice of objective thought', as Merleau-Ponty often labels the most fundamental intellectual prejudice shared by empiricists and intellectualists alike, is not simply an opinion which Merleau-Ponty takes to be false (not a *mistake, pace* Priest 1998: 6). It goes far deeper than that, in three connected senses. First, it lies deeper than a mere mistake in the prejudiced thinker's intellect. Secondly, it possibly implicates his 'will' as well as his intellect: there is some sense in which someone in the grip of this prejudice *wants* to see things in accordance with it. Thirdly, the aim of combating it pervades the whole style of Merleau-Ponty's writing, in a way that the simple correction of a mistake could not possibly. I will identify three 'levels' of prejudice, with the usual caveats about inseparability; the labels for the first two ('naiveté' and 'dishonesty') come from Merleau-Ponty's initial critique of empiricism and intellectualism in the Preface (PP viii-xi/ix-xii); the third, 'bad faith', is my own (taken from Sartre) but captures a great deal that is implicit in Merleau-Ponty.

- *'Naïveté'*. The charge of naiveté stems from the fact that these psychologists and philosophers in the grip of objective thought 'take for granted, without explicitly mentioning it, the other point of view, namely that of consciousness, through which from the outset a world forms itself around me and begins to exist for me' (*PP* ix/ix; cf. *PP* 57/66: 'classical science is a form of perception which loses sight of its origins and believes itself complete'). Again, 'the philosopher describes sensations and their substratum as one might describe the fauna of a distant land – without being aware that he himself perceives . . . and that perception as he lives it belies everything that he says of perception in general'

(*PP* 207/240). And again, having criticized 'classical psychologists' for their failure to recognize that the body is not an object, Merleau-Ponty notes that the subject-matter studied by the psychologist, unlike that of the physicist or the chemist, 'was himself: he lived it while he thought about it' (*PP* 96/110).

There is a kind of 'perversity' about such naïveté. It leads scientific psychologists simply to ignore their own proper subject-matter: since 'intellectualism is blind to the mode of existence and co-existence of perceived objects, to the life which steals across the visual field and secretly binds its parts together' (*PP* 35/40), it misses important aspects of what it has set out to study.[47] To put the point otherwise, it elevates to centre-stage what is in fact simply a 'second-order expression' (*PP* viii/ix) of the life-world, while ignoring what that second-order expression *expresses*. Again, 'causal thought' 'blinds us to that dimension of behaviour which is precisely the one with which psychology is concerned' (*PP* 120/138) – though the phrase '*blinds us*' brings us to the next level of prejudice, as does the charge of 'hypocrisy' here: 'Rationalism and scepticism draw their sustenance from an actual life of consciousness which they both hypocritically take for granted' (*PP* 296/345).

- '*Dishonesty*'. Objective thought does not simply ignore the life-world: it positively *conceals* it from us, by constructing *simulacra* of the life-world and presenting them to us as the real thing. Empiricist constructions 'make incomprehensible' and 'conceal' or 'hide from us' ' "the cultural world" or "human world" in which nevertheless almost our whole life is led' (*PP* 23/27). Empiricism 'excludes from perception the anger or pain which I nevertheless read in a face' (*PP* 23-4). Likewise, the intellectualist makes the world 'the outcome of a series of syntheses which link . . . sensations, then aspects of the object . . . when both are nothing but products of analysis, with no sort of prior reality' (*PP* x/xi). Cf. Köhler: 'So far removed from common experience is [the Introspectionist's] true sensory world that, if we should ever learn its laws, all of them together would not lead us back to the world we actually live in' (*GP* 51). 'Science enjoins [the child] . . . to turn away from the living and meaningful world . . . for which science tries to substitute a universe of frozen objects, independent of all gaze and all thought' (Beauvoir 2004: 159). Cf. also Husserl's reference to 'the surreptitious substitution of the mathematically substructed world of idealities for . . . our everyday life-world' (*Crisis* 48-9). Again, empiricism 'can always build up, with psychic atoms, near equivalents of all these structures [e.g., the horizons of perceived objects]. But the inventory of the perceived world . . . will increasingly show it up as a kind of mental blindness' (*PP* 25/29). This term 'mental blindness' begins to get us to the third level of intellectual prejudice.

- '*Bad faith*'.[48] Sartre's conception of 'bad faith' is often loosely rendered as 'self-deception'.[49] This goes beyond 'dishonesty' (i.e., other-deception) in more than the obvious respect: first, Sartre characterizes bad faith in terms of a particular attitude to evidence and argument, an attitude which shows up in characteristic *patterns* of thinking which may be called 'perverse'; secondly, these patterns of thinking imply that bad faith cannot be *eradicated* simply by adducing contrary evidence and counter-argument; and thirdly, there is a sense in which bad faith is a (self-imposed) limitation on one's own *freedom*. All three implications also show up in this passage from Wittgenstein. (He here uses the term 'dogma' rather than 'prejudice' or 'bad faith'; but, again, the term is not the important thing).

Dogma is expressed in the form of an assertion, and is unshakable, but at the same time any practical opinion *can* be made to harmonize with it; admittedly more easily in some cases than in others . . . This is how dogma becomes irrefutable and beyond the reach of attack . . . [A] dogma is not a wall setting limits to what can be believed, but more like a brake which, however, practically serves the same purpose; it is almost as though someone were to attach a weight to your foot to restrict your freedom of movement. (1980: 28)[50]

We can see all three of these aspects reflected in the intellectual prejudices treated by Merleau-Ponty and an understanding of them in his treatment of those prejudices.

i) The perverse attitude to evidence and argument shows up time and time again. As just one instance, we saw in Ch. 2 that '[t]he relationships "figure" and "background", "thing" and "non-thing", and the horizon of the past appear . . . to be structures of consciousness irreducible to the qualities which appear in them'. One might think that it would be sufficient to refute empiricism simply to point this out; but:

Empiricism will always retain the expedient of treating this *a priori* as if it were the product of some mental chemistry. The empiricist will concede that every object is presented against a background which is not an object, the present lying between two horizons of absence, past and future. But, he will go on, these significations are derivative . . . [and he will attempt to] reconstruct theoretically these structures with the aid of the impressions whose actual relationships they express. (*PP* 22-3/26)

The movement of thought which he here ascribes to the empiricist is characteristic of bad faith: the empiricist makes use of the 'expedient' of explaining the apparently 'contrary' phenomena *away* – 'reconstructing' them as 'derivative' of items whose existence he recognizes (e.g., impressions and their 'chemical combinations'). (Cf. the Coda to Ch. 2 on 'Inappropriate use of "auxiliary hypotheses"'.)

ii) This entails that there is a sense in which no prejudice can be *refuted.* And Merleau-Ponty repeatedly makes this very point: 'On this footing empiricism cannot be refuted. Since it rejects the evidence of reflection . . . there is no phenomenon which can be adduced as a crucial proof against it . . . the description of phenomena does not enable one to refute thought that is not alive to its own existence . . . [And] empiricism can always retort that it *does not understand*' (*PP* 23/26-7). He repeats this idea that there is no such thing as a 'crucial proof' or a 'decisive experiment' in psychology on a number of occasions (for instance, there is 'no fact capable of decisively bearing out that the tactile experience of patients is or is not identical with that of normal people, and [a particular] conception . . . can always be reconciled with the facts, given some auxiliary hypothesis', *PP* 117/135). Moreover, as long as the psychologist confines himself to objective thinking, different hypotheses cannot even recommend themselves as 'more plausible' or 'more probable' because he is blind to them. This might encourage the psychologist, not to keep searching for a crucial experiment, but at least to consider the *possibility* of stepping outside objective thinking (cf. *PP* 118/135-6). Blindness to alternative possibilities is one of the deepest and most worrying aspects of an intellectual prejudice, and this observation begins to encroach on the third aspect.

iii) Intellectual prejudices restrict our freedom of thought, especially our freedom to look at things differently – which was, as we saw in §iv above, what marked 'symbolic' forms of behaviour and hence 'the human order'. It is significant that prejudices are characteristically expressed with modal language ('must', 'cannot', etc.) or via such language as 'all' or 'every', 'really', 'nothing but' or 'only' and so on; these terms all serve to screen out alternative ways of looking at things. Merleau-Ponty constantly uses such language here to express the mental outlook of the empiricist: '[s]eeing a figure can be only simultaneously experiencing all the atomic sensations which go to form it . . . A shape is nothing but a sum of limited views (*PP* 14/16); again 'the constancy hypothesis forces us to admit that the "normal sensations" are already there. They must then be unperceived' (*PP* 26/30). Empiricism is 'not concerned with what we see, but what we ought to see, according to the retinal image' (*PP* 31/36). Likewise, intellectualism 'describes *de facto* perception according to the data of "analytic" and attentive perception, in which the moon in fact resumes its *true* apparent diameter . . . the moon on the horizon should never appear bigger than it is' (*PP* 31/36).

It is therefore *liberating* to rid oneself of an intellectual prejudice. And this too Merleau-Ponty acknowledges: 'If we abandon the empiricist postulate . . . we are *free to recognize* the strange mode of existence enjoyed by the object behind our back' (*PP* 25/29, italics added), as well as the 'miracles' immanent in 'my glance toward the goal' (*Signs* 66-7) and the 'magic' by which the body 'confer[s] its own spatial particularizations on the landscape without ever appearing in it' (PP 254/296).

NOTES

PREFACE

1 Primary biographical sources include Sartre's posthumous tribute to Merleau-Ponty (Sartre 1998) and a number of Beauvoir's autobiographical works and collections of letters. There are useful biographical sketches in, e.g., the introduction to Stewart ed. 1998 and Carman 2008.

2 This conference is famous for an event which never happened. The story is told (and repeated, e.g., by Hems 1976: 55 n.1) that Merleau-Ponty's suggestion 'Is our enterprise not the same?' was met with Ryle's 'I hope not'. (*'Notre programme n'est-il pas le meme?'* – *'J'espère que non'*, Leslie Beck's introduction to Wahl ed. 1962: 7). In fact, Merleau-Ponty asked Ryle whether he saw *himself* as engaged in the same programme as *Russell and Wittgenstein*, to which Ryle responded 'I very much hope not!' (Ryle 1962: 98). What Ryle goes on to say changes the sense of the response in any case: he added that the very idea of complete agreement with another philosopher – *any* other philosopher – would be 'a death-blow to the whole philosophical enterprise' (Ryle 1962: 98). Nonetheless the exchange between Ryle and Merleau-Ponty produced little in the way of a meeting of minds; it is referred to on several occasions in this book.

3 I exclude his political works; I also exclude *VI*, his posthumously published unfinished work in which many have found inspiration. Much interest has been generated by the publication in 2003 of an English translation of his lecture notes on *Nature*, representing Merleau-Ponty's critical engagement with biology, to which I refer briefly in Ch. 6. I expect that the even more recent (2010) publication of a complete English translation of his lectures on child psychology and pedagogy will likewise generate considerable interest; I refer to these from time to time as well.

4 This is why I give more quotations from *PP* than is usual in introductory books, which some will no doubt find annoying: not only do these quotations provide evidence for my interpretation, but they enable the reader to begin to learn Merleau-Ponty's unique 'language'.

5 This order is not strict; for instance, the final chapter of *PP* Part I is so relevant to Merleau-Ponty's treatment of others and intersubjectivity that discussion of it is postponed until my own Chapter 5. Moreover, I have not explicitly included a chapter on *PP* Part

III, although elements of Part III are incorporated in a number of chapters. I think the vision I am here putting forward can be seen clearly without explicitly focusing on Part III; in any case, this 'unseen side' of *PP* is 'present in its own way'.

6 Merleau-Ponty's theoretical interest in perception was long-standing: witness the fact that in 1933 he put forward two research proposals (in *TD* as 'The nature of perception: two proposals') on the nature of perception for the *Caisse National des Sciences* (what became in 1939 the CNRS) from which he received a scholarship.

7 Merleau-Ponty's interest in Gestalt psychology actually preceded his interest in Husserl and Heidegger; it is clearly an important factor in his thinking.

CHAPTER 1

1 Jean-Paul Sartre is clearly in the background as well, but I will not discuss him until Ch. 5. (The intellectual relationship between Merleau-Ponty and Sartre is vexed, and Merleau-Ponty's less than sympathetic reading of Sartre has sometimes been taken for granted as correct, and at other times, vigorously challenged. See Whitford 1982, Stewart ed. 1998.) Of use for a basic understanding of these phenomenologists are Hammond et al. 1991, which covers Husserl, Sartre and Merleau-Ponty; and Cerbone 2006, which covers these three as well as Heidegger. For more scholarly and in-depth reading on phenomenology, see Spiegelberg 1969 and Moran 2000. See Toadvine and Embree (eds) 2002 on Merleau-Ponty's reading of Husserl; the interpretation I present here is my own.

2 Husserl was certainly not the first to use the *term*; see Spiegelberg 1969, Vol. I, Introduction.

3 Although Merleau-Ponty attended these lectures, he cannot have understood much as he did not speak much German then (Schmidt 1985: 18). For our purposes, *CM* has the great advantage of being short.

4 The very fact that such a thesis was supervised by *psychologists* may strike us as bizarre today, but it reflects the predominance of the view at that time that to analyse a concept is to describe how – through what psychological acts – we form that concept; this is one aspect of what became known as 'psychologism' and is widely held by Anglo-American philosophers to have been definitively refuted by Frege; Husserl himself (at Frege's instigation) came to repudiate it as well. Merleau-Ponty's relationship to psychologism is more nuanced, but cannot be discussed here. The Coda to Ch. 2 is however relevant.

5 'Husserl wrote as if he had never met a scientist – or a joke' (Ryle 1971: 181). The first part at least is clearly unfair.

6 These are presented in a different order in Merleau-Ponty's preface and in §§ii and iii below. Both Merleau-Ponty's summary and my own omit reference to Husserl's transcendental ego.

7 See Zirión 2006 for an illuminating deflationary discussion of this 'battle-cry'.

8 Indeed Ryle uses the word 'Führer' – a singularly insensitive term in the historical context especially of the Jewish-born Husserl, as Glendinning (2006: 72) points out.

9 Husserl also transformed Brentano's conception, but this is not the place to detail those transformations; see, for example, Spiegelberg 1969: 107–08.

10 If yet more Husserlian terminology be needed, he calls the former 'noematic' descriptions or descriptions of 'noemata' (singular: noema), the latter 'noetic' descriptions or descriptions of noeses (singular: 'noesis').

11 Also called the transcendental reduction. Note that 'reduction' is meant in its original Latin sense of 'leading back' and that *epoché* (according to Moran 2000: 148) is taken from the Greek skeptics and means a 'cessation'. These two terms have been argued not to be strictly equivalent in Husserl's usage (see, e.g., Zahavi 2003: 46) but they are closely linked and present purposes do not warrant a more technical discussion.

12 It was important to Husserl that we could achieve an 'intuition' of essences, just as we can achieve an 'intuition' of individual things; the term 'intuition' (used here in a broadly Kantian sense) is correlative with the term 'object', and essences were for Husserl objects, that is, 'subjects of possibly true predications' (*Ideas* §3). The idea that essences are objects has commonly been read as a form of Platonism or Meinongianism (see, e.g., Ryle 1971: 170), a view that meets with considerable resistance in modern Anglo-American philosophy.

13 A term that originally came from Uexküll (Spiegelberg 1969: 161), about whom more in Ch. 6iv.

14 Many Heidegger scholars will see this as a rather narrow characterization of *BT* (cf. Moran 2000: 412).

15 It is not my purpose here to assess the plausibility of Merleau-Ponty's reading of Husserl.

16 See Ch. 5 for a full discussion of the problem of others.

17 As Sartre does in the Introduction to *BN*.

18 Merleau-Ponty actually begins with a critique of the logical positivists' way of thinking about essence, namely simply as the meaning of the word (say, the word 'consciousness', hardly an arbitrarily chosen example); I want to postpone discussion of this critique to the Coda to Ch. 4, since it has implications for a number of distinctions, which many analytic philosophers hold dear.

19 Husserl scholars divide on the issue of whether Husserl was a transcendental idealist. It is worth noting that similar arguments divide scholars on the issue of whether, in the *Tractatus Logico-Philosophicus*, Wittgenstein expressed a form of transcendental idealism (see, e.g., Sullivan 2003 and Moore 2007). I suspect that the exegetical issues would be mutually illuminating.

20 Let us also take note of those scare-quotes here: 'Phenomenology is *eo ipso "transcendental idealism"*' (*CM* 86).

21 As we will, see, not only familiarity, but intellectual prejudices, may interfere with our recognition of phenomena.

22 Heidegger has a somewhat similar strategy: he highlights cases where a piece of equipment is inadequate to the task or breaks, thereby becoming suddenly and obtrusively present-at-hand, which forcefully demonstrates that readiness-to-hand is our normal way of encountering equipment. As Mooney (2011) comments, whereas Heidegger focuses on unreadiness-*to*-hand, Merleau-Ponty's emphasis is on 'unreadiness-*of*-hand'.

23 'Analytical reflection believes that it can trace back the course followed by a prior constituting act and arrive, in the "inner man" – to use Saint Augustine's expression – at a constituting power which has always been identical to that inner self'. Since Husserl ends *CM* with the quotation from Augustine 'Truth dwells in the inner man', and since the term 'constitution' is a central Husserlian term, one might be forgiven for inferring that Husserl is one of the *targets* of this attack on intellectualism.

24 Cf. the title of Waelhen's Foreword to the second French edition of *SB*: 'A philosophy of the ambiguous'.

25 I should also mention that many sociologists including Bourdieu (see Ch. 6iii) associate the term 'phenomenology' with the approach called 'ethnomethodology' (founded by the late Harold Garfinkel); this has some clear historical connections with phenomenology 'proper', but I will not attempt to say anything about it here.

26 See Ch. 2; there is an excellent discussion of this notion of phenomenology and its incompatibility with the phenomenology of Husserl and Merleau-Ponty in Overgaard and Zahavi 2009.

27 See Hass 2008: 5–10 for a useful presentation of the phenomenological method as a method of *reasoning* which he, following Heidegger, calls 'saying to show', as well as a rebuttal of the supposition that phenomenology is essentially subjectivistic.

28 See Carman 2005; Cerbone 2006: 164–69; Morris 2008: 28–9, 70–2; and Overgaard and Zahavi 2009 for robust defences of phenomenology against the Dennettian attack.

CHAPTER 2

1 I am for the present using terms like 'assumption' and 'presupposition'; Merleau-Ponty's favourite term, strikingly, is 'prejudice'. It occurs in the title of the Introduction and it recurs throughout the book; I think it needs to be taken fully seriously. See the Coda to Ch. 6.

2 He had evidently read Guillaume's books on Gestalt psychology, which brought this psychology to the attention of French intellectuals, even prior to hearing Aron Gurwitch's lectures on Gestalt psychology and phenomenology in the 1930s. His 'two proposals' on the nature of perception (in *TD*) date back to 1933 and draw heavily on Gestalt psychology.

3 See Ash 1998, esp. Chs. 3 and 5; Spiegelberg 1969: 54 on Husserl's mentor Stumpf's influence on the Gestalt psychologists; Heinämaa 2008, who also highlights the importance of Gurwitch.

4 '[S]cience seemed incapable of dealing with the most significant human problems. Rather than abandoning natural science', the Gestalt psychologists 'proposed that the difficulty was not with science itself, but with the current conception of natural science among psychologists'. Their reformed conception, they hoped, 'would do justice to the intrinsic meaning and value in human experience' (Ash 1998: 2, embedded quotation from M. Henle).

5 This Picture bears comparison to what Charles Taylor (2005) calls 'the epistemological picture', but Taylor's picture, I think, captures only a part of the picture against which Merleau-Ponty is inveighing. Taylor (2005: 26) takes from Wittgenstein the idea that 'pictures can hold us captive'. I take it that 'being held captive' is part of what is involved in the notion of a prejudice (see the Coda to Ch. 6), and that Merleau-Ponty and Wittgenstein share a conception that (at least part of) the task of philosophy is to free people from their intellectual prejudices (see Morris 2007).

6 Romdenh-Romluc (2011) identifies many of the same assumptions (see esp. pp. 24–34). I see some advantages in representing them graphically.

7 As Fisher notes, '[i]t is often asserted . . . that existentialism is anti-scientific'. He explicitly rebuts this charge in the case of Merleau-Ponty (Fisher 1969: 9), as will I.

8 Some analytic philosophers speak of 'natural meaning' in this context, although normally only to dismiss it as Ryle does here.

9 For present purposes, I am not distinguishing between Husserl's and Merleau-Ponty's conceptions of such horizons; see Kelly (2005) for an admirable discussion of the issues between them.

10 There is discussion in the literature about the relationship between the term 'structure' (as, for example, in the title of *SB* but also in its frequent occurrence in *PP*) and the term 'Gestalt'. Some commentators simply assume that the two are equivalent; I agree with Embree (1980: 94) that structure, for example, 'figure-ground' structure, is better understood as 'the way in which the Gestalt is organized'.

11 Objects that unfold *through* time (melodies, films . . .) are themselves temporal *Gestalten*. 'The melody is a figure of sound which does not mingle with the background noises . . . which may accompany it. The melody is not a sum of notes, since each note only counts by virtue of the function it serves in the whole' (*SNS* 49). Merleau-Ponty illustrates a parallel point about film by reciting an experiment in which *one and the same shot* of a man was shown first after a shot of a bowl of soup, then after a shot of young woman lying in a coffin and finally after a shot of a child playing. The audience saw that the man 'was looking pensively at the dish, that he wore an expression of sorrow when looking at the woman, and that he had a glowing smile for the child . . . The meaning of the shot therefore depends on what precedes it in the movie' (*SNS* 54).

12 See also Ch. 1 of Köhler's *GP* and more recently Taylor's seminal *The Explanation of Behaviour* (1964). The critique of behaviourism is expanded slightly in Ch. 6iv.

NOTES

13 As Köhler brings out here, their idea of scientific psychology involves choosing a subject of a certain type 'as the system to be investigated. Certain conditions . . . are given and objectively controlled. And the resulting reaction [overt behaviour, physiological response] . . . is registered or measured' (*GP* 14); what happens between the stimulus and the response is in their view beyond the scope of scientific investigation: what is in between (presumably including perception) is simply treated as a 'black box'.

14 See Ch. 4 for more about this important notion of the 'analytical attitude'.

15 Ch. 3 of *PP*: Introduction also considers the empiricist notion of attention, but its main focus is intellectualism; see below.

16 We may be said to experience sensations when adopting the 'analytical attitude'; but such experiences, to put it crudely, are not *perceptual* experience. See Ch. 4.

17 A fair chunk of *PP* Part I.1 ('Sense experience') is devoted to the question of the unity of the senses. The context for this in turn is 'the notorious problem of the contribution of the senses to our experience of space' (*PP* 217/252), often put it in the form of the question of whether a blind man can have experience of space (cf. *PP* 221/258). This issue is connected to what has become known as 'Molyneux's problem'. Molyneux famously asked Locke whether a man who has been born blind and who has learnt to distinguish between a globe and a cube by touch would be able to distinguish these objects simply by sight, once he had been enabled to see. As we might expect, the empiricist Locke said no, whereas the intellectualist Leibniz said yes, through making just the assumptions which Merleau-Ponty criticizes. See Carman (2008), Ch. 2 §5; also, more remotely, Gallagher (2005), Ch. 7.

18 Whether they fully respect their insights in their experimental procedures is another matter; see Mirvish 1983.

19 When Merleau-Ponty says on the one hand that the latter are 'new objects', and on the other that this 'constitution' of a new object makes 'explicit and articulate' what was previously an 'indeterminate horizon', he is simply saying that the 'new' object is *internally related* to the old horizon; see §i above.

20 The idea of the 'objective world' also includes the notion that all relations are external. Hence Merleau-Ponty says that intellectualism 'leaves the starting-point unaffected': '[w]e started off from a world in itself'; we now have 'thought about the world, but the nature of this world remains unchanged: it is still defined by the absolute mutual exteriority of its parts' (*PP* 39/45).

21 Tiemersa is of the few scholars to thematize the field-theoretical terminology in Merleau-Ponty.

22 Lewin also called it 'hodological space', a term embraced by Sartre (although Sartre rejected the notion of 'determining': see Morris 2008: ch. 6; cf. Merleau-Ponty's critique of Lewin, *CPP* 352f.). Although Merleau-Ponty hardly mentions Lewin in *PP*, he draws on him heavily later (*CPP*), and many aspects of Lewin's conception seem utterly at home in *PP*.

23 Koffka identified a further category of what *he* called 'physiognomic characters', which, despite not being of 'practical use', 'exert a powerful influence on our behaviour': for example, the 'very strong character of gruesome awe' which a corpse has to the ordinary person (1935: 359).

24 Many Merleau-Ponty commentators have latched onto the term 'solicitation' to express demand characters and onto J. J. Gibson's term 'affordance' to express functional characters. Koffka's term 'demand character' translates what Lewin called *Aufforderungscharakter*, which appears in English translations of Lewin as 'valence' or 'invitation character'. A little confusingly, Gibson's term 'affordance' (which looks like it ought to be his own translation of *Aufforderungscharakter*) approximates more closely to Koffka's 'functional character'. Gibson himself notes that, unlike demand characters, affordances are 'invariant', that is, they do not change from moment to moment with the needs of the observer (1979: 138-9); however, as he does not mention functional characters, he does not recognize that this very feature brings affordances close to functional characters.

25 Cf.: naturalism is 'a philosophical position, empirical in method, that regards everything that exists or occurs to be conditioned in its existence or occurrence by causal factors within one all-encompassing system of nature, however spiritual or purposeful or rational some of these things and events may in their functions and value prove to be' (Lamprecht quoted by Lauer in a translator's footnote, *PRS* 79 n.13).

26 He makes the telling remark that the philosopher who is interested in the findings of the human sciences 'is not the one who wants to explain or construct the world, but the one who seeks to deepen our insertion in being' (*Signs* 123): in other words, empiricist and intellectualist philosophers will see no value in the human sciences, but phenomenologists (at least proper phenomenologists) will.

27 Anthropologists will find this completely anodyne. We must remember, however, that imagination is a *methodological tool for investigating possibilities* for the phenomenologists (see Ch. 1), in somewhat the spirit of Bourdieu, whose whole project is 'inspired by the conviction that one cannot grasp the logic of the social world . . . without emerging oneself in the particularity of a historically situated and dated empirical reality but in order to construe it as a "particular case of the possible", in Gaston Bachelard's phrase'. (Quoted in Earle 1999: 187 n.6; cf. *Signs* 105.)

CHAPTER 3

1 The German phenomenologist Max Scheler had also contrasted the *Leib* with *Körper*. See Mirvish 1983 for a discussion of Scheler's conception of the body and its influence on Merleau-Ponty.

2 From this perspective, I find unhelpful – in an otherwise admirable book – Romdenh-Romluc's claim that for Merleau-Ponty 'the body is a form of consciousness' (2011: 62).

3 Merleau-Ponty regularly contrasts 'classical psychology' with the 'new psychology', that is, Gestalt psychology (cf. *SNS* 48).

4 It is only relatively recently that Anglo-American philosophers have even begun to focus their attention on the body to any appreciable degree; this is in part, no doubt, because it is all but invisible because of its familiarity.

5 I am for the moment postponing consideration of *PP* I.6, 'The body as expression, and speech'; this anticipates a number of the themes that come out in *PP* Part II.4 and it is considered in Ch. 5 below.

6 This term was invented by Sherrington in 1906; Bell, considerably earlier, described the senses of joint position and movement (Cole and Paillard 1995: 246).

7 There is much discussion in the literature about how to translate Merleau-Ponty's term '*schéma corporel*'; it is translated as 'body image' in *PP* 1962, as 'body schema' in *PP* 2002. In the end, I have gone with the latter, partly because (cf. Gallagher 1995) the term 'body image' is on everybody's lips these days to refer to the ways in which someone thinks and feels about his or her body, for instance as thin or fat, masculine or feminine, attractive or unattractive and so on. This usage has little to do with the present topic.

8 I return to the idea that the body is 'constantly perceived' in Ch. 4, and that the body as 'affective object' in Ch. 6. The body's 'power to give me double sensations' is strictly inseparable from its kinaesthetic aspect. See Moran 2010 for a detailed treatment of the double sensation, that is, the fact – deliberately tendentiously described here – that when I touch one hand with the other, the second hand 'has the strange property of being able to feel too' (*PP* 93/106). Moran's immensely scholarly article explores Husserl and Sartre as well as Merleau-Ponty on the double sensation, as well as many classical and Gestalt psychologists' discussions of the double sensation and of touch.

9 Merleau-Ponty's actual targets here are likely to include Husserl, for whom kinaesthetic sensations provide the answer to the question: In virtue of what do we experience the changing appearance of a perceived object as appearances of the same object?

10 Wittgenstein's criticisms of James on kinaesthetic sensations (see Morris 1992) have some parallels with Merleau-Ponty's arguments.

11 James offers the argument that someone who, through anaesthesia or neurological disorder, lacks kinaesthetic impressions is unable to say how his limbs are situated or to perform movements to order (1890 II: 489). Clearly this argument commits a fallacy ('suppose it happens that when the limb is no longer ticklish I can't tell where it is? Shall I say that I know where it is by its ticklishness?', Wittgenstein 1988: 78).

12 This argument involves, among other things, an atomization of *time*, as Merleau-Ponty brings out: in fact, '[a]t each successive instant of a movement, the preceding instant is not lost sight of. It is, as it were, dovetailed into the present . . . the impending position is also covered by the present, and through it all those which will occur throughout the movement' (*PP* 140/162).

13 Jonathan Cole made the phenomenologically resonant observation that when Ian (described below), who due to his neurological condition must

attend both to the 'action' and the 'goal', focuses on body while acting, 'he thinks in terms of joints or limbs and not muscle spindles or angles'.

14 O'Shaughnessy (e.g., 1980 and 1995) should be credited with initiating Anglo-American focus on proprioception independently of these neurological case-histories. It may be surprising, given Merleau-Ponty's strategy of using abnormal cases for philosophical purposes (see below, esp. §§iv and v), that he did not consider cases like Sacks' 'disembodied lady', but these are extremely rare, and Cole and Paillard suggest that such cases were not described until relatively recently (1995: 245).

15 Cole's patient is simply called 'IW' in Cole 2009; Cole 1995 (an entire book about this patient) names him as Ian Waterman.

16 Descartes' internal senses are not often thematized; see Baker and Morris 1996: 124ff for a rare exception. He distinguished between the external senses – the usual suspects: sight, hearing, touch, taste and smell – and the internal senses, of which he identifies two, one whose proper objects are pain, hunger, thirst and so on; the other whose proper objects are joy, anger, fear and so on.

17 There is much more to be said about proprioception, some of which is touched on in Ch. 4.

18 This notion is introduced at the end of *PP* I.2 and treated it in more depth at the beginning of *PP* I.3, with some important addenda in *PP* I.4.

19 Many of today's neuroscientists reduce consciousness to the brain and the body to its representation in the somatosensory cortex (see Gallagher 1995: 225).

20 There are honourable exceptions to this, including the aforementioned Sacks and Cole.

21 Recent studies of phantom limbs (e.g., Ramachandran and Blakeslee 1998) have shown up varieties that do not sit happily with Merleau-Ponty's account outlined in this section, for example, congenital phantoms (in which the person is born missing an arm or even both arms but still develops a phantom). Such discoveries do not invalidate Merleau-Ponty's account of phantom limbs in amputees, but do present a challenge to the phenomenologist. (Might the 'bodily reciprocity' elaborated in Ch. 5iv be pressed into service, for example?) I am grateful both to Jonathan Cole and Komarine Romdenh-Romluc on a separate occasion for pressing this question.

22 See Mooney (2011). Merleau-Ponty's terminology of 'abstract' and 'concrete' is not altogether helpful.

23 See, for example, Jensen 2009: 7–10; and Romdenh-Romluc 2011: 64–73 for detailed accounts of Merleau-Ponty's arguments here.

24 The origins of the notion of the 'power of projection' were intellectualist (see *PP* 121/139, where it is listed alongside 'a "symbolical function"' and 'a "representative function"'); needless to say, when Merleau-Ponty uses this phrase *in propria persona* (e.g., *PP* 112/129, 120/138, 127/146, 156/181) it is not an intellectualist notion.

25 The crudity of this will be ameliorated below. This topic has been discussed in considerable detail (kicked off by Zaner 1964) by, for example, Dreyfus 2007; Romdenh-Romluc 2007 and 2011; Jensen 2009;

and Mooney (2011). I cannot hope to do the issues justice here but have learned much from these authors.

26　Jensen (2009) has called attention to some peculiarities in the history of Merleau-Ponty's descriptions of Schneider's performance of such tasks.

27　Hence Dreyfus speaks of 'absorbed coping' (Dreyfus 2000): our capacity simply to perform motor tasks without having to think about them, while taking unexpected obstacles in our stride.

28　Cf. Mooney (2011); as he points out, the experiments to demonstrate these deficiencies in Schneider were never done, nor does Merleau-Ponty moot them.

29　Schneider's quasi-motor intentionality is what he calls in *SB* an 'amovable' form of behaviour; see Ch. 6iv.

30　Merleau-Ponty does not always make this qualification, but it surely is implicit given his descriptions of Schneider's performance of familiar tasks.

31　Up to a point, this echoes the title case of Sacks' (1985) *The Man who Mistook his Wife for a Hat*, who could not recognize faces (i.e., literally 'physiognomies') or any other ordinary objects. Yet, Schneider has no difficulty recognizing his needles and scissors when engaged in the wallet-making for which he is trained.

32　Strictly, they cannot possess demand characters *just* as they do for normal people; the distinction between demand characters and functional characters is no sharper than the distinction between actual and possible; see §iii.

33　Cf. Jensen (2009).

34　There is scope for fruitful comparison between Merleau-Ponty's remarks on habits and Ryle's on 'knowing how'; note that Ryle too saw his principal target as 'intellectualism', the idea 'that the intelligent execution of an operation must embody two processes, one of doing and the other of theorizing' (1949: 32).

35　Jonathan Cole tells me that this example comes from James.

36　'Care [is] the Being of Dasein [human reality]' (*BT* 180), and '[t]emporality [is] the ontological meaning of care' (*BT* 65).

37　Many see Merleau-Ponty as a 'philosopher of space'; he is equally a philosopher of time. This is an aspect of his thinking that Beauvoir (2004) not only picks up on but also identifies as a fundamental point of difference between Merleau-Ponty and Sartre: the subject, for Merleau-Ponty, is never a pure for-itself, and the reason for this is temporality, which explains both 'the opacity of the world' and 'the opacity of the subject' (the latter is explained in Ch. 5ii). Sartre too identifies Merleau-Ponty's sense of 'primordial historicity' (1998: 567) as the leitmotif of his thinking from his earliest student days.

38　See *PP* III.2 for Merleau-Ponty's conception of time and temporality more generally; Romdenh-Romluc (2011, Ch. 8) has a good discussion of this.

39　Many dancers and sportspersons speak of 'muscle memory', an apparently oxymoronic concept that echoes a term which Merleau-Ponty uses: 'motor memory' (*PP* 140/161).

40 Weiss 2008 elegantly elaborates this double-sidedness of habit (focusing on James, Merleau-Ponty and Bourdieu).

41 This has implications for the very concept of freedom: 'we must recognize a sort of sedimentation in our life' (*PP* 441/513). If I have been 'content to live' in an inferiority complex for the past twenty years, it is difficult to change and improbable that I will change: 'I have committed myself to inferiority . . . made it my abode', and 'this past, though not a fate, has at least a specific weight' (*PP* 442/514). This point is one of Merleau-Ponty's most telling criticisms of Sartre's conception of freedom: because Sartre does not thematize habit, he is unable to accord a phenomenological reality to the sort of 'probability' – for example, the probability of changing one's 'fundamental project' – that only a notion of habit can make sense of. Bourdieu too makes this criticism (1977: 215 n. 18). Cf. also Ostrow 1990.

42 Cf. Romdenh-Romluc 2011: 93f.

43 The only author explicitly to make this connection to my knowledge is Franzese (2002). Foucault himself drew a sharp line between two phenomenological traditions, placing Canguilhem on one side and Merleau-Ponty on the other, and subsequently taking no interest in the latter (in his introduction to Canguilhem's *On The Normal and the Pathological,* 1978: ix-x). This does Merleau-Ponty an injustice, as many have pointed out (see, e.g., the introduction to Carmen and Hansen (eds), 2005: 20).

44 Mol 1998: 275. As she brings out here, the relationships in practice between clinical and laboratory norms and between vital and social norms are far more polyvalent than this might suggest.

45 Merleau-Ponty says surprisingly little about the actual process of skill acquisition. Dreyfus 1996 usefully supplements Merleau-Ponty (although his account is not without its critics) by distinguishing and describing the stages of 'novice', 'advanced beginner', 'competent', 'proficient' and 'expert'.

46 See, for example, Shusterman 2005; Morris 2010b.

CHAPTER 4

1 I cannot, in this context, avoid homogenizing the views of the different Gestalt psychologists. Nor can I assess the fairness of Merleau-Ponty's interpretations of Gestalt psychology.

2 As Embree (1980: 97–8) highlights.

3 As Cerbone's box (2006: 98) might lead us to imagine.

4 One might even identify a fourth assumption: that the body is a *stationary* object.

5 One striking manifestation of their continued adherence to naturalism is the doctrine of 'isomorphism', according to which 'in a given case the organisation of experience and the underlying physiological facts have the same structure' (*GP* 177); for instance, 'when the visual field exhibits a thing as a detached entity, the corresponding process in the

brain is relatively segregated from surrounding processes' (*GP* 201-2). (Cf. *CPP* 147: having introduced the valuable notion of the perceptual field, Köhler then 'attempts to find the equivalent of the perceptual spectacle and its configuration in *physical forms* . . . of which the nervous system is the seat'.) No doubt, Gestalt neurophysiology will strike today's neurophysiologists as hopelessly naïve and outdated; Merleau-Ponty's criticisms are deeper and may apply equally to much more up-to-date neurophysiology. (Dreyfus 2005: 142–23 seems to me to have misunderstood the import of Merleau-Ponty's arguments here.) Merleau-Ponty makes two points: one is that here the Gestalt psychologist has *changed the subject*: having given us 'a glimpse of "lived depth"', he then 'interrupts' the *description* and switches to *explanation*, attempting to 'derive organization in depth from a chain of observed facts' (cf. *CPP* 352). Secondly, as an explanation of 'lived depth', this *could not possibly work*: even if there were 'somewhere in the brain a functional structure homologous with . . . organization in depth', this would be nothing but a *factual* depth, something measurable, and could not possibly explain – short of 'some cerebral alchemy' – our lived experience of depth, our 'taking it up, 'assuming it', 'discovering its immanent significance' (*PP* 258/300-1, cf. *CPP* 353).

6 *PP* 49 n.1/57 n.44 suggests that this concept of motivation is one of Husserl's 'fluid' notions. Heinämaa (2008) observes that for Husserl, the term 'motivation' signals his turn to 'genetic' phenomenology (thence pursued by Merleau-Ponty, as he himself indicates, *PP* vii/vii-viii); it is beyond the scope of the present study to develop this.

7 Wrathall's otherwise useful article is marred by the account he gives of action-motivation; seems to suppose that in our ordinary use 'a motive is the intentional state that prompts or moves us to act', for instance a desire, and hence finds odd the idea that 'states of affairs in the world' (in my example, the phone call from my uncle) might move us to act (2005: 115-16). See Morris 2010a on Sartre's (much more phenomenologically accurate) account, which is far more developed than Merleau-Ponty's but has close affinities with the account on *PP* 259/301-2.

8 As philosophers of art will recognize, there are some here analogies (as well as disanalogies) with Sibley (e.g., 1965); these cannot be explored in this context.

9 Within such objectivism, Merleau-Ponty suggests (in a rare moment of humour), 'depth is tacitly equated with *breadth seen from the side,* and this is what makes it invisible'; he adds that '[f]or God, who is everywhere, breadth is immediately equivalent to depth', but that just shows that these thinkers can give no account of *human* experience (*PP* 255/297-8).

10 The intellectualist philosopher Malebranche even helps us understand ocular convergence as a 'sign' of distance –that is, a *reason for inferring* distance – by getting us to 'visualize my gaze as the blind man's two sticks, which run more sharply together as the object is brought nearer' (*PP* 257/299; cf. *WP* 42).

11　This is shown, *inter alia*, by the 'visual cliff' devised b J. J. Gibson's wife E. J. Gibson. Merleau-Ponty argues on the basis of Gestalt evidence that 'infantile perception is structured from its first moment'; this implies neither that 'the infant's perception and the adult's the same' (*CPP* 148), nor that Gestalt structures are 'innate' (*CPP* 149-50).

12　This is also why 'lived perspective' is not the same as 'geometrical perspective', as Cézanne above all other artists noticed. (See, e.g., *SNS* 14, *WP* 41.)

13　This is strikingly demonstrated by the fact that a 'subject whose oculo-motor muscles are paralyzed sees objects moving to his left whenever he believes that he is turning his eyes to the left' (*PP* 47/55).

14　No doubt Merleau-Ponty has particular genres of painting primarily in mind here; his great love was always Cézanne. Other painters and other genres play in various ways with the motives of perception.

15　It is significant that it took painters centuries to discover these 'motives'; as Merleau-Ponty notes, a reflection on the eye, although 'not seen as such', makes the face a living face, as painters eventually discovered; without it, 'the eye remains dull and sightless as in the paintings of the early masters' (*PP* 309/360). Gombrich 1950 may be seen as a history of the discovery by painters of the motives of perception.

16　Harrison, in a magnificent demonstration that scientism lives on, quotes this and comments: 'An interesting perspective on the issue, but we scientists don't have the luxury of simply asserting [such things] . . . ; we have to come up with a little more in the way of evidence. Meanwhile, back with our theory' (2001: 19).

17　It follows that those classical psychologists who identified, as peculiarities of the body, that it is 'an object which does not leave me' (*PP* 90/103), that the 'perspective' from which we perceive it is 'unvarying' (*PP* 91/104), have inverted the truth: '[w]hat prevents the body from ever being an object . . . is that it is that by which there are objects' (*PP* 92/105), it is *that by which* the factual permanence of (say) Mont Blanc to the residents of Annecy is factually permanent, it is *that by which* there is perspective.

18　Stephen Mulhall (at a seminar) made this point, for which I am grateful.

19　From Robert Downey, 'Wine snob scandal', in the *Seattle Weekly*, 20 February 2002.

20　I am grateful to Jonathan Cole for sending me the following passages from Sir Charles Bell, which express something of the same spirit: 'There is inconsistency and something of the child . . . in mankind . . . We use the limb without being conscious of the thousand parts which must conform to a single act . . . by an effort of the cultivated mind as must rouse ourselves to observe things and actions of which the sense has been lost through long familiarity.' Also: 'We stand by so fine an exercise of this power . . . and the muscles are from habit so directed with so much precision that we do not know how we stand.'

21　We might also mention the related dichotomy between conceptual and factual investigations, as it played a role in the exchange between Merleau-Ponty and Ryle at Royaumont. Merleau-Ponty pointed out that Ryle seemed simply to assume, 'as an established thing, which there was no need to discuss', a distinction between factual investigations and conceptual investigations, and asked him to clarify this (Merleau-Ponty 1962: 93). Ryle's reply was to point out some paradigms of factual investigations: those of the chemist, or the astronomer, who makes use of instruments ('for the one telescope, spectroscope, examination of photographs; for the other scales, test tubes, Bunsen burner') – '[n]othing very mysterious, as you see' – and to assert that 'questions of fact of this sort aren't in the competence of philosophy' (Ryle 1962: 96-7) – as if that clarified everything.

22 The latter expression is used by Husserl (*Crisis* III.A §36); although Merleau-Ponty does not employ the expression, his challenge to the *a priori/a posteriori* dichotomy – sketched below – may be seen as alluding to it.

23 Husserl had earlier proposed the notion of a 'material *a priori*'; he rejected the idea that synthetic *a priori* propositions should concern only the 'form' of experience, and thus introduced the idea of synthetic *a priori* propositions which concerned its 'matter'. This notion too was heavily attacked by the logical positivists (see Schlick 1949). Schlick expended considerable effort to show that the allegedly material *a priori* proposition 'A surface cannot be simultaneously red and green' (1949: 280-85) fit neatly into the positivists' 'analytic *a priori*/ synthetic *a posteriori*' distinction; readers must judge for themselves whether he succeeded. The interchange between Taylor and Ayer (both 1976) is instructive on many of the issues in this Coda.

24 We can see the positivists' influence even on such Merleau-Ponty commentators as Priest, who insists that talk of 'defining' anything other than 'linguistic items' is 'loose' (1998: 17) or 'confused' (1998: 196). See Morris 2003.

25 From Merleau-Ponty's point of view, their enterprise involves a misunderstanding of *language,* on which more in the Coda to Ch. 5.

26 Those who make a distinction between essence and accident see truths ascribing essential properties as necessary, truths ascribing accidental properties as contingent; it does not follow that all necessary truths are truths ascribing essential properties, nor that all contingent truths are truths ascribing accidental properties. Merleau-Ponty's claim here really does need to be understood against the background of his conception of essence; it is misleading to see him as claiming that the figure-ground structure is *logically* necessary truth, as Matthews (2002: 51) does. Romdenh-Romluc (2011: 40f.) does an excellent job of making Merleau-Ponty's claim plausible. She does not thematize 'concrete essence', but she does use the related term 'nature'; however, her claim that 'the actual nature of vision' is 'discovered empirically' is in need of elucidation.

27 A number of Merleau-Ponty commentators, most notably Kelly (2005), highlight this normativity without, however, directly linking it to Merleau-Ponty's notion of concrete essence.

28 Once again, Husserl is clearly in the background.

29 Cf. also Husserl's *The Origins of Geometry*.
30 See also his later reflections, clearly incited by Sartre's assertion that the actual arrangement of our sense-organs (e.g., the fact that we have hands which can touch each other) is 'a purely factual given' , that is, contingent (*BN* 358): 'What if our eyes were made in such a way as to prevent our seeing any part of our body, or if some baneful arrangement of the body were to let us move our hands over things, while preventing us from touching our own body? . . . There would be no humanity' (*PrP* 163).

CHAPTER 5

1 Remember from Ch. 1 that it was in part because Husserl recognized a problem of others that he showed himself *not* to be a true transcendental idealist.
2 Note, however, that the term 'object' is having to work overtime for Sartre: the Other-as-object is an *object in virtue of being the 'intentional object'* of my look, and the Other-as-object is the other's body (*BN* 346), but the other's body is *not* an object – that is, not a physiological or physical object, as the prejudice of objective thought takes it to be. Sartre's promiscuous use of the term 'object' is unfortunately the source of much misunderstanding. It has certainly misled commentators, for example, Hass, under Sartre's system 'the other's body is defined essentially the same as a rock or a toaster' (2008a: 105); it may have misled Merleau-Ponty as well.
3 To the extent that he is simply arguing that even within such conflict situations, I and the other recognize each other as subjects, Sartre will hardly disagree. (Again, Sartre can be his own worst enemy: his promiscuous use of the term 'object' may disguise this basic point of agreement.)
4 Moreland 1998 is an insightful treatment of *PP* III.1; he, however, speaks of the 'opacity' of consciousness for Merleau-Ponty, which goes just a little far. It is neither entirely transparent nor entirely opaque.
5 Cf. Husserl *Crisis* 150: 'To live as a person is to live in a social framework, wherein I and we live together in community and have the community as a horizon'.
6 Mauss (1973 [1935]) had shown that even seemingly 'natural' types of conduct (walking, running and urinating as well as swimming, dancing and eating) were performed differently in different cultures; Merleau-Ponty was familiar with Mauss' work on 'body techniques' (see *CPP* 235), although he seems to have been more interested in his conception of sociology than in this particular observation. However, given Merleau-Ponty's resistance to identifying a 'natural' layer of behaviour upon which is superimposed a cultural layer (*PP* 189/220), one might expect him to embrace Mauss' finding.
7 Even a highly 'reciprocal' personal project (e.g., my 'resolve' 'to live in an interworld in which I accord as much place to others as to myself')

is fraught with possibilities of hypocrisy, 'since this very attachment to another's interest still has its source in me' (*PP* 357/415).

8   See McGinn 1998 for a careful discussion of this 'solipsism'.

9   Although clearly there is scope for social and cultural misunderstandings, where the 'one' of, for example, '*One* uses a spoon thus' differs, not to mention much more radical intercultural failures of comprehension.

10 It may be argued that his blindness to the pre-personal and impersonal layers of shared existence rests on the inadequacy of his treatment of the body. It may also be argued that this inadequacy in turn lies in his basic ontology of in-itself and for-itself, where the in-itself is conceived of as (in itself) unstructured (see Moreland 1998).

11 Alternatively, I could justify the analogy on the basis of a point-by-point correspondence between my *own* body 'from the inside' and my *own* body 'from the outside' – between, say, 'the visible smile' and 'what we may call the "motor smile"'– and then move on to connecting my visible smile with the other's; but there is no such point-by-point correspondence (*PrP* 116).

12 This requires multiple qualifications: first, we can *come* to a bodily understanding of the expressive gestures of other species (see, e.g., Cole 1995, Ch. 5, on understanding great apes' facial expressions). And it is far from clear that *all* such understanding of other species even begins as intellectual; one brought up with cats may never go through the stage of understanding their expressive gestures intellectually, and the bodies of children raised by wolves evidently respond to their caregivers with what I call below the 'I can do that too'. Thirdly, it is doubtful that Merleau-Ponty would (or anyway should) want to see bodily reciprocity confined by boundaries defined by biology, and in any case the very notion of 'species' is contestable even within biology. See Ch. 6. Cf. Wittgenstein: 'Only of a living human being and what resembles (behaves like) a living human being can we say: it sees; is blind; hears; is deaf; is conscious or unconscious . . .' (1968: §281).

13 Again, I can imitate someone facing me without expressly thinking 'the hand which appears on the right side of my visual field is for my partner the left one' (*PP* 141/163).

14 Merleau-Ponty was presumably unfamiliar with autism; according to Sacks, it was described more or less simultaneously by Kanner and Asperger in the 1940s (1995: 245).

15 These autistic individuals do not argue from analogy; rather (cf. *BN* 223), they simply use one set of bodily manifestations (say, the frowning and redness) to predict the likely occurrence of another (say, the shouting). Perhaps this confirms the practical difficulties (noted earlier) in getting an argument from analogy off the ground.

16 See, for example, Baron-Cohen et al. 1993.

17 Oliver Sacks borrowed this phrase for the title and title essay of his 1995 book. Cf. Bourdieu on anthropologists in an unfamiliar culture who are 'condemned' to adopt 'the representation of action which is forced on agents or groups when they lack practical mastery of a highly valued competence' (1977: 2)

18 A recently documented 'abnormal' phenomenon has been dubbed 'mirror-touch synaesthesia': a young girl with this condition, when asked by her mother why she was limping, replied that her leg still hurt from having witnessed her friend hurt her foot the day before (Radio 4, 'All in the Mind', 26 April 2011). She felt pain where her friend did, and had assumed that everyone else was the same way. A study of such mirror-touch synaesthetes demonstrated that they, but not the controls, felt *both* cheeks being touched when they were touched on one cheek but watched another being touched on the opposite cheek (Banissy & Ward 2007). Might Merleau-Ponty say of this phenomenon as what he said of synaesthesia (Ch. 4iii), that it also is the rule and not the exception, although most of us 'unlearn' it?

19 At this early stage, one cannot even speak of 'communication', since there is no sharp boundary between individuals: rather we should speak of 'pre-communication' (*PrP* 119; cf. *CPP* 258). In his lectures on child psychology, Merleau-Ponty describes the process of individuation (i.e., becoming a bounded individual) in much more detail (see *PrP* lecture 4 and *CPP* lecture 5).

20 See Eilan 2007 for a thoughtful discussion of these issues.

21 On this point, Merleau-Ponty cites Husserl's notion of 'coupling', which is 'anything but a metaphor. In perceiving the other, my body and his are coupled . . . [T]his conduct which I am only able to see, I live somehow from a distance' (*PrP* 118).

22 Möbius' syndrome was first described around the turn of the twentieth century.

23 Of course, the face is not the only part of the body by which we express emotions and respond to others' emotions (although it is peculiarly important); it is, however, noteworthy that many Möbius patients have difficulty in understanding or producing even those nonverbal signals that do not involve the face (Cole 1999: 119). We might make sense of this by taking note of Merleau-Ponty's striking claim (once again derived from the Gestalt psychologists) that there is an internal relation between the *various* gestures that express an emotion; these gestures do not form a disconnected 'array' of disparate manifestations, each one caused independently by the inner emotion. 'In ordinary experience we find a fittingness and a meaningful relationship between the gesture, the smile and the tone of a speaker' (*PP* 55/64; cf. *PP* 281/327, *WP* 63); likewise, the frown, the clenched fist and the growling tone of the angry man form a kind of Gestalt unity.

24 See Ch. 6 for a bit more about the embodied cognition approach; its explicit ontology remains naturalistic, but just as Merleau-Ponty could accept the Gestalt psychologists' experimental findings while refusing their ontology, so too could he do with this approach.

25 Strictly, these were photographs that only showed the upper part of the face including the eyes and forehead; the test used is called the 'Reading the mind in the eyes test' or RMET. A parallel study involved smearing the expressive parts of subjects with a gel which shrank when it dried, so that their facial muscles had to work against resistance and thus

contracted harder than they would normally; thus, their bodies 'from the inside' were exaggerating their emotional facial expression. Such subjects were *more* accurate at identifying facial expressions, using RMET again, than the control situation in which the gel was smeared on their arm rather than on their face. Neal and Chartrand (2011) also tested these individuals using the 'Reading the mind in the voice test' (RVET), which uses brief clips of emotional speech. There was again a difference between the subjects' ability to read emotions dependent on whether the gel was on their face or on their arm, as the Gestalt nature of emotional expression would lead us to predict; this effect was not, however, statistically significant.

26 From 'Botox: blocking emotions and wrinkles?', http://beauty.doctissimo.com. It has also been suggested, although the evidence here is more mixed, that BOTOX® recipients experience their own emotions less acutely (Davis et al. 2010); there is even some preliminary evidence that BOTOX® may benefit sufferers of major depression (Finzi & Wasserman 2006), a finding that would be at least *prima facie* bizarre unless one acknowledged the internal relation between emotion and its expression.

27 This is a criticism made of Merleau-Ponty by Levinas. Hass 2008b provides a delicately balanced discussion of their debate about 'alterity'. See also Sanders 2008, which includes Husserl in the dialogue. Stawarska 2006 takes note of an apparent analogy between bodily reciprocity and the reversibility of the so-called 'double sensation' (e.g., my touching my own hand with the other), but cautions rightly that it would be a mistake to confuse the intracorporeity of the latter with the intercorporeity of the former.

28 See also Wacquant's (2006) sociological study of being an apprentice boxer.

29 The affinities between Merleau-Ponty and the later Wittgenstein on these issues will be obvious to anyone who knows Wittgenstein and I will not try to spell them out here; recall that it was the recognition of gesture-meaning that first got Wittgenstein off of his earlier conception of language. (The story is told that Sraffa made a rude gesture and then asked him 'What's the logical form of this?')

30 There is some consideration of Merleau-Ponty's critique of 'structuralist' approaches to language in Ch. 6iii.

31 He qualifies this, however, by saying that only in the case of 'first-hand speech' (see below) is speech 'identical to thought' (*PP* 178 n.1/207 n.4).

32 Aphasics who are incapable of understanding what is said to them may still be attuned to the emotional content of words and gestures, as Sacks discovered when he heard 'a roar of laughter from the aphasia ward' during a televised speech by Ronald Reagan: they could not understand his words but were responding to his overdone tonalities, inflections, and hand gestures (Sacks 1985: 76).

33 Baldwin sees Merleau-Ponty in *PP* as having overvalued 'speaking' as opposed to 'spoken' speech; it is not clear to me that he does so consistently.

Baldwin is, however, right to call attention to Merleau-Ponty's focus on spoken as opposed to *written* language (2007: 100-102).

34 Adams 2008 stresses this angle; see also Hass 2008a: 177f.

35 Csordas, we should add, resists the idea that glossolalia is just nonsense: it 'bears a global meaning as an inspired form of praise to God' – a global meaning that 'can be apprehended immediately' – and its 'speakers' take it as 'a basic tenet that the expressive powers of glossolalia transcend the inadequacies of natural languages' (2002: 74-5). At a more abstract level, '[t]he stripping away of the semantic dimension in glossolalia is not an absence, but rather the drawing back of a discursive curtain to reveal the grounding of language in natural life' (2002: 76)

CHAPTER 6

1 Dreyfus charges McDowell with succumbing to 'the myth of the mental', that is, a version of intellectualism; McDowell resists this charge. The discussion of animals (§iv below) is relevant for making sense of what is at issue. As Marie McGinn ('The role of conceptual abilities in the objective purport of experience', unpublished, presented at a conference in York in 2011) argues, McDowell sees a 'dualism' between mere sensitivity to features of the environment (revealed in what Merleau-Ponty will call 'syncretic' forms of behaviour) and a comprehension of the world, which depends on conceptual capacities. This leaves out both the 'amovable' forms of behaviour and the 'symbolic' forms of behaviour possessed by a young child (as exhibited in the bodily reciprocity though which it enters into the social and cultural interworld; see Ch. 5ii) prior to a point at which we would say of it that it possesses concepts.

2 See Gallagher 2008 for a more sympathetic assessment. According to Wilson and Foglia (2011: 1), 'Cognition is embodied when it is deeply dependent upon features of the physical body of an agent, that is, when aspects of the agent's body beyond the brain play a significant causal or physically constitutive role in cognitive processing', which makes it clear that this approach takes the body to be *Körper* rather than *Leib*. Their article is a good place to begin; those who wish to know more might look at Varela, Thompson and Roach 1991, Damasio 1997, Clark 2008, and Noë 2008.

3 The influence of the Gestalt psychologists is openly acknowledged in Gibson's writings. We owe our awareness of the direct influence of Merleau-Ponty principally to Dreyfus (2007: 69 n.1).

4 Bermúdez et al. 1995 is a good place to look for early manifestations of both trends.

5 Ingold is an anthropologist but has (I am told) a following among geographers. The guiding Merleau-Pontyan idea that makes this influence intelligible is *lived space*.

6 I am alluding to what feminists sometimes call 'the problem of difference'. It is suggested (see §ii below) that men and women live in their bodies and the world differently; and even within the category

of human beings called 'women', there are important differences (class, race, age, ethnicity, sexual orientation, etc.), which suggest different 'worlds'; to pursue this too far, however, ultimately leads to solipsism (Kruks 2006: 27, who offers an eminently sane approach to 'the problem of difference' and sees Merleau-Ponty as playing an important role in such an approach). See Fanon 1967 for a classic treatment of the 'raced' body, and more recently, with a feminist perspective, Alcoff 2006. See Moore 1988 Ch. 1 for a feminist anthropologist's angle on 'difference'.

7 Merleau-Ponty asserts that 'the situation of the object of study' '[i]n child psychology (as in psychopathology, the psychology of primitives, and the psychology of women) . . . is so different from that of the observer that it cannot be grasped on its own terms' (cf. also *CPP* 346). (As Welsh 2008: 47 notes, this seems to suggest that only a man could be a psychologist.) To group children, 'primitives', the mentally ill and women together seems to classify all of them as somehow *defective* – an inference apparently confirmed when Merleau-Ponty asserts that '[a] dult thought, normal and civilised, is *better* than childish, morbid or barbaric [as well as 'feminine'?] thought' (*WP* 56, italics added). There is, however, a saving grace: he immediately adds 'one condition': that we recognize that even 'adult thought, normal and civilised' is rooted in the *irrational*, and is shot through with 'fantasies, dreams, patterns of magical behaviour and obscure phenomena' (*WP* 56; cf. *Signs* 122); 'Are we not also sometimes prelogical?' (*CPP* 376). (Cf. Wittgenstein: on 'kissing the picture of one's beloved', 1979: 64.)

8 Some of the feminist literature engages with *VI* more than with *PP*; I will not comment on this angle here. The literature on animals tends to pick up on *SB* (whose results are presupposed in and occasionally referred to in *PP*) and on Merleau-Ponty's lecture notes *Nature*, published in 1994, but only made available in an English translation in 2003.

9 Merleau-Ponty is much less well-known in the field of child psychology than his successor to the chair in child psychology and pedagogy at the Sorbonne, Jean Piaget. I will not here be talking about the world of children, but see Merleau-Ponty's Sorbonne lectures (*CPP*), including his critiques of Piaget.

10 See, however, the work of the feminist historian of biology Donna Haraway (1992, 2003), although her writings cannot be called phenomenological. See also Ingold 1988, which makes use of Uexküll (see §iv) and Gibson.

11 Part of Levinas' critique of Merleau-Ponty is the charge that he underplays vulnerability (see e.g., Hass 2008b).

12 I do not mean to *identify* pain with illness; as Leder rightly points out, one may have pain without illness and conversely. However, as he also notes, 'disease tends to effect many of the same experiential shifts as does pain' (1990: 79). Thus, there is a point in treating them in the same section.

13 The term 'biomedicine' is used by anthropologists, who argue that simply to call it 'medicine' would have the ethnocentric implication that

systems of medicine not based on Western scientific biology are *not* really medicine, but are rather mere 'ethnomedicine' or 'folk medicine' based on 'beliefs' rather than 'knowledge' (see Gaines and Davis-Floyd 2004). Biomedicine is as much an ethnomedicine as shamanic healing is; and its 'deep cultural logic' is as rooted in Western culture as that of shamanic healing is in the culture of Siberian and other hunter-gatherer societies (see Kleinman et al. 1994: 8).

14 The focus in this section is on individuals who are 'physically' rather than 'mentally' ill (Merleau-Ponty's 'madmen'), difficult though is to draw such a distinction. There are, however, a number of interesting phenomenological studies in the field of philosophy of psychiatry, which draw on Merleau-Ponty; here I will simply refer the reader to the journal *Philosophy, Psychiatry, Psychology* and the OUP series *International Perspectives in Philosophy and Psychiatry*, where phenomenology in general and Merleau-Ponty in particular often figure significantly.

15 Their descriptions of pain and illness have been taken up by phenomenologically oriented medical anthropologists; DelVecchio Good et al. 1994 is a paradigm example. These anthropologists also draw on Elaine Scarry's classic 1985 study *The Body in Pain*, particularly her subtitle *The Making and Unmaking of the World*.

16 Leder's qualification is relevant for illness but not for congenital 'disability'. There is a whole 'disability' literature, which space considerations preclude developing here; Silvers 2009 gives a useful overview from a feminist perspective as well as a useful bibliography. See also Inahara 2009b.

17 There is a potential problem here, which parallels 'the problem of difference' in feminism (see n.8 above), as Inahara 2009a brings out; such descriptions may be charged with homogenizing the varieties of 'bodily' illness.

18 Havi Carel (2008) has been especially influential; she is a philosopher who has been remarkably successful in bringing together phenomenologists and health-care professionals, e.g., at a recent workshop entitled 'Phenomenology and the Vulnerable Body: The Experience of Illness' (University of Hull 2010).

19 Moreover, Beauvoir sees in *PP*, and Merleau-Ponty sees in *L'Invitée, ethical* possibilities that may not immediately meet the eye (e.g., Beauvoir affirms that we can build an ethics 'to which man can totally and sincerely adhere' on the solid basis of a phenomenological account of human existence, 2004 [1945]: 160, and sees *PP* as contributing to this solid basis). See, for example, Bergoffen 1997, Heinämaa's introduction to Beauvoir 2004.

20 See Heinämaa 2003 (also Cavallaro 2003: 15; like many feminists, she is not entirely fair to Sartre). Beauvoir 2004 gives a clear indication of how she sees (or saw at the time) the fundamental ontological differences between Sartre and Merleau-Ponty.

21 Up to a point this remark anticipates the move, visible in the sociological literature over the past couple of decades, to speak of 'femininities' and

'masculinities' in the plural; most, however, would not see one 'femininity' or 'masculinity' per 'civilisation' as Merleau-Ponty does, but multiple intersecting ones.

22 See also Weiss 2006, which explores the multiple meanings of embodied city life through the lenses of Irigaray and Merleau-Ponty's later notion of flesh.

23 Some have found more inspiration in Merleau-Ponty's later unfinished work *VI*, about which I will say nothing here.

24 Andrews 2006 defends Merleau-Ponty against some misunderstandings in this area. This snippet cannot possibly do justice to the influence that Irigaray has had both on feminism in general and on the feminist reception of Merleau-Ponty. (See Whitford 1991 for a good introduction to Irigaray.) Irigaray is difficult in her own right; moreover, her response to Merleau-Ponty (1993: 151-84) and feminist responses to that focus on *VI*. For these reasons, further treatment of this strand of the feminist reception of Merleau-Ponty is beyond the scope of this study, but see Halsema 2008 and Young 2008 as recent examples.

25 See Lennon 2010 for a useful overview of feminist perspectives on the body more generally.

26 This provides a certain kind of *post facto* justification for Merleau-Ponty's grouping-together of women with the ill.

27 I will not, in this section, differentiate between sociology and social and cultural anthropology; the distinction remains contestable even today, and has a different history in France and in the Anglophone world.

28 Although the anthropologist Csordas runs with Merleau-Ponty's example: 'a smile for the American and the Japanese is grounded in the same anatomical apparatus, but transcends it by being appropriated or thematized in the one case as friendship and in the other as anger' (2002: 77).

29 Cf. *Signs* 112, which uses his favoured metaphor of 'centripetal' and 'centrifugal' movement to characterize individual and culture respectively, adding that the compossibility of both movements is 'unthinkable' 'from a causal point of view'.

30 In later work, he would do the same thing with biology; see *Nature*, and, for example, Barbaras 2005.

31 One might also mention Marcel Mauss, whose lectures at the Collège de France Sartre and Merleau-Ponty attended (Hayman 1987: 237). Merleau-Ponty found in Mauss' work 'a contribution [to sociology] which in effect paralleled that of Gestalt psychology' (Schmidt 1985: 49), but (like Gestalt psychology) one that fell short of a radical critique of the positivist sociology which preceded him. See 'From Mauss to Lévi-Strauss' (1959; in *Signs*).

32 Merleau-Ponty says a great deal more about structural linguistics in 'Indirect language and the voices of silence' in *Signs*.

33 Some will see this as a conflation of very different notions of structure, just as some will see Merleau-Ponty's reconciling project in the Preface (see Ch. 1) as eliding the differences between Husserlian and Heideggerean phenomenology. One might prefer to see here a deep-rooted desire on

Merleau-Ponty's part for dialogue and an insightful appreciation of shared ground.

34 ' "Kinship systems", like "phonemic systems", are built up by the mind on the level of unconscious thought', from Lévi-Strauss' *Structural Anthropology*, quoted by Bourdieu (1977: 28). Lévi-Strauss drew not only on structural linguistics but also on cybernetics, which was being developed in the 1940s. Cybernetics in a general way stressed the inter-relation between elements in a system and underlay the development of computers. The notion that the workings of the brain could be mod-elled on those of computers was an early application of cybernetics.

35 Another of Bourdieu's teachers was Canguilhem (see the Coda to Ch. 3). Bourdieu is often counted as a sociologist, but often also as an anthropologist. He was trained in philosophy; moreover, he explic-itly engages with recognizably philosophical questions, so much so that some are prepared to count him *as* a philosopher (Shusterman 1999: 2), and even as a metaphilosopher (Shusterman 1999: 10).

36 No doubt Foucault's dismissal of Merleau-Ponty was also influential (see Ch. 3 n.38). Bourdieu's disparaging references to 'lived experience', 'subjectivism' and 'the phenomenologists' refer to Sartre, Schutz and Garfinkel, rather than Merleau-Ponty. See Ostrow 1990 for, *inter alia*, a critique of Bourdieu's narrow view of phenomenology. Bourdieu does refer favourably to Merleau-Ponty's *SB* on several occasions.

37 There is an enormous literature on rules and rule-following by Wittgenstein scholars. One of the few to link this literature with Merleau-Ponty is Wrathall (2007). Taylor (1999), Bouveresse (1999) and Earle (1999) all link the Wittgensteinian rule-following literature to Bourdieu, who explicitly invites such a comparison (e.g., Bourdieu 1977: 29: 'Wittgenstein effortlessly brings together all the questions evaded by structural anthropology and no doubt more generally by all intellectualism').

38 There are prior uses of this term 'habitus' in Husserl and also in Mauss. Bourdieu is best-known by the reading public for his notion of 'capital' (economic, social, cultural and symbolic); but this notion cannot fully be understood without recognizing its intertwining with habitus and field.

39 Weiss (2008: 232 ff.) powerfully expresses a discomfort which many of us must feel at the virtual disappearance of the individual into the group habitus.

40 Merleau-Ponty was 'faced with the task of taming an excessively subjec-tivist theory with a knowledge of the opacity and density of the world of structures. Contemporary social theorists are faced with the task of overcoming an excessively objectivist understanding of structures with the knowledge that structures do not simply constrain agents, they also allow agents to act in ways which frequently lead to the transformation of the structures themselves' (Schmidt 1985: 166–67).

41 Bourdieu actually *dismisses* the idea that understanding another's actions involves a ' "reactivation" of the "lived intention" of the agent who performs them' (Bourdieu 1977: 80), a view that could sound like

Merleau-Ponty's notion, but his target here is evidently *not* Merleau-Ponty.

42 Berthoz and Christen (2009: 1-2) contrast the 'Continental' approach to studying animals – the approach that developed into ethology – with the 'Anglo-Saxon' style, which focused on laboratory experiments, typically from a behaviourist or 'learning-theory' perspective. This is a useful generalization, but there are exceptions; indeed, one of Merleau-Ponty's criticisms of the Gestalt psychologists was precisely that they tended to confine their work to the laboratory: in their eagerness for 'precision in their formulas', their 'favorite subject of study was those forms whose appearance, especially in the laboratory, was more or less regular, given a certain number of external conditions' (*SNS* 85).

43 Cf. Gibson 1979: 141: although affordances are invariants, they may not be 'valid' for everyone; an affordance may be 'valid for all the animals of a species as when it is part of a niche'.

44 *SB* Part III distinguishes between the physical, the vital and the human 'orders'. *PP* 78 alludes to this: a drop of oil 'adapts itself to given external forces' (physical order); an insect 'projects the norms of its environment and itself lays down the terms of its vital problem' (vital order); but, he adds, 'it is a question of an *a priori* of the species and not a personal choice' (human order). Like Uexküll, he offers his conception of the 'vital order' as a way of steering *between* the mechanism and vitalism of his age (*SB* 158ff.).

45 Thus, once again we can see a kind of justification for his bracketing animals with the ill.

46 See also some of the articles in Berthoz and Christen (eds) (2009), which take off from Uexküll on animals.

47 Compare Husserl: 'that which is in principle the most essential' 'escapes psychology . . . The true method follows the nature of the things to be investigated and not our own prejudices and preconceptions' (*PRS* 101-2); and because modern psychology has not done this, it fails to be 'psychology in the true, fully scientific sense' (*PRS* 119).

48 Taylor (2005: 27–8) describes the prejudice of objective thought as 'a structuring framework understanding that guided their questioning and reasoning about these matters . . . it just went on shaping the thoughts that were in the foreground, without our really being aware of its action'. This too suggests some similarities to the notion of bad faith.

49 There is a vast literature on Sartre's conception of bad faith. It is noteworthy that Sartre analysed everyday prejudices such as racism or anti-Semitism in terms of bad faith.

50 Wittgenstein is another philosopher in whom these terms 'prejudice', 'dogma' and the like need to be taken fully seriously (see Baker 2004, Morris 2007).

BIBLIOGRAPHY

Adams, H. (2008). 'Expression'. In R. Diprose and J. Reynolds, (eds), pp. 152–62.

Alcoff, L. M. (2006). *Visible Identities: Race, Gender and the Self*. Oxford University Press: New York.

Andrews, J. (2006). 'Vision, violence and the other: a Merleau-Pontyan ethics'. In D. Olkowski and G. Weiss, (eds), pp. 167–82.

Ash, M. G. (1998). *Gestalt Psychology in German Culture 1890–1967*. Cambridge University Press: Cambridge, New York and Melbourne.

Austin, J. L. (1962). *Sense and Sensibilia*. G. J. Warnock, (ed.) Clarendon: Oxford.

Ayer, A. J. (1976). 'Phenomenology and linguistic analysis II'. In H. A. Durfee, (ed.), pp. 232–42.

—(1977). *Part of My Life: The Memoirs of a Philosopher*. Harcourt Brace Jovanovich: New York and London.

Bair, D. (1990). *Simone de Beauvoir: A Biography*. Summit Books: New York.

Baker, G. (2004). *Wittgenstein's Method: Neglected Aspects*. K. J. Morris, (ed.) Blackwell: Oxford.

Baker, G. and K. J. Morris (1996). *Descartes' Dualism*. Routledge: London and New York.

Baldwin, T. (2007). 'Speaking and spoken speech'. In T. Baldwin, (ed.), pp. 87–103.

—(2007). (ed.) *Reading Merleau-Ponty on Phenomenology of Perception*. Routledge: London and New York.

Banissy, M. J. and J. Ward (2007). 'Mirror-touch synesthesia is linked with empathy'. *Nature Neuroscience* 10, pp. 815–16.

Barbaras, R. (2005). 'A phenomenology of life'. In T. Carman and M. B. N. Hansen, (eds), pp. 206–30.

Baron-Cohen, S., H. Tager-Flausberg and D. J. Cohen (1993). *Understanding Other Minds: Perspectives from Autism*. Oxford Medical Publications: Oxford.

Bartky, S. (1990). *Femininity and Domination: Studies in the Phenomenology of Oppression*. Routledge: New York and London.

de Beauvoir, S. (1992). *The Prime of Life*. Trans. P. Green. André Deutsch and Weidenfeld & Nicolson: London. (Original French publication 1960.)

—(1998). '*Merleau-Ponty and Pseudo-Sartreanism*.' In J. Stewart, (ed.), pp. 448–91. (Original French publication 1955.)

—(2004). A review of *The Phenomenology of Perception* by Maurice Merleau-Ponty. Trans. M. Timmermann with notes by S. Keltner. In M. A. Simons, (ed.) *Simone de Beauvoir: Philosophical Writings*, pp. 159–64. (Original French publication 1945.)

—(2011). *The Second Sex*. Trans. C. Borde and S. Malovany-Chevallier. Vintage Books: London. (This translation first appeared in 2009. Original French publication 1949.)

Bergoffen, D. (1997). *The Philosophy of Simone de Beauvoir: Gendered Phenomenologies, Erotic Generosities*. State University of New York Press: New York.

Bermúdez, J. L., A. Marcel and N. Eilan (eds) (1995). *The Body and the Self*. Bradford/MIT: Cambridge, MA and London.

Berthoz, A. and Y. Christen, (eds) (2009). *Neurobiology of "Umwelt"*. Springer: Berlin and Heidelberg.

Block, N. (1980). 'Troubles with functionalism.' In N. Block, (ed.), *Readings in the Philosophy of Psychology*, Vol. 1. Harvard University Press: Cambridge, MA, pp. 268–305.

Bordo, S. (1993). *Unbearable Weight: Feminism, Western Culture and the Body*. University of California Press: Berkeley, CA.

Bourdieu, P. (1977). *Outline of a Theory of Practice*. Trans. R. Nice. Cambridge University Press: Cambridge.

—(1984). *Distinction*. Routledge: London.

—(1990). *The Logic of Practice*. Trans. R. Nice. Stanford University Press: Stanford.

—(1992). *Language and Symbolic Power*. Polity: Cambridge.

Bouveresse, J. (1999). 'Rules, dispositions, and the *habitus*'. In R. Shusterman, (ed.), pp. 45–63.

Buchanan, B. (2008). *Onto-Ethologies: The Animal Environments of Uexküll. Heidegger, Merleau-Ponty, and Deleuze*. State University of New York Press: Albany, NY.

Butler, J. (1989). 'Sexual ideology and phenomenological description'. In J. Allen and I. M. Young, (eds), *The Thinking Muse: Feminism and Modern French Philosophy*. Indiana University Press: Bloomington, IN, pp. 85–100.

—(1990). *Gender Trouble: Feminism and the Subversion of Identity*. Routledge: New York and London.

Calarco, M. (2008). *Zoographies: The Question of the Animal from Heidegger to Derrida*. Columbia University Press: New York and Chichester.

Canguilhem, G. (1978). *On the Normal and the Pathological*. Trans. C. R. Fawcett. Reidel: Dordrecht, Boston and London. (Original French publication 1966.)

Carel, H. (2008). *Illness*. Acumen: Stocksfield.

Carman, T. (2005). 'On the inescapability of phenomenology'. In D. W. Smith and A. L. Thomasson, (eds), *Phenomenology and Philosophy of Mind*. Oxford University Press: Oxford, pp. 67–89.

—(2008). *Merleau-Ponty*. Routledge: London and New York.

Carman, T. and M. B. N. Hansen, (eds) (2005). *The Cambridge Companion to Merleau-Ponty*. Cambridge University Press: Cambridge.

Cataldi, S. L. and W. S. Hamrick (2007). *Merleau-Ponty and Environmental Philosophy: Dwelling on the Landscapes of Thought.* State University of New York Press: Albany, NY.

Cerbone, D. R. (2006). *Understanding Phenomenology.* Acumen: Stocksfield.

Chisholm, D. (2008). 'Climbing like a girl: An exemplary adventure in feminist phenomenology'. *Hypatia* 23(1), pp. 9–40.

Clark, A. (2008). *Supersizing the Mind: Embodiment, Action, and Cognitive Extension.* Oxford University Press: New York.

Cole, J. (1995). *Pride and a Daily Marathon.* MIT Press: Cambridge, MA and London.

—(1998). *About Face.* MIT Press: Cambridge, MA.

—(2009). 'Impaired embodiment and intersubjectivity'. *Phenomenology and the Cognitive Sciences* 8, pp. 343–60.

Cole, J. and J. Paillard (1995). 'Living without touch and peripheral information about body position and movement: Studies with deafferented subjects'. In J. Bermúdez et al., (eds), pp. 245–66.

Crossley, N. (1996). 'Body-subject/body-power: agency, inscription and control in Foucault and Merleau-Ponty'. *Body and Society* 2, 99.

—(2000). 'Maurice Merleau-Ponty'. In B. Turner and A. Elliott, (eds), *Profiles in Contemporary Social Theory.* Sage: London, pp. 30–42.

—(2001). 'The phenomenological habitus and its construction'. *Theory and Society* 30(1), pp. 81–120.

—(2005). 'Mapping reflexive body techniques.' *Body and Society* 11(1), pp. 1–35.

—(2008). 'Sociology'. In R. Diprose and J. Reynolds, (eds), pp. 228–39.

Crowther, P. (2001). *Art and Embodiment: From Aesthetics to Self-Consciousness.* Oxford University Press: Oxford.

Csordas, T. J. (2002). *Body/Meaning/Healing.* Palgrave Macmillan: Basingstoke and New York.

Damasio, A. (1999). *The Feeling of What Happens: Body and Emotion in the Making of Consciousness.* Harcourt Brace & Co.: New York.

Davis, J. I., A. Senghas, F. Brandt and K. N. Ochsner (2010). 'The effects of BOTOX injections on emotional experience'. *Emotion* 10(3), pp. 433–40.

DelVecchio Good, M.-J., P. E. Brodwin, B. J. Good and A. Kleinman, (eds) (1994). *Pain as Human Experience: An Anthropological Perspective.* University of California Press: Berkeley, CA (paperback edition).

Dennett, D. C. (1991). *Consciousness Explained.* Little, Brown & Co.: Boston.

Descartes, R. (1991). *The Philosophical Writings of Descartes*, Vol. III. Trans. J. Cottingham, R. Stoothoff, D. Murdoch and A. Kenny. Cambridge University Press: Cambridge. (Correspondence dating from 1619–1650.)

Dillard-Wright, D. B. (2009a). *Ark of the Possible: The Animal World in Merleau-Ponty.* Lexington Books: Lanham, MD.

—(2009b). 'Thinking across species boundaries: general sociality and embodied meaning'. *Society and Animals* 17(1), pp. 53–71.

Dillon, M. C. (1988). *Merleau-Ponty's Ontology.* Indiana University Press: Bloomington, IN.

Diprose, R. and J. Reynolds, (eds) (2008). *Merleau-Ponty: Key Concepts.* Acumen: Stocksfield.

Dolezal, L. (2010). 'The (in)visible body: feminism, phenomenology, and the case of cosmetic surgery'. *Hypatia* 25(2), pp. 357–75.

Dreyfus, H. (1996). 'The current relevance of Merleau-Ponty's phenomenology of embodiment'. Available at http://ejap.louisiana.edu/EJAP/1996. spring/dreyfus.1996.spring.html.

—(2000). 'A Merleau-Pontyian critique of Husserl's and Sartre's representationalist accounts of action'. *Proceedings of the Aristotelian Society* 100(3), pp. 287–302.

—(2005). 'Overcoming the myth of the mental: how philosophers can profit from the phenomenology of everyday expertise'. American Philosophical Association Pacific Division Presidential Address. Available at http:// socrates.berkeley.edu/~hdreyfus/pdf/Dreyfus%20APA%20Address%20%20 10.22.05%20.pdf.

—(2007a). 'The return of the myth of the mental'. *Inquiry* 50(4), pp. 352–65.

—(2007b). 'Response to McDowell'. *Inquiry* 50(4), pp. 371–77.

—(2007c). 'Reply to Romdenh-Romluc'. In T. Baldwin, (ed.), pp. 59–69.

Durfee, H. A. (ed.) (1976). *Analytic Philosophy and Phenomenology*. Martinus Nijhoff: The Hague.

Earle, W. (1999). 'Bourdieu *nouveau*'. In R. Shusterman, (ed.), pp. 175–91.

Eilan, N. (2007). 'Consciousness, self-consciousness and communication'. In T. Baldwin, (ed.), pp. 118–38.

Embree, L. (1980). 'Merleau-Ponty's examination of Gestalt psychology'. *Research in Phenomenology* 10, pp. 89–121.

Fallaize, E., (ed.) (1998). *Simone de Beauvoir: A Critical Reader*. Routledge: London and New York.

Fanon, F. (1967). *Black Skin, White Masks*. Trans. C. L. Markmann. Grove Press: New York. (Original French publication 1952.)

Finzi, E. and E. Wasserman (2006). 'Treatment of depression with botulinum toxin A: a case series'. *Dermatologic Surgery* 32, pp. 645–50.

Fisher, A. L. (1969). 'Introduction' to *The Essential Writings of Merleau-Ponty*. A. L. Fisher, (ed.) Harcourt, Brace & World, Inc.: New York.

Flanagan, O. (1992). *Consciousness Reconsidered*. Bradford/MIT Press: Cambridge, MA and London.

Flynn, B. (2004). 'Merleau-Ponty'. In the *Stanford Encyclopedia of Philosophy*. http://plato.stanford.edu/entries/merleau-ponty/.

Foucault, M. (1979). *Discipline and Punish: The Birth of the Prison*. Trans. A. Sheridan. Vintage Books: New York.

Franzese, S. (2002). '*Ripensare la "normalità": la nozione strutturale di normalità in Merleau-Ponty*'. In *Segni i Comprensione* XVI: 45.

Gaines, A. D. and R. Davis-Floyd (2004). 'Biomedicine'. In C. R. Ember and M. Ember, (eds), *Encyclopedia of Medical Anthropology*, Vol. I. Springer: New York, pp. 95–109.

Gallagher, S. (1995). 'Body schema and intentionality'. In J. Bermúdez et al., (eds), pp. 225–44.

—(2005). *How the Body Shapes the Mind*. Oxford University Press: New York.

—(2008). 'Cognitive science'. In R. Diprose and J. Reynolds, (eds), pp. 207–17.

Gibson, J. J. (1979). *The Ecological Approach to Visual Perception*. Houghton Mifflin: Boston.

Glendinning, S. (2006). *The Idea of Continental Philosophy*. Edinburgh University Press: Edinburgh.

Goldman, A. I. and C. S. Sripida (2005). 'Simulationist models of face-based emotion recognition'. *Cognition* 94, pp. 193–213.

Gombrich, E. (1950). *The Story of Art*. Phaidon: London.

Good, B. J. (1994). *Medicine, Rationality, and Experience*. Cambridge University Press: Cambridge.

Grimshaw, J. (1999). 'Working out with Merleau-Ponty'. In J. Arthurs and J. Grimshaw, (eds) *Women's Bodies: Discipline and Transgression*. Cassell: London, pp. 91–116.

Grosholz, E. T., (ed.) (2004). *The Legacy of Simone de Beauvoir*. Clarendon Press: Oxford.

Grosz, E. (1994). *Volatile Bodies: Toward a Corporeal Feminism*. Indiana University Press: Bloomington, IN.

Guillaume, P. (1937). *La Psychologie de la Forme*. Flammarion: Paris. (All translations mine.)

Halsema, A. (2008). 'Phenomenology in the feminine: Irigaray's relationship to Merleau-Ponty'. In G. Weiss, (ed.), pp. 63–84.

Hammond M., J. Howarth and R. Keat (1991). *Understanding Phenomenology*. Blackwell: Oxford.

Haraway, D. (1992). *Primate Visions: Gender, Race and Nature in the World of Modern Science*. Verso: London and New York.

—(2003). *The Companionate Species Manifesto: Dogs, People and Significant Otherness*. Prickly Paradigm Press: Chicago.

Harrison, J. (2001). *Synaesthesia: The Strangest Thing*. Oxford University Press: Oxford.

Hass, L. (2008a). *Merleau-Ponty's Philosophy*. Indiana University Press: Bloomington and Indianapolis.

—(2008b). 'Elemental alterity: Levinas and Merleau-Ponty'. In G. Weiss, (ed.), pp. 31–44.

Hayman, R. (1987). *Sartre: A Biography*. Simon & Schuster: New York.

Heinämaa, S. (2003). *Phenomenology of Sexual Difference*. Rowman and Littlefield: Lanham, MD.

—(2008). 'Phenomenological reactions to Gestalt psychology'. In S. Heinämaa and M. Reuter, (eds) *Psychology and Philosophy: Inquiries into the Soul from Late Scholasticism to Contemporary Thought*. Springer: Dordrecht, pp. 263–84.

Hems, J. M. (1976). 'Husserl and/or Wittgenstein'. In H. A. Durfee, (ed.), pp. 55–86.

Inahara, M. (2009a). 'This body which is not one: femininity and disability'. *Body and Society* 15(1), pp. 47–62.

—(2009b). *Abject Love: Undoing the Boundaries of Physical Disability*. VDM Verlag: Saarbrücken.

Ingold, T. (1988). *What is an Animal?* Unwin Hyman: London.

—(2000). *The Perception of the Environment: Essays on Livelihood, Dwelling and Skill*. Routledge: London.

Irigaray, L. (1987). *An Ethics of Sexual Difference*. Trans. C. Burke and G. C. Gill. Continuum: London and New York.

—(1993). *The Ethics of Sexual Difference.* Trans. C. Burke and G. C. Gill. Athlone Press: London.

James, W. (1890). *The Principles of Psychology*, 2 vols. Dover Publications: New York.

Jensen, R. T. (2009). 'Motor intentionality and the case of Schneider'. *Phenomenology and the Cognitive Sciences* 8, pp. 371–88.

Kahane, G., E. Kanterian and O. Kuusela, (eds) (2007). *Wittgenstein and his Interpreters.* Blackwell: Oxford.

Kelly, S. D. (2005). 'Seeing things in Merleau-Ponty.' In T. Carman and M. B. N. Hansen, (eds), pp. 74–110.

Kleinman, A., P. E. Brodwin, B. J. Good and M.-J. DelVecchio Good (1994). 'Pain as human experience: an introduction'. In M.-J. DelVecchio Good et al., (eds), pp. 1–28.

Koffka, K. (1935). *Principles of Gestalt Psychology.* Routledge & Kegan Paul: London.

Kruks, S. (2006). 'Merleau-Ponty and the problem of difference in feminism'. In D. Olkowski and G. Weiss, (eds), pp. 25–48.

Leder, D. (1990). *The Absent Body.* Chicago University Press: Chicago and London.

Lennon, K. (2010). 'Feminist perspectives on the body'. In *Stanford Encyclopedia of Philosophy.* http://www.seop.leeds.ac.uk/entries/feminist-body/.

Lewin, K. (1936). *Principles of Topological Psychology.* Trans. F. Heider and G. M. Heider. McGraw-Hill: New York

Luria, A. R. (1987). *The Mind of a Mnemonist.* Trans. L. Solotaroff. Harvard University Press: Cambridge, MA and London. (First English publication 1968.)

Matthews, E. (2006). *Merleau-Ponty: A Guide for the Perplexed.* Continuum: London and New York.

Mauss, M. (1973). 'Techniques of the body'. Trans. B. Brewster. *Economy and Society* 2, pp. 70–88. (Original French publication 1935.)

McCann, R. (2008). 'Entwining the body and the world: architectural design and experience in light of "Eye and Mind"'. In G. Weiss, (ed.), pp. 265–81.

McDowell, J. (1994). *Mind and World.* Harvard University Press: Cambridge, MA.

—(2007a). 'What myth?' *Inquiry* 50(4), pp. 338–51.

—(2007b). 'Response to Dreyfus'. *Inquiry* 50(4), pp. 366–70.

McGinn, M. (1998). 'The real problem of others: Cavell, Merleau-Ponty and Wittgenstein on scepticism about other minds'. *European Journal of Philosophy* 6(1), pp. 45–58.

Merleau-Ponty, M. (1962). Contribution to the discussion of Ryle. In J. Wahl, (ed.), pp. 93–6. (This discussion appears in English in *TD* as 'Phenomenology and analytic philosophy'.)

Mirvish, A. M. (1983). 'Merleau-Ponty and the nature of philosophy'. *Philosophy and Phenomenological Research* 43(4), pp. 449–76.

Moi, T. (1990). *Feminist Theory and Simone de Beauvoir.* Blackwell: Oxford and Cambridge, MA.

Mol, A. (1998). 'Lived reality and the multiplicity of norms: a critical tribute to Georges Canguilhem'. *Economy and Society* 27(2/3), pp. 274–84.

Mooney, T. (2011). 'Plasticity, motor intentionality and concrete movement in Merleau-Ponty'. *Continental Philosophy Review* 44(4), pp. 359–81.

Moore, A. W. (2007). 'Wittgenstein and transcendental idealism'. In G. Kahane et al., (eds), pp. 174–99.

Moore, H. L. (1988). *Feminism and Anthropology*. Polity: Cambridge.

Moran, D. (2000). *An Introduction to Phenomenology*. Routledge: London and New York.

— (2010). 'Husserl, Sartre and Merleau-Ponty on embodiment, touch and the "double sensation"'. In K. J. Morris, (ed.), pp. 41–66.

Moreland, J. M. (1998). 'For-itself and in-itself in Sartre and Merleau-Ponty'. In J. Stewart, (ed.), pp. 16–24.

Morris, K. J. (1992). 'Wittgenstein on knowledge of posture'. *Philosophical Investigations* 15(1), pp. 30–50.

—(2003). 'Merleau-Ponty and out-of-body experiences'. *Journal of the British Society for Phenomenology* 34(2), pp. 157–67.

—(2007). 'Wittgenstein's method: ridding people of philosophical prejudices', in G. Kahane et al., (eds) pp. 66–87.

—(2008). *Sartre*. Blackwell (Great Minds series): Oxford.

—(2010). (ed.) *Sartre on the Body*. Palgrave Macmillan: London.

—(2010a). 'Sartre on action'. In T. O'Connor and C. Sandis, (eds) *A Companion to the Philosophy of Action.* Wiley-Blackwell: Malden, MA, Oxford and Chichester.

—(2010b). 'The phenomenology of clumsiness'. In K. J. Morris, (ed.), pp. 161–82.

Nagel, T. (1974). 'What is it like to be a bat?' *Philosophical Review* 83(4), pp. 435–50.

Neal, D. T. and T. L. Chartrand (2011). 'Embodied emotion perception: amplifying and dampening facial feedback modulates emotion perception accuracy'. *Social Psychological and Personality Science* (online: Sage Journals).

Niedenthal, P. M., M. Mermillod, M. Maringer and U. Hess (2010). 'The simulation of smiles (SIMS) model: embodied simulation and the meaning of facial expression'. *Behavioral and Brain Sciences* 33, pp. 417–80.

Noë, A. (2008). *Out of Our Heads: Why You Are Not Your Brain and Other Lessons from the Biology of Consciousness*. Farrar, Straus and Giroux: New York.

Okely, J. (1986). *Simone de Beauvoir: A Re-Reading*. Virago: London.

Oksala, J. (2006). 'Female freedom: Can the lived body be emancipated?' In D. Olkowski and G. Weiss, (eds), pp. 209–28.

Olkowski, D. (2006). 'Only nature is mother to the child'. In D. Olkowski and G. Weiss, (eds), pp. 49–70.

Olkowski, D. and G. Weiss, (eds) (2006). *Feminist Interpretations of Merleau-Ponty*. Pennsylvania University Press: University Park, PA.

O'Shaughnessy, B. (1980). *The Will*. 2 vols. Cambridge University Press: Cambridge.

—(1995). 'Proprioception and the body image'. In J. Bermúdez et al., (eds), pp. 175–204.

Ostrow, J. (1990). *Social Sensitivity: A Study of Habit and Experience*. State University of New York Press: Albany, NY.

Overgaard, S. and D. Zahavi (2009). 'Understanding (other) minds: Wittgenstein's phenomenological contribution'. In E. Zamunev and D. Levy, (eds), *Wittgenstein's Enduring Arguments*. Routledge: London.

Pandya, R. (2008). 'The borderlands of identity and culture'. In G. Weiss, (ed.), pp. 241–64.

Priest, S. (1998). *Merleau-Ponty*. Routledge: London and New York.

Ramachandran, V. S. and S. Blakeslee (1998). *Phantoms in the Brain*. Harper Collins: London.

Romdenh-Romluc, K. (2007). 'Merleau-Ponty and the power to reckon with the possible'. In T. Baldwin, (ed.), pp. 44–58.

—(2011). *Merleau-Ponty and Phenomenology of Perception*. Routledge: London and New York.

Rothfield, P. (2008). 'Living well and health studies'. In R. Diprose and J. Reynolds, (eds), pp. 218–27.

Ryle, G. (1949). *The Concept of Mind*. Hutchinson: London.

—(1962). '*La phenomenologie contre the Concept of Mind*'. Trans. A. Gombay. In J. Wahl, (ed.), pp. 65–84, and his response to Merleau-Ponty in discussion, pp. 96–100. (The English version of this lecture can be found in Ryle [1971], pp. 171–96. The discussion appears in English in *TD* as 'Phenomenology and analytic philosophy'.)

—(1971). *Collected Papers I: Critical Essays*. Hutchinson & Co.: London.

Sacks, O. (1985). *The Man Who Mistook His Wife for a Hat*. Summit Books: New York.

—(1995). *An Anthropologist on Mars*. Alfred A. Knopf: New York.

Safranski, R. (1998). *Martin Heidegger: Between Good and Evil*. Trans. E. Osers. Harvard University Press: Cambridge, MA and London.

Sanders, M. (2008). 'Intersubjectivity and alterity'. In R. Diprose and J. Reynolds, (eds), pp. 142–51.

Sartre, J. P. (1998). 'Merleau-Ponty *vivant*'. In J. Stewart (ed.), pp. 565–626. (Original French publication 1961).

Schiebinger, L., (ed.) (2000). *Feminism and the Body*. Oxford University Press: Oxford and New York.

Schlick, M. (1949). 'Is there a factual a priori?' In H. Feigl and W. Sellars, (eds) *Readings in Philosophical Analysis*. Appleton-Century-Crofts Inc.: New York, pp. 277–85. (Original German publication 1930/1.)

Schmidt, J. (1985). *Merleau-Ponty: Between Phenomenology and Structuralism*. MacMilllan: Basingstoke and London.

Shusterman, R., (ed.) (1999a). *Bourdieu: A Critical Reader*. Blackwell: Oxford and Malden, MA.

Shusterman, R. (1999b). 'Introduction: Bourdieu as philosopher'. In R. Shusterman, (ed.), pp. 1–13.

—(2005). 'The silent, limping body of philosophy'. In T. Carman and M. B. N. Hansen, (eds), pp. 151–80.

Sibley, F. (1965). 'Aesthetic and non-aesthetic'. *Philosophical Review* 74(2), pp. 135–59.

Silvers, A. (2009). 'Feminist perspectives on disability'. In the *Stanford Encyclopedia of Philosophy*. http://www.seop.ledac.uk/entries/feminism-disability/.

Spiegelberg, H. (1969). *The Phenomenological Movement: A Historical Introduction*, 2nd edn, 2 Vols. Martinus Nijhoff: The Hague.

Stawarska, B. (2006). 'From the body proper to flesh: Merleau-Ponty on intersubjectivity'. In D. Olkowski and G. Weiss, (eds), pp. 91–106.

Steeves, H. P. (1999). *Animal Others: On Ethics, Ontology and Animal Life*. State University of New York Press: Albany, NY.

Stewart, J., (ed.) (1998). *The Debate Between Sartre and Merleau-Ponty*. Northwestern University Press: Evanston, IL.

Stratton, G. M. (1896). 'Some preliminary experiments on vision without inversion of the retinal image'. *Psychological Review* 3, pp. 611–17.

—(1897). 'Vision without inversion of the retinal image'. *Psychological Review* 4, pp. 441–81.

Sullivan, P. (2003). 'Ineffability and nonsense'. *Proceedings of the Aristotelian Society*, supp. vol. 76, pp. 195–223.

Taylor, C. (1964). *The Explanation of Behaviour*. London: Routledge.

—(1976). 'Phenomenology and linguistic analysis I'. In H. A. Durfee, (ed.), pp. 217–31.

—(1999). 'To follow a rule ...'. In R. Shusterman, (ed.), pp. 29–44.

—(2005). 'Merleau-Ponty and the epistemological picture'. In T. Carman and H. B. N. Hansen, (eds), pp. 26–49.

Tiemersma, D. (1987). 'Merleau-Ponty's philosophy as a field theory: Its origins, categories and relevance'. *Man and World* 20, pp. 419–46.

Toadvine, T. (2007). '"Strange kinship": Merleau-Ponty on the human-animal relation'. In A.-T. Tymieniecka, (ed.), *Phenomenology of Life: From the Animal Soul to the Human Mind. Book I: In Search of Experience. Analecta Husserliana* XCIII, pp. 17–32.

—(2009). *Merleau-Ponty's Philosophy of Nature*. Northwestern University Press: Evanston.

Toadvine, T. and L. Embree, (eds) (2002). *Merleau-Ponty's Reading of Husserl*. Springer: Dordrecht, London and Boston.

Toombs, S. K. (1988). 'Illness and the paradigm of lived body'. *Theoretical Medicine* 9, pp. 201–26.

—(1993). *The Meaning of Illness: A Phenomenological Account of the Different Perspectives of Physician and Patient*. Kluwer: Dordrecht.

Uexküll, J. V. (2010). *A Foray into the Worlds of Animals and Humans, with a Theory of Meaning*. Trans. J. D. O'Neil. University of Minnesota Press: Minneapolis, MN. (Original publication 1934.)

Varela, F. J., E. Thompson and E. Roach (1991). *The Embodied Mind: Cognitive Science and Human Experience*. MIT Press: Cambridge, MA.

Wacquant, L. (2006). *Body and Soul: Notebooks of an Apprentice Boxer*. Oxford University Press: New York.

Wahl, J., (ed.) (1962). *Cahiers de Royaumont: La Philosophie Analytique*. Les Éditions de Minuit: Paris. (Translations of the Introduction and the discussion of Ryle mine.)

Warnock, G. J. (1973). 'Saturday mornings'. In G. J. Warnock, (ed.) *Essays on J. L. Austin*. Clarendon: Oxford, pp. 31–45.

Warnock, M. (2002). *A Memoir: People and Places*. Duckbacks (Duckworth): London.

Weiss, G. (1999). *Body Images: Embodiment as Intercorporeality*. Routledge: New York and London.

—(2008). 'Can an old dog learn new tricks? Habitual horizons in James, Bourdieu, and Merleau-Ponty'. In G. Weiss, (ed.), pp. 223–240.

Weiss, G., (ed.) (2008). *Intertwinings: Interdisciplinary Encounters with Merleau-Ponty*. State University of New York Press: Albany, NY.

Welsh, T. (2008). 'The developing body: A reading of Merleau-Ponty's conception of women in the Sorbonne lectures'. In G. Weiss, (ed.), pp. 45–62.

Widdershoven, G. A. M. (1998). 'Commentary on "a phenomenology of dyslexia"'. In *Philosophy, Psychiatry and Psychology* 5(1), pp. 29–31.

Wierzbicka, A. (1997). *Understanding Cultures Through Their Key Words*. Oxford University Press: New York and Oxford.

Wilson, R. A. and L. Foglia (2011). 'Embodied cognition'. In the *Stanford Encyclopedia of Philosophy*. http://www.seop.leeds.ac.uk/entries/embodied-cognition.

Wittgenstein, L. (1968). *Philosophical Investigations*. Trans. G. E. M. Anscombe. Basil Blackwell: Oxford.

—(1979). 'Remarks on Frazer's *Golden Bough*'. Trans. J. Beversluis. In C. G. Luckhardt, (ed.), *Wittgenstein: Sources and Perspectives*. Cornell University Press: Ithaca.

—(1980). *Culture and Value*. G. H. Von Wright and H. Nyman, (eds) P. Winch, trans. Blackwell: Oxford.

—(1988). *Lectures on the Philosophy of Psychology 1947–47*. Notes by P. T. Geach, K. J. Shah and A. C. Jackson. Edited by P. T. Geach. Harvester/Wheatsheaf: Hemel Hempstead.

Wolfe, C. (2003). *Zoontologies: The Question of the Animal*. University of Minnesota Press: Minneapolis, MN.

Wrathall, M. A. (2005). 'Motives, reasons and causes'. In T. Carmen and H. B. N. Hansen, (eds), pp. 111–28.

—(2007). 'The phenomenology of social rules'. In T. Baldwin, (ed.), pp. 70–86.

Young, B. (2008). 'The language of the lips, Merleau-Ponty and Irigaray: Toward a culture of difference'. In G. Weiss, (ed.), pp. 85–96.

Young, I. M. (1990). 'Throwing like a girl.' In I. M. Young, (ed.), *Throwing Like a Girl and Other Essays in Feminist Philosophy and Social Theory*. Indiana University Press: Bloomington and Indianapolis, pp. 141–59.

—(2005). *On Female Bodily Experience: 'Throwing like a Girl' and Other Essays*. Oxford University Press: New York.

Zahavi, D. (2003). *Husserl's Phenomenology*. Stanford University Press: Stanford.

Zaner, R. M. (1964). *The Problem of Embodiment: Some Contributions to a Phenomenology of the Body*. Martinus Nijhoff: The Hague.

—(1981). *The Context of Self: A Phenomenological Inquiry Using Medicine as a Clue*. Ohio University Press: Athens, OH.

Zirión, A. (2006). 'The call "back to the things themselves" and the notion of phenomenology'. *Husserl Studies* 22, pp. 29–51.

INDEX

The bold page numbers throughout this index indicate the central places where the related topic is discussed.